PENGUIN (Penguin logo) CLASSICS

FOUNDING EDITOR: T. J. B. SPENCER
GENERAL EDITOR: STANLEY WELLS
SUPERVISORY EDITORS: PAUL EDMONDSON, STANLEY WELLS

THE WINTER'S TALE

T. J. B. SPENCER, sometime Director of the Shakespeare Institute of the University of Birmingham, was the founding editor of the New Penguin Shakespeare, for which he edited both *Romeo and Juliet* and *Hamlet*.

STANLEY WELLS is Honorary President of the Shakespeare Birthplace Trust, Emeritus Professor of Shakespeare Studies at the University of Birmingham, and General Editor of the Oxford Shakespeare. His many books include *Shakespeare: For All Time*, *Shakespeare & Co.*, *Shakespeare, Sex, and Love* and *Great Shakespeare Actors*.

ERNEST SCHANZER was a Shakespeare scholar who taught at the Universities of Liverpool and Munich. Author of a book on *Shakespeare's Problem Plays*, he also had a special interest in Shakespeare's sources and in his late plays. He edited *Pericles* for the Signet edition.

RUSS MCDONALD is Professor of English Literature at Goldsmiths, University of London. His publications include the widely-adopted *Bedford Companion to Shakespeare*, *Shakespeare's Late Style*, and, most recently, *The Bedford Shakespeare*, a teaching edition prepared with Lena Cowen Orlin. Having taught at five American universities, he has received multiple awards for distinguished teaching.

PAUL EDMONDSON is Head of Research at the Shakespeare Birthplace Trust and an Honorary Fellow of the Shakespeare Institute. His publications include *Shakespeare's Sonnets*; *A Year of Shakespeare: Re-living the World Sh... ...peare Festival*; *Shakespeare Beyond ... The Shakespeare Circle: An Alternat... ...*.

D1334137

WILLIAM SHAKESPEARE

The Winter's Tale

Edited with a Commentary by
ERNEST SCHANZER
and with an Introduction by
RUSS MCDONALD
The Play in Performance by
PAUL EDMONDSON

PENGUIN BOOKS

PENGUIN CLASSICS

UK | USA | Canada | Ireland | Australia
India | New Zealand | South Africa

Penguin Books is part of the Penguin Random House group of companies
whose addresses can be found at global.penguinrandomhouse.com.

This edition first published in Penguin Books 1986
Reissued in the Penguin Shakespeare series 2005
Reissued in Penguin Classics 2015

004

This edition copyright © Penguin Books, 1986
Account of the Text and Commentary copyright © Ernest Schanzer, 1986
General Introduction and Chronology copyright © Stanley Wells, 2005
Introduction and Further Reading copyright © Russ McDonald, 2005
The Play in Performance copyright © Paul Edmondson, 2005
All rights reserved

The moral rights of the editors have been asserted

Set in PostScript Monotype Fournier
Typeset by Palimpsest Book Production Limited, Falkirk, Stirlingshire
Printed in Great Britain by Clays Ltd, St Ives plc

ISBN: 978-0-141-39656-9

www.greenpenguin.co.uk

Penguin Random House is committed to a
sustainable future for our business, our readers
and our planet. This book is made from Forest
Stewardship Council® certified paper.

Contents

General Introduction

Every play by Shakespeare is unique. This is part of his greatness. A restless and indefatigable experimenter, he moved with a rare amalgamation of artistic integrity and dedicated professionalism from one kind of drama to another. Never shackled by convention, he offered his actors the alternation between serious and comic modes from play to play, and often also within the plays themselves, that the repertory system within which he worked demanded, and which provided an invaluable stimulus to his imagination. Introductions to individual works in this series attempt to define their individuality. But there are common factors that underpin Shakespeare's career.

Nothing in his heredity offers clues to the origins of his genius. His upbringing in Stratford-upon-Avon, where he was born in 1564, was unexceptional. His mother, born Mary Arden, came from a prosperous farming family. Her father chose her as his executor over her eight sisters and his four stepchildren when she was only in her late teens, which suggests that she was of more than average practical ability. Her husband John, a glover, apparently unable to write, was nevertheless a capable businessman and loyal townsfellow, who seems to have fallen on relatively hard times in later life. He would have been brought up as a Catholic, and may have retained

Catholic sympathies, but his son subscribed publicly to Anglicanism throughout his life.

The most important formative influence on Shakespeare was his school. As the son of an alderman who became bailiff (or mayor) in 1568, he had the right to attend the town's grammar school. Here he would have received an education grounded in classical rhetoric and oratory, studying authors such as Ovid, Cicero and Quintilian, and would have been required to read, speak, write and even think in Latin from his early years. This classical education permeates Shakespeare's work from the beginning to the end of his career. It is apparent in the self-conscious classicism of plays of the early 1590s such as the tragedy of *Titus Andronicus*, *The Comedy of Errors*, and the narrative poems *Venus and Adonis* (1592–3) and *The Rape of Lucrece* (1593–4), and is still evident in his latest plays, informing the dream visions of *Pericles* and *Cymbeline* and the masque in *The Tempest*, written between 1607 and 1611. It inflects his literary style throughout his career. In his earliest writings the verse, based on the ten-syllabled, five-beat iambic pentameter, is highly patterned. Rhetorical devices deriving from classical literature, such as alliteration and antithesis, extended similes and elaborate wordplay, abound. Often, as in *Love's Labour's Lost* and *A Midsummer Night's Dream*, he uses rhyming patterns associated with lyric poetry, each line self-contained in sense, the prose as well as the verse employing elaborate figures of speech. Writing at a time of linguistic ferment, Shakespeare frequently imports Latinisms into English, coining words such as abstemious, addiction, incarnadine and adjunct. He was also heavily influenced by the eloquent translations of the Bible in both the Bishops' and the Geneva versions. As his experience grows, his verse and prose become more supple, the patterning less apparent, more ready to accommodate the rhythms of ordinary speech, more colloquial in diction, as in the speeches of the Nurse in *Romeo and Juliet*, the characterful prose of Falstaff and Hamlet's soliloquies. The effect is of increasing psychological realism, reaching its greatest heights in *Hamlet*, *Othello*, *King Lear*, *Macbeth* and *Antony and Cleopatra*. Gradually he discovered ways of adapting the regular beat of the pentameter to make it an infinitely flexible instrument for matching thought with feeling. Towards the end of his career, in plays such as *The Winter's Tale*, *Cymbeline* and *The Tempest*, he adopts a more highly mannered style, in keeping with the more overtly symbolical and emblematical mode in which he is writing.

So far as we know, Shakespeare lived in Stratford till after his marriage to Anne Hathaway, eight years his senior, in 1582. They had three children: a daughter, Susanna, born in 1583 within six months of their marriage, and twins, Hamnet and Judith, born in 1585. The next seven years of Shakespeare's life are virtually a blank. Theories that he may have been, for instance, a schoolmaster, or a lawyer, or a soldier, or a sailor, lack evidence to support them. The first reference to him in print, in Robert Greene's pamphlet *Greene's Groatsworth of Wit* of 1592, parodies a line from *Henry VI, Part III*, implying that Shakespeare was already an established playwright. It seems likely that at some unknown point after the birth of his twins he joined a theatre company and gained experience as both actor and writer in the provinces and London. The London theatres closed because of plague in 1593 and 1594; and during these years, perhaps recognizing the need for an alternative career, he wrote and published the narrative poems *Venus and Adonis* and *The Rape of Lucrece*. These are the only works we can be

certain that Shakespeare himself was responsible for
putting into print. Each bears the author's dedication to
Henry Wriothesley, Earl of Southampton (1573–1624),
the second in warmer terms than the first. Southampton,
younger than Shakespeare by ten years, is the only person
to whom he personally dedicated works. The Earl may
have been a close friend, perhaps even the beautiful and
adored young man whom Shakespeare celebrates in his
Sonnets.

The resumption of playing after the plague years saw
the founding of the Lord Chamberlain's Men, a company
to which Shakespeare was to belong for the rest of his
career, as actor, shareholder and playwright. No other
dramatist of the period had so stable a relationship with a
single company. Shakespeare knew the actors for whom
he was writing and the conditions in which they performed.
The permanent company was made up of around twelve
to fourteen players, but one actor often played more than
one role in a play and additional actors were hired as
needed. Led by the tragedian Richard Burbage (1568–1619)
and, initially, the comic actor Will Kemp (d. 1603), they
rapidly achieved a high reputation, and when King James
I succeeded Queen Elizabeth I in 1603 they were renamed
as the King's Men. All the women's parts were played by
boys; there is no evidence that any female role was ever
played by a male actor over the age of about eighteen.
Shakespeare had enough confidence in his boys to write
for them long and demanding roles such as Rosalind (who,
like other heroines of the romantic comedies, is disguised
as a boy for much of the action) in *As You Like It*, Lady
Macbeth and Cleopatra. But there are far more fathers
than mothers, sons than daughters, in his plays, few if any
of which require more than the company's normal comple-
ment of three or four boys.

The company played primarily in London's public playhouses – there were almost none that we know of in the rest of the country – initially in the Theatre, built in Shoreditch in 1576, and from 1599 in the Globe, on Bankside. These were wooden, more or less circular structures, open to the air, with a thrust stage surmounted by a canopy and jutting into the area where spectators who paid one penny stood, and surrounded by galleries where it was possible to be seated on payment of an additional penny. Though properties such as cauldrons, stocks, artificial trees or beds could indicate locality, there was no representational scenery. Sound effects such as flourishes of trumpets, music both martial and amorous, and accompaniments to songs were provided by the company's musicians. Actors entered through doors in the back wall of the stage. Above it was a balconied area that could represent the walls of a town (as in *King John*), or a castle (as in *Richard II*), and indeed a balcony (as in *Romeo and Juliet*). In 1609 the company also acquired the use of the Blackfriars, a smaller, indoor theatre to which admission was more expensive, and which permitted the use of more spectacular stage effects such as the descent of Jupiter on an eagle in *Cymbeline* and of goddesses in *The Tempest*. And they would frequently perform before the court in royal residences and, on their regular tours into the provinces, in non-theatrical spaces such as inns, guildhalls and the great halls of country houses.

Early in his career Shakespeare may have worked in collaboration, perhaps with Thomas Nashe (1567–c. 1601) in *Henry VI, Part I* and with George Peele (1556–96) in *Titus Andronicus*. And towards the end he collaborated with George Wilkins (*fl.* 1604–8) in *Pericles*, and with his younger colleagues Thomas Middleton (1580–1627), in *Timon of Athens*, and John Fletcher (1579–1625), in *Henry*

VIII, *The Two Noble Kinsmen* and the lost play *Cardenio*. Shakespeare's output dwindled in his last years, and he died in 1616 in Stratford, where he owned a fine house, New Place, and much land. His only son had died at the age of eleven, in 1596, and his last descendant died in 1670. New Place was destroyed in the eighteenth century but the other Stratford houses associated with his life are maintained and displayed to the public by the Shakespeare Birthplace Trust.

One of the most remarkable features of Shakespeare's plays is their intellectual and emotional scope. They span a great range from the lightest of comedies, such as *The Two Gentlemen of Verona* and *The Comedy of Errors*, to the profoundest of tragedies, such as *King Lear* and *Macbeth*. He maintained an output of around two plays a year, ringing the changes between comic and serious. All his comedies have serious elements: Shylock, in *The Merchant of Venice*, almost reaches tragic dimensions, and *Measure for Measure* is profoundly serious in its examination of moral problems. Equally, none of his tragedies is without humour: Hamlet is as witty as any of his comic heroes, *Macbeth* has its Porter, and *King Lear* its Fool. His greatest comic character, Falstaff, inhabits the history plays and *Henry V* ends with a marriage, while *Henry VI, Part III*, *Richard II* and *Richard III* culminate in the tragic deaths of their protagonists.

Although in performance Shakespeare's characters can give the impression of a superabundant reality, he is not a naturalistic dramatist. None of his plays is explicitly set in his own time. The action of few of them (except for the English histories) is set even partly in England (exceptions are *The Merry Wives of Windsor* and the Induction to *The Taming of the Shrew*). Italy is his favoured location. Most of his principal story-lines derive from printed writings; but the structuring and translation of these narratives into dramatic terms is Shakespeare's own, and he invents much additional material. Most of the plays contain elements of myth and legend, and many derive from ancient or more recent history or from romantic tales of ancient times and faraway places. All reflect his reading, often in close detail. Holinshed's *Chronicles* (1577, revised 1587), a great compendium of English, Scottish and Irish history, provided material for his English history plays. The *Lives of the Noble Grecians and Romans* by the Greek writer Plutarch, finely translated into English from the French by Sir Thomas North in 1579, provided much of the narrative material, and also a mass of verbal detail, for his plays about Roman history. Some plays are closely based on shorter individual works: *As You Like It*, for instance, on the novel *Rosalynde* (1590) by his near-contemporary Thomas Lodge (1558–1625), *The Winter's Tale* on *Pandosto* (1588) by his old rival Robert Greene (1558–92) and *Othello* on a story by the Italian Giraldi Cinthio (1504–73). And the language of his plays is permeated by the Bible, the Book of Common Prayer and the proverbial sayings of his day.

Shakespeare was popular with his contemporaries, but his commitment to the theatre and to the plays in performance is demonstrated by the fact that only about half of his plays appeared in print in his lifetime, in slim paperback volumes known as quartos, so called because they were made from printers' sheets folded twice to form four leaves (eight pages). None of them shows any sign that he was involved in their publication. For him, performance was the primary means of publication. The most frequently reprinted of his works were the nondramatic poems – the erotic *Venus and Adonis* and the more moralistic *The Rape of Lucrece*. The *Sonnets*, which appeared in 1609, under his name but possibly without his consent, were less successful, perhaps because the vogue for sonnet sequences, which peaked in the 1590s, had passed by then. They were not reprinted until 1640, and then only in garbled form along with poems by other writers. Happily, in 1623, seven years after he died, his colleagues John Heminges (1556–1630) and Henry Condell (d. 1627) published his collected plays, including eighteen that had not previously appeared in print, in the first Folio, whose name derives from the fact that the printers' sheets were folded only once to produce two leaves (four pages). Some of the quarto editions are badly printed, and the fact that some plays exist in two, or even three, early versions creates problems for editors. These are discussed in the Account of the Text in each volume of this series.

Shakespeare's plays continued in the repertoire until the Puritans closed the theatres in 1642. When performances resumed after the Restoration of the monarchy in 1660 many of the plays were not to the taste of the times, especially because their mingling of genres and failure to meet the requirements of poetic justice offended against the dictates of neoclassicism. Some, such as *The Tempest* (changed by John Dryden and William Davenant in 1667 to suit contemporary taste), *King Lear* (to which Nahum Tate gave a happy ending in 1681) and *Richard III* (heavily adapted by Colley Cibber in 1700 as a vehicle for his own talents), were extensively rewritten; others fell into neglect. Slowly they regained their place in the repertoire, and they continued to be reprinted, but it was not until the great actor David Garrick (1717–79) organized a spectacular jubilee in Stratford in 1769 that Shakespeare began to be regarded as a transcendental genius. Garrick's idolatry prefigured the enthusiasm of critics such as Samuel Taylor Coleridge (1772–1834) and William Hazlitt (1778–1830). Gradually Shakespeare's reputation spread abroad, to Germany, America, France and to other European countries.

During the nineteenth century, though the plays were generally still performed in heavily adapted or abbreviated versions, a large body of scholarship and criticism began to amass. Partly as a result of a general swing in education away from the teaching of Greek and Roman texts and towards literature written in English, Shakespeare became the object of intensive study in schools and universities. In the theatre, important turning points were the work in England of two theatre directors, William Poel (1852–1934) and his disciple Harley Granville-Barker (1877–1946), who showed that the application of knowledge, some of it newly acquired, of early staging conditions to performance of the plays could render the original texts viable in terms of the modern theatre. During the twentieth century appreciation of Shakespeare's work, encouraged by the availability of audio, film and video versions of the plays, spread around the world to such an extent that he can now be claimed as a global author.

The influence of Shakespeare's works permeates the English language. Phrases from his plays and poems – 'a tower of strength', 'green-eyed jealousy', 'a foregone conclusion' – are on the lips of people who may never have read him. They have inspired composers of songs, orchestral music and operas; painters and sculptors; poets, novelists and film-makers. Allusions to him appear in pop songs, in advertisements and in television shows. Some of his characters – Romeo and Juliet, Falstaff, Shylock and Hamlet – have acquired mythic status. He is valued for his humanity, his psychological insight, his wit and humour, his lyricism, his mastery of language, his ability to excite, surprise, move and, in the widest sense of the word, entertain audiences. He is the greatest of poets, but he is essentially a dramatic poet. Though his plays have much to offer to readers, they exist fully only in performance. In these volumes we offer individual introductions, notes on language and on specific points of the text, suggestions for further reading and information about how each work has been edited. In addition we include accounts of the ways in which successive generations of interpreters and audiences have responded to challenges and rewards offered by the plays. The Penguin Shakespeare series aspires to remove obstacles to understanding and to make pleasurable the reading of the work of the man who has done more than most to make us understand what it is to be human.

                                                    Stanley Wells

The Chronology of Shakespeare's Works

A few of Shakespeare's writings can be fairly precisely dated. An allusion to the Earl of Essex in the chorus to Act V of *Henry V*, for instance, could only have been written in 1599. But for many of the plays we have only vague information, such as the date of publication, which may have occurred long after composition, the date of a performance, which may not have been the first, or a list in Francis Meres's book *Palladis Tamia*, published in 1598, which tells us only that the plays listed there must have been written by that year. The chronology of the early plays is particularly difficult to establish. Not everyone would agree that the first part of *Henry VI* was written after the third, for instance, or *Romeo and Juliet* before *A Midsummer Night's Dream*. The following table is based on the 'Canon and Chronology' section in *William Shakespeare: A Textual Companion*, by Stanley Wells and Gary Taylor, with John Jowett and William Montgomery (1987), where more detailed information and discussion may be found.

The Two Gentlemen of Verona	1590–91
The Taming of the Shrew	1590–91
Henry VI, Part II	1591
Henry VI, Part III	1591

Introduction

The Winter's Tale is a product of Shakespeare's late career, and it bears the distinctive markings of that period. Like the plays with which it is normally grouped, *Pericles*, *Cymbeline* and *The Tempest*, it is a hybrid, a complex mixture of disparate parts. Both innovatory and old-fashioned, responsive to contemporary trends in theatrical form yet reliant on familiar Shakespearian episodes and ideas, it shares with his other late works fundamental properties of structure, tone and subject matter. While controversy persists about how to label these plays, whether they are best described as tragicomedies or romances, their resemblances to one another and their differences from most of Shakespeare's other work, especially the tragedies that immediately precede them, justify a separate category and signify a major shift in his thinking about the world, particularly his attitude towards the theatre.

If the first audiences found *The Winter's Tale* a curious assortment of familiar and novel elements, they themselves represented a mixture of social and economic classes. The play was given at the Globe on Wednesday, 15 May 1611, a performance witnessed by the London physician-alchemist Simon Forman and described in his diary; it was also performed at the banqueting house at

Whitehall Palace in London for the court in the autumn of that year; and it was almost certainly played at the indoor theatre in Blackfriars as well, since the King's Men were using both the indoor and outdoor playhouses at the time. These are the earliest known performances of *The Winter's Tale*, which then remained in the repertory: the company presented it again as part of the festivities for the marriage of King James's daughter, Princess Elizabeth, in 1612–13. The text may have undergone some revision between these early runs, but we have only one version, that printed in the Folio of 1623. Exactly when Shakespeare composed the play is unclear. It could have been written anytime between 1609 and early 1611: twentieth-century scholarship tended to favour the later date, but recent thought, reflected in the Chronology published here, has tentatively placed it earlier, before *Cymbeline*. It is possible, of course, that Shakespeare worked on both plays at the same time.

Although generalizations about cultural taste are risky, it is fair to say that Jacobean playgoers thought of themselves as 'modern', up to date and distinct from their Elizabethan predecessors. Ironically, part of the evidence for this conclusion is a perceptible nostalgia for the glories (real or imagined) of the earlier age and the now-beloved queen who had presided over it. Accompanying such rosy retrospection and sense of distance was the conviction that tastes had become more sophisticated, that the primitive pleasures of that earlier age, represented in the theatre by such bombastic crowd-pleasers as Thomas Kyd's *The Spanish Tragedy* (1587?) and Christopher Marlowe's two-part *Tamburlaine* (1587–8?), had been properly discarded. There is reason to think that the first audiences would have considered *The Winter's Tale* an example of a new kind of play that was becoming fashionable, a mode imported from Italy and adapted expressly for London: tragicomedy. At the same time there is reason to think that those audiences would have considered the play somewhat outmoded. Shakespeare took as his source an Elizabethan prose novella by Robert Greene called *Pandosto, or The Triumph of Time*. Published in 1588 and reprinted three times before 1611, it would have been known to some, perhaps many, members of Shakespeare's audience. Therefore, as both an adaptation of a familiar story from a simpler era and an exemplar of the very latest in dramatic form, *The Winter's Tale* probably struck its original audiences as simultaneously backward-looking and sophisticated.

Modern readers and spectators approaching the play, especially those acquainted with some of Shakespeare's other dramas, will probably discern another kind of hybridity. The reappearance of favourite plot devices, character types and thematic material makes the play seem familiar and identifiably Shakespearian. At the same time, however, his treatment of those conventions, particularly the new mode to which they contribute, imparts an air of novelty and experimentation to the drama. Shakespeare has ventured into new artistic territory, and an introduction to this realm properly begins with his revised perspective on human experience, especially his revaluation of the place of theatrical fictions – and of art generally – in that experience. Such concerns lead logically to a discussion of dramatic modes, particularly the play's affiliations with the generic categories of tragicomedy and romance. Like the other late dramas, *The Winter's Tale* is shaped by a new authorial attitude towards theatre, a viewpoint that accounts for its exceptional self-consciousness, its numerous surprises, the originality of its ending and the playful difficulty of its poetic style.

This new freedom also governs Shakespeare's articulation of ideas: some of the most significant are the complex relation of art and nature, the destructive and consoling effects of time, the creative powers of women, and the problem of belief. In its representation of human experience *The Winter's Tale* seems exceptionally ambitious: much seems to be at stake, and so complex is the treatment of thematic material that over time people have responded to it in vastly different ways. What is practically indisputable, however, especially in performance, is its extraordinary affective power.

EXPANDED VISTAS

In the fourth act of *King Lear*, the old Earl of Gloucester, traumatized physically and mentally – he has just been brutally blinded for his loyalty to the King – seeks to commit suicide. He begs 'poor Tom', the vagrant madman who is actually his son Edgar in disguise, to lead him to Dover so that he can hurl himself from the cliffs into the sea, and when the old man doubts that they have arrived at the cliffs, Edgar seeks to convince him by devising a verbal picture of what Gloucester cannot see.

                                    How fearful
      And dizzy 'tis to cast one's eyes so low!
      The crows and choughs that wing the midway air
      Show scarce so gross as beetles. Halfway down
      Hangs one that gathers sampire – dreadful trade!
      Methinks he seems no bigger than his head.
      The fishermen that walk upon the beach
      Appear like mice, and yon tall anchoring bark
      Diminished to her cock; her cock, a buoy

Almost too small for sight. The murmuring surge
That on th'unnumbered idle pebble chafes
Cannot be heard so high. I'll look no more,
Lest my brain turn, and the deficient sight
Topple down headlong. (IV.6.11–24)

Edgar's speech is an exercise in visual perspective, the
trick of foreshortening that the eye naturally performs
when surveying a distant field. With the two characters,
we look from above, noting objects in order from near
to distant. Everything is reduced in size, and by the end
of the sequence, the description of the distant ship, the
components of the visible space have been arranged in
exact relation to one another: A seems as small as B
normally does, which now seems as small as C usually
would, and so on. At the conclusion of the passage,
Gloucester attempts to kill himself, 'falling' from what
he thinks are the heights. But since Edgar's description
is a visual fiction, the blind old man has merely tumbled
on to the ground – the actor has simply toppled over on
to the flat stage – and the experience results in his
'salvation', providing him with a fresh perspective on
human suffering.

Edgar's survey of the imagined landscape constitutes
a kind of thematic pun, an exercise in optical perspective
calculated to promote philosophical perspective, especially the consolations of patience and distance. Visually
speaking, what we see, particularly the magnitude of what
we see, depends on where we stand. Similarly, in terms of
experience, how we understand what has happened to us
depends on what we know, on 'where we are' in relation
to that experience. The aim of this highly unrealistic
episode is to teach Gloucester perspective and patience.
Etymologically, the word 'per-spective' suggests the need

to 'look through' present suffering to a more enduring and potentially comforting reality beyond it. The Dover scene, composed no more than four or five years before *The Winter's Tale*, is vital to comprehension of Shakespeare's late work because it forecasts a development in his thinking about mortality, a transformation that will determine the distinctive form of the last plays.

The thematic value of such perspective, although implicit in Shakespeare's early drama, becomes explicit in the mature tragedies, notably in the combination of sympathy and ironic distance with which we are encouraged to regard the tragic heroes. Each of them finally discovers a wider perspective than that displayed initially, an awareness of the self in time and appreciation of the value of such awareness. Coriolanus, at the scene of his fatal reconciliation before the gates of Rome, declares that 'the heavens do ope, | The gods look down, and this unnatural scene | They laugh at' (V.3.184–6). That passage describes the expanded vistas also perceived by such figures as Antony, in his rumination on the polymorphous, shifting clouds that 'mock our eyes with air' (*Antony and Cleopatra*, IV.14.7), or Macbeth, who recognizes in his 'Tomorrow, and tomorrow, and tomorrow' speech (V.5.19–28) the distance between the man he was and the monster he has become. In that most problematic of the late tragedies, *Timon of Athens*, part of the difficulty is that the shattered Timon, ruined financially and abandoned by all his former friends, cannot achieve consolation – that is, cannot look beyond his immediate misery to a philosophical understanding of his fall. In each play the force of the tragedy depends upon the brevity of this recognition: the hostile environment destroys the visionary who comprehends it. Philosophical perspective represents a form of imaginative reflection, a creative response to the conditions of mortality, and thus the dramatist's passage from tragedy to tragicomedy or romance entails another form of adjusted vision – artistic perspective.

Shakespeare moves into his post-tragic phase by reconceiving the stage as a space where the consolations of such temporal awareness may be enjoyed, sustained (at least temporarily) and repeated. Rather than deplore the falsity and corruption of the material world, he imagines a theatrical alternative, embracing its unreality and accepting its pleasures as temporary but powerful solace. This commitment to a virtual reality accounts for the abundant self-consciousness of the last plays, especially those moments in which, as the actors watch a stage performance within the performance, the stage becomes the reality. The most memorable such analogy occurs in *The Tempest*: Prospero's speech about the dissolution of the 'gorgeous palaces' and the 'great globe itself' (IV.1.147–58) identifies the world with the play and asserts that both are, in a sense, no more than illusions. Such a concentric structure, art within art, implies that the theatrical realm is no less real than the material, the actual world no less bogus than the stage. In reality, dead wives and outcast daughters do not return; in the realm of the theatre, they may. The imaginative relief afforded by *The Winter's Tale* and the other romances may be temporary, but it is as actual as what we are accustomed to calling 'reality'.

TRAGICOMIC ROMANCE

Broadly speaking, the first half of *The Winter's Tale* is tragic, the second comic. The first three acts are dominated by grievous error, suffering and even death;

the fourth and fifth acts depict the wooing of young lovers, forgiveness of sin and reunited families. The action begins when Leontes, King of Sicilia, suspects his wife Hermione of adultery with his long-time friend Polixenes, King of Bohemia. Acting without proof, Leontes swiftly removes his son Mamillius from Hermione's care, orders his faithful servant Camillo to poison Polixenes, pronounces his infant daughter a bastard and banishes her to the wilderness, and arraigns the innocent Hermione in a humiliating public inquisition. The trial scene – the culmination of the first half – comes to a sudden halt with the judgement of Apollo's oracle:

OFFICER (*reads*) *Hermione is chaste; Polixenes blameless; Camillo a true subject; Leontes a jealous tyrant; his innocent babe truly begotten; and the King shall live without an heir, if that which is lost be not found* (III.2.131–4).

Immediately a messenger enters to announce the death of the boy Mamillius, Hermione faints and is taken from the stage, and Paulina, her confidante, re-enters to announce and accuse Leontes of the Queen's death. Now acknowledging his wrongs, the stricken King commits himself to a life of penance, and in a kind of coda to the tragic half of the play, Leontes' courtier Antigonus is seen leaving the baby on the coast of Bohemia, where she is discovered by an aged shepherd. But not before Antigonus loses his life: '*Exit, pursued by a bear*' (III.3.57).

Ironically, that episode initiates the play's turn towards the comic, which gains momentum when the personified figure of Time enters to announce the passage of sixteen years. Polixenes, having learned that his son Florizel, disguised as a commoner, has fallen in love with a shepherd's daughter named Perdita, disguises himself, with his adviser Camillo, and joins the sheep-shearing festival at the home of the old Shepherd. Also attending is the rogue Autolycus, who sells knick-knacks and ballads and dupes the countryfolk. When Polixenes angrily reveals himself and forbids the marriage, Camillo privately helps the young couple to elope back to Leontes' court in Sicilia, where they are followed by Polixenes and Camillo, the old Shepherd and his son, and Autolycus. The penitent, still-grieving Leontes receives the young couple, Perdita's birth is revealed, her marriage to Florizel sanctioned, the Shepherd and his son rewarded, and the two kings reunited. Then, in the extraordinary final scene, everyone assembles in Paulina's chapel to see a statue of Hermione, and while they admire its verisimilitude, the statue slowly comes to life. Although Mamillius is dead and sixteen years have been wasted, this restoration of the lost daughter and wife, supplemented by the marriage of Camillo and Paulina, brings about an affirmative ending that in generic terms feels comic, despite the shadow cast by the first three acts of the play.

The two halves of *The Winter's Tale* thus correspond to the comic and tragic emphases that Shakespeare had been developing and adjusting over the previous two decades. Like all the late plays, especially *The Tempest*, *The Winter's Tale* seems to be a storehouse for many of Shakespeare's favourite narrative and theatrical conventions. Most obviously, it restages the tragic jealousy of *Othello*, although in this version Leontes combines the traits of both the instigator and the jealous husband, Iago and Othello. Paulina becomes the female servant who speaks out early rather than late, her tirade against her king and master a much expanded version of Emilia's 'O gull! O dolt! | As ignorant as dirt!' (V.2.162–3). The disguise plot, allowing Polixenes and Camillo to spy on

Florizel and his low-born beloved, is a paternal variation on the dress-up plots of such comedies as *The Merchant of Venice* or *Twelfth Night* and on Edgar's machinations in *King Lear*. Camillo repeats the part of Kent, Lear's faithful servant who remains surreptitiously loyal in spite of his master's folly. The sheep-shearing festival in Bohemia re-creates the green world of the comedies, and the joys of that refuge are augmented by the sharp contrast with the tragic environment of the play's first half. The final episode, especially the mysterious, almost sacred reappearance of Hermione, intensifies the narrative device familiar from *Much Ado About Nothing*, *Twelfth Night* and *Measure for Measure*, in which an apparently lost lover or family member is restored and a happy ending ensured.

The retrospective Shakespeare borrowed not only from himself but also from others. Scholars have established that from about 1605 the plays attest to his engagement with literary texts of the bygone Elizabethan era – Sidney's *Arcadia* (pub. 1590) for one, the prose romance containing the story of the Paphlagonian king that becomes the Gloucester family sub-plot of *King Lear*. Obviously he had been rereading the great works of history and translation from the Tudor years, Raphael Holinshed's *Chronicles* (2nd edn 1587) and Sir Thomas North's translation of Plutarch's *Lives* (2nd edn 1595). Ovid he had always loved, and the mingling of mortal and immortal realms that distinguishes the late plays may signify a renewed interest in those Roman tales of metamorphosis: *The Winter's Tale* invokes the myth of Ceres and Proserpina as well as that of Pygmalion and Galatea. The playwright's own sonnets, many composed during the 1590s, were published for the first time in 1609. Whether or not the author assisted with or even consented to their publication, the collection represents his development of one of the most distinctive Elizabethan literary forms, and the tortured sexuality that marks so many of those lyric poems is visible in some refracted form in all the last plays. The most immediate of the Elizabethan influences is, of course, Greene's *Pandosto*. Either as cause or effect, this apparent process of retrospection seems to have refreshed Shakespeare's thinking about the pleasures of fiction.

Even as Shakespeare was looking back to Elizabethan favourites he was also looking around him, specifically at the new form of tragicomedy that had suddenly become popular in the first decade of the seventeenth century. The term 'tragicomedy' was hardly new, having been employed to describe certain ancient texts: Plautus' *Amphitruo* (c. 195 BC) was said to be the great classical example of the form, and Shakespeare himself had drawn upon that Roman play in composing *The Comedy of Errors*. In 1604 John Marston's *The Malcontent*, a play with a keen satiric edge, was designated a 'Tragicomoedia' in the Stationers' Register. But the event that dignified the new mode occurred in 1608–9, when the young John Fletcher produced *The Faithful Shepherdess*, his version of Guarini's *Il Pastor Fido* (1590). In prefacing the published text with a brief discursive introduction to tragicomedy, Fletcher articulated the formal terms of a style in which he may have been dabbling for two or three years. (*The Woman Hater* (1606–7) and *Cupid's Revenge* (1607–8) display some freedom with the conventions of genre, and while these plays are mostly by Francis Beaumont, some scholars believe that Fletcher may have assisted with them, making them perhaps the earliest of the pair's collaborations.) The printed definition may have been the young playwright's attempt to distance his work from the old-fashioned sense of the term: some thirty years before, in *The Defence of Poetry* (*c.* 1580; pub. 1595), Sir Philip Sidney had condemned 'mongrel tragicomedy' as marred by 'mingling kings and clowns'. Fletcher, by contrast, elegantly defined pastoral tragicomedy as a play that 'wants deaths, which is enough to make it no tragedy, yet brings some near it, which is enough to make it no comedy'.

In practice, what this means is that the tragicomic mode entails extremes of tone, incorporating both the threats of tragedy and the warmth and affirmation of comedy. Although *The Faithful Shepherdess* was apparently not a hit, Fletcher and Beaumont produced two more tragicomedies, *Philaster, or Love Lies a Bleeding* (1609–10) and *A King and No King* (1611), and audiences seem to have developed a taste for the form. For the next three decades, until the closing of the theatres, the major commercial playwrights attempted either independently or collaboratively to supply the public playhouses with fresh examples of it. Shakespeare himself must be numbered among the early experimenters in tragicomedy, whether or not the generic term is finally applied to this and his other late plays. By the time he wrote *The Winter's Tale*, he had already collaborated on one conforming generally to Fletcher's definition: in *Pericles* the hero suffers the apparent death of his wife and murder of his daughter, but in the last act, after the passage of some sixteen years, both are restored to him. Similar narrative forms and devices appear in *Cymbeline* and *The Tempest*, where families are reunited, disaster is narrowly averted, and the joy of the ending is augmented by the potential tragedy. In thinking about Shakespeare's interest in tragicomedy it is worth remembering that the Folio of 1623, our only source for the text, contains no such category:

The Winter's Tale is included with the comedies. Still, it seems likely that Jacobean audiences reacted to a play like *Cymbeline* much as they responded to *Philaster*; that the plays would have been grouped together; and that when first presented *The Winter's Tale* would have been deemed Shakespeare's effort in the new style.

To many later critics the category of tragicomedy, however historically appropriate, seemed inadequate to account for much of the extraordinary narrative material in Shakespeare's late plays, and thus they came to be known as 'romances', a rubric devised by the nineteenth-century poet and critic Edward Dowden. Romance is a broader category than tragicomedy, more often applied to prose fictions such as Sidney's *Arcadia* or to narrative poems such as Edmund Spenser's *The Faerie Queene* (1590–95) than to drama. Probability is neglected, magical events abound, space and time expand to accommodate the multiple components of a tall tale. Although tragicomedy also breaches the boundaries of the probable, romance does so in a distinctive way, relying on resurrection, theophany (the appearance of a divine being) and other such supernatural events. The geographical scope of romance fiction, most apparent in the wanderings of the hero, is related etymologically, through the Latin verb for 'wander', *vagare*, to the extravagant narrative, style and tone common to the romance form. Shipwrecks, oracular pronouncements, incest, wicked stepmothers, stolen princes, foundlings, bears – this is the stuff of romance. One of the most enduring of literary forms, romance began with the Greeks and manifests itself nowadays in the form of supermarket romance novels, Westerns, and fantasies such as *The Lord of the Rings* and *Star Wars*. Whether or not we accept 'romance' as the preferred descriptor, the romance tradition undeniably furnished Shakespeare with much of his narrative material and influenced the tone of his final theatrical efforts.

Romance is sometimes considered a little too popular. Late in his career Shakespeare's longer-lived contemporary Ben Jonson defended the failure of one of his own comedies by blaming the public for preferring 'No doubt some mouldy tale, | Like *Pericles*' ('Ode to Himself', ll. 21–2). In his conversations with William Drummond he derided Shakespeare for endowing Bohemia with a sea coast in *The Winter's Tale*, a detail the playwright took from *Pandosto*, and when Jonson complained, in the Induction to *Bartholomew Fair* (1614), about playwrights 'that beget *Tales*, *Tempests*, and such like *Drolleries*', he was apparently scoffing at two of Shakespeare's late plays, mocking the fantastic dimension that makes them distinctive. All these complaints derive from Jonson's contempt for the popularity and conventionality – what he considered the vulgarity – of dramatic romance, and they represent a moral objection. He seems to have felt that Shakespeare was squandering his talent by peddling entertaining fantasies; he believed that fiction ought to be instructive, ought to expose the follies and errors of the society for which it was written by showing 'an image of the times', ought to employ 'deeds and language such as men do use' (Prologue to *Every Man in His Humour*; composed *c.* 1604–16). To such a neoclassical sensibility, the moral function of drama depended on a credible representation of familiar experience, an illusion of the world in which spectators could recognize themselves and their own culture. Thus Jonson set *Epicoene, or the Silent Woman* and *The Alchemist* in the very London neighbourhoods through which the audience had travelled to the theatre.

Significantly, these two comedies were written in 1609
and 1610, at just the moment when Shakespeare was
turning away from dramatic realism and adopting a more
liberal approach to theatrical illusion.

In his criticism of Shakespeare's later plays, Jonson
may be said to have fallen into a Shakespearian trap: *The
Winter's Tale*, like much romance fiction, slyly conceals
its moral or intellectual ambitions. A 'winter's tale' to
Shakespeare's audience suggested a yarn or trifle, a
dubious story appealing particularly to children or other
credulous folk, something not to be taken seriously. The
play is a fantasy, an improbable fiction in which the
unlikely narrative material makes the suspension of dis-
belief especially challenging, and this incredibility is
characteristic of romance. Shakespeare constructs an
illusory realm while pointedly reminding the viewer of
its unreality, its distance from the familiar world. Herein
lies the paradox of the most sophisticated romances, of
which *The Winter's Tale* is certainly one: the pleasures
of romance are challenged throughout by a powerful
strain of anti-romance, the implication that such pleasures
are quixotic and that it is naive to credit foolish fancies.

FROM TRAGIC TO COMIC

In taking up the new form Shakespeare found a vehicle
for his revised understanding of the relation between
stage and world. This reorientation gives *The Winter's
Tale* and the other late plays their extraordinary self-
consciousness, a frank theatricality that can puzzle
someone coming to them for the first time. Shakespeare's
earlier work is predominantly 'representational', in that
the audience is invited to immerse itself in the fiction,

pretending (within the limits of the early modern theatrical space) that the stage faithfully represents the material world and that the characters are 'real'. The emotional effects of *Much Ado About Nothing* or *Othello* derive from such identification or absorption. The playwright is absent. In the late plays, however, he seems practically to be a presence at the side of the stage, advertising his audacity, encouraging the spectator to relish the theatricality of the show, and underscoring improbabilities rather than disguising them. Thus these late dramas are said to be 'presentational', a term denoting their playful self-consciousness. A famous instance of the presentational style is the final scene of *Cymbeline*, in which several characters' real identities are disclosed one after another, and the audience, already aware of the truth, delights in the process of revelation. Another is found in *The Tempest*, as Prospero confides to the audience his marital plans for Miranda and Ferdinand. Throughout this phase Shakespeare's fresh commitment to theatricality appears in his blatant manipulation of time and space, the frequent lack of motivation discernible in character, the intervention of supernatural forces, the abundance of asides and choruses, and the new freedom with which he handles the dramatic verse.

The sequence of episodes that reverses the direction of *The Winter's Tale* at its mid-point is typical of Shakespeare's histrionic bravura in these tragicomedies. The shift is so abrupt as to be almost risible; in fact, for many years it was considered a fault, as if the playwright couldn't be bothered to conceal the joints in his structure. Although the shape of the play resembles the form of the word 'tragi-comedy', its construction is strikingly original. In Beaumont and Fletcher's prototypical tragi-comedies, *A King and No King* and *Philaster*, the clever

resolution that averts catastrophe is withheld from the
audience until the final moments, although well-placed
clues generate expectations of a positive outcome.
Cymbeline also delays most of its resolution until the end,
even though the audience knows from the start that
Innogen is guiltless and learns in the third act that the
two Welsh boys are the sons of the King and brothers
of the heroine. At early performances of *The Winter's
Tale* those spectators acquainted with Greene's *Pandosto*
would have expected a dark ending: although the marriage
of the two kings' children helps to ameliorate the bleak-
ness of the story, the death of the Queen and especially
Pandosto's suicide, sprung on the reader in the last
sentence of the novella, make for a disturbing conclusion.
But Shakespeare, in adapting the story for the stage,
reverses direction in Act III. The change of scene, the
new story of young love, the mischief of Autolycus with
the rustics, the singing and dancing at the country festival
– all these features refresh and reorient the audience after
the bleak intensity of the first half. The festive tone,
combined with the length of the sheep-shearing, helps
to put the tragic events of the play into a larger perspective. Some humour leavens the first half, particularly
the comically authoritative manner of Paulina, while
the second half is not without potential peril, notably
Polixenes' threats against Florizel and Perdita. But even
the deliberate contrasts in mood within the larger two-
part structure underscore the unreality, the theatrical
knowingness of the drama.

The pivot on which the mood of the play turns and
to which the dramatist delights in calling attention is made
up of three contiguous episodes at the end of Act III and
beginning of Act IV. First Antigonus arrives on the coast
of Bohemia, describes a dream in which Hermione has

appeared to him, places the royal infant on the ground, and exits the stage – and indeed the world – '*pursued by a bear*'. The bear was perhaps not as surprising to the Jacobean spectator as it is to the modern. *Mucedorus*, an exceedingly popular Elizabethan play of unknown authorship, revived frequently between *c*. 1590 and 1610, contains one. Nevertheless, the device is an especially piquant example of the mature Shakespeare's playful attitude towards the stage. Theatre history does not tell us whether the King's Men employed a live bear or a man in a bear's suit to chase Antigonus and devour him offstage. While playing at the Globe, they might have obtained a live animal from the bear-baiting arena nearby on the Bankside. Whether such an arrangement would have been possible at Blackfriars is less certain, although the Banqueting House at court was sometimes used as an arena for both plays and bear-baiting, and pet bears were kept in London at the time (one of the most famous, mentioned enthusiastically by a character in *The Merry Wives of Windsor*, was named Sackerson). It seems more plausible, however, that the company used an actor dressed as a bear, an exercise in counterfeiting consistent with the other special effects. The audience would probably have reacted with horror on first seeing the creature and then with relief and laughter upon recognizing the trick, thus experiencing physically the play's shift from the tragic to the comic mode.

Antigonus' notorious departure is followed immediately by two entrances that constitute the second phase of the turn. The old Shepherd, entering with complaints about teenagers frightening his flock, comes upon the bundle containing the child, while his son arrives to describe the sinking of the ship and the dismemberment of Antigonus. Shakespeare takes pains, in the summary words of the old Shepherd, to juxtapose and link such opposites as birth and death, youth and age, joy and sorrow: 'Heavy matters, heavy matters! But look thee here, boy. Now bless thyself: thou met'st with things dying, I with things new-born' (III.3.108–10). As the two rustics depart with the foundling, Time the Chorus enters to announce and explain the jump forward of sixteen years. Justification of his authority to manipulate the dramatic time-scheme gives way to a clunky summary of the plot: 'remember well, | I mentioned a son o'th'King's, which Florizel | I now name to you' (IV.1.21–3). Such a short cut is normally associated with artistic ineptitude or indolence, the equivalent of an unexpected voice-over in a film. But it is typical of the casual, knowing approach characteristic of the mature Shakespeare.

Such apparent carelessness provides a context for other problematic cases of dramatic surprise. Leontes' jealousy, for example, is often unsettling to readers and spectators because it appears to be unmotivated. Some scholars, troubled by the implausibility of the King's behaviour, have searched for clues to his suspicion in the hundred lines that precede his first passionate soliloquy, but the straws at which they grasp seem extremely insubstantial: as has been frequently pointed out, had Shakespeare wanted to worry the audience about infidelity between Hermione and Polixenes he might have done so clearly. But there is no evidence of adultery, only Leontes' fantasy of it. That this is how Shakespeare intended the audience to understand the jealousy, as unmotivated and sudden, is suggested by his earlier jealousy narratives and his adaptation of his source. In both *Much Ado About Nothing* and *Othello*, although jealousy emerges quickly and is acted upon almost immediately, the man who imagines himself aggrieved is given 'reasons', false though they be, to suspect the woman: Don John deceives Claudio just as Iago does Othello, and both victims are given 'proofs' – a witnessed tryst, a handkerchief – to validate their suppositions. The lack of such verbal and material evidence in *The Winter's Tale* is consistent with Shakespeare's transformation of his immediate source.

In Greene's fiction, Pandosto (Leontes' counterpart) develops a suspicion which intensifies over time: 'These and suchlike doubtful thoughts a long time smothering in his stomach began at last to kindle in his mind a secret mistrust which, increased by suspicion, grew at last to a flaming jealousy that so tormented him as he could take no rest. He then began to measure all their actions . . .' Not only does Shakespeare withhold any motive or development and deprive Leontes of allies and sympathizers, but he also invites the audience to deplore and to scoff at the King's infected mind, chiefly with the intervention of Paulina in the second act. Disapproval, however, stops short of contempt. Despite the King's arrogance, misogyny, stubbornness and cruelty, few directors prompt the audience to abandon him emotionally. Perhaps this is one benefit of the unmotivated jealousy: to some extent Leontes seems as much a victim as those he victimizes, the onslaught of jealousy like a sudden illness or stroke of lightning, devastating but inescapable and undeserved.

The statue scene, the 'resurrection' of Hermione, is the last and most thrilling of the play's surprises. Here it is instructive to compare the ending with those of two similar plays, *Pericles* and *Cymbeline*, because the differences in structure indicate that Shakespeare was experimenting with various ways of concluding the same kind of story. (As I have indicated, the chronological priority of *Cymbeline* and *The Winter's Tale* is uncertain, but *Pericles* is almost surely earlier than either.) The last act of *Pericles* splits into two joyous finales, the first being the King's reunion with his daughter whom he believed dead, and the second the reunion with Thaisa, wife and mother, also supposed dead. The end of *Cymbeline* is notoriously diffuse, with serial revelations, misunderstandings, clarifications, reversals and surprises. The last scene of *The Winter's Tale*, by contrast, is deliberately concentrated: the stage is dominated by, and the spectators on- and offstage focus their attention entirely upon, the statue of Hermione. Shakespeare's treatment of the statue signifies an original approach to the problem of the ending, implying an authorial desire to experiment with the related and complementary effects of irony and surprise.

Pericles presents two reunions in the last act, but the first, between Pericles and his daughter, is so movingly shaped that the second, between husband and wife and daughter, seems anticlimactic. That miscalculation, perhaps, accounts for the brilliant originality of the penultimate scene in *The Winter's Tale* two or three years later. In this long prose interlude three Gentlemen and Autolycus describe a recognition scene between Leontes and his daughter, not to mention the reconciliations of Leontes and Polixenes, Leontes and Camillo, and Polixenes and his son. The unexpected summary, delivered by nobodies, may at first seem disappointing, in that we have been led to hope for this celebratory gathering and now appear to have been deprived of it. Indeed Shakespeare seems deliberately to have stimulated disappointment. The narrators exaggeratedly lament the inadequacy of their efforts to communicate the satisfactions of the event: the meeting of the two kings was 'a sight which was to be seen, cannot be spoken of' (V.2.41–2), the meeting of father and daughter an 'encounter, which lames report to follow it and undoes description to do it' (55–6). By thus suppressing the expected conclusion, Shakespeare contrives to magnify the surprise of the statue scene. Hermione's revival generates immense theatrical force because we do not anticipate it. Rarely does Shakespeare withhold such vital information from his audience, usually preferring the ironic satisfactions that come with knowledge. Here he does toss out a couple of clues, notably Paulina's insistence that Leontes' new queen, should there be one, must equal Hermione in beauty, but 'That | Shall be when your first queen's again in breath; | Never till then' (V.1.82–4). Even with such hints, however, the first-time spectator is not prepared for the 'wonder' that the statue scene evokes in the theatre.

The emotional potency of the conclusion owes much to the mystery surrounding it. Is the statue that comes to life not a statue at all? Is Hermione merely standing in an immobile pose, pretending to be petrified? Has she, in cahoots with Paulina, hidden herself for sixteen years, emerging to greet her lost daughter? On these questions the play is dumb. 'I . . . have preserved | Myself to see the issue' (V.3.125–8), the Queen declares, suggesting that her 'death' was a hoax and the 'revival' a staged performance. One of the courtiers reports having noticed that Paulina 'hath privately, twice or thrice a day, ever since the death of Hermione, visited that removed house' (V.2.103–5), as if she were hiding something. And yet Paulina's announcement at the end of the trial scene had been unambiguous: 'I say she's dead; I'll swear't' (III.2.201). Although she disavows 'wicked powers' (V.3.91), beneficent gods appear to be supervising and perhaps intervening in mortal affairs.

This is a play in which Apollo's oracle answers a human query with a gnomic prediction that comes true, in which Time is personified as a character, in which the son and daughter of estranged childhood friends from distant shores meet and marry. We have had no trouble accepting these improbabilities; the coming to life of a statue is hardly more incredible. As Dr Johnson, in the Preface to his edition of the plays, said about the process of theatrical perception generally, 'Surely he that imagines this may imagine more.' Ultimately, of course, whatever an audience concludes, the 'statue' is in fact a woman pretending to be a statue – and in 1611, a boy pretending to be a woman pretending to be a statue. Still, the equivocations of the episode reflect Shakespeare's deliberate confounding of art and reality: we have difficulty deciding whether what we see is a statue or a woman pretending to be a statue for the same reasons we have difficulty distinguishing between the world of the stage and the stage of the world. In the playhouse, nothing is certain.

'YOU SPEAK A LANGUAGE THAT I UNDERSTAND NOT'

Shakespeare's new attitude towards the stage and its components affects not only what we see but also what we hear. By this point in his career the playwright had modified his poetic style so thoroughly that the poetry of *The Winter's Tale*, like that of the other late works, is uncommonly challenging. Actors frequently puzzle over how to convey the sense of some of their speeches, particularly given the abundance of metrically irregular and syntactically tangled lines; readers, enjoying the leisure to stop and contemplate an especially clotted sentence, have difficulty paraphrasing what a character has said, although they have a general idea of the meaning; even editors admit to being baffled by the literal sense of certain passages. The technical factors that create such a complicated style represent a further development of poetic tendencies that Shakespeare had been experimenting with in the late tragedies, especially tactics such as omission and repetition. But the metamorphosis in his handling of blank verse at the end of his career is also partly attributable to his shift in theatrical perspective. Listening to *The Winter's Tale* or *Cymbeline* requires patience, mental persistence and faith that semantic clarity will eventually be forthcoming. The distance from which the spectator observes the tragicomic action corresponds to the position the listener occupies in relation to the spoken language.

The irregular and often knotty syntax derives from a distinctive combination of inclusion and omission. Shakespeare's most obvious trait is his penchant for ellipsis, for skipping over whatever verbal material he can. He discards vowels and elides consonants into a single sound ('of the' becomes 'o'th'), omits subjects and pronouns, especially relative pronouns, dispenses with participles and verbs, drops conjunctions, and eliminates as many elements as he can, as a few examples will indicate.

But once before I spoke to th'purpose? When?
Nay, let me have't; I long. (I.2.100–101)

We are yours i'th'garden. Shall's attend you there?
    (I.2.178)

                    Not noted, is't,
But of the finer natures? (I.2.225–6)

> Nor was't much
> Thou wouldst have poisoned good Camillo's honour
> To have him kill a king – poor trespasses,
> More monstrous standing by . . . (III.2.185–8)

The listener is expected to fill in the gaps, to supply the missing words or phrases, and then to confront even more demanding clauses and sentences. Amid these omissions the alert auditor perceives the complementary tactic of inclusion, even of extreme repetition. 'Too hot, too hot!' begins Leontes' first soliloquy (I.2.108), and not only he but everyone else insistently repeats words and phrases.

Even as Shakespeare eliminates syllables, words and longer elements, he also protracts the length of sentences and clauses, and these longer sentences are extremely concentrated, as if he wishes to pack as much as possible into his speakers' lines. Conclusions based on punctuation can be misleading because we punctuate more consistently than they did in the early seventeenth century, so that any modern edition will be more thoroughly pointed than the version in the Folio. But in both modern and early editions the verse lines in *The Winter's Tale* and the surrounding plays seem very heavily punctuated: commas, dashes and semicolons make lines choppy and irregular; numerous semantic intrusions retard momentum; a sentence will start in one direction, stop suddenly, then reverse itself. Many of the interpolated phrases are parenthetical, and while we know that Ralph Crane, the scribe who copied *The Winter's Tale* for its publication in the first Folio, apparently had a special affection for parentheses, still many sentences seem to demand them.

The poetic rhythms, like the syntax, are highly irregular, owing to the poet's exceptionally liberal approach towards the blank-verse pattern. In other words, perfectly regular lines of blank verse, such as Paulina's

Thĕ kéepĕr óf thĕ prísŏn, cáll tŏ hím. (II.2.1)

are much less frequent than in most of Shakespeare's earlier work. The iambic pentameter is maintained, but only barely. Various forms of irregularity contribute to the complex sound palette.

Trochees:

Skúlkĭng in corners? (I.2.289)

Spondees:

Hóurs mínŭtes? Nóon mídnĭght? (I.2.290)

Unexpected caesurae (pauses):

                                  Lower messes
Perchance are to this business púrblĭnd? //Sáy. (I.2.227–8)

Reversed feet:

Hĭs cúpbéarĕr – whom I from meaner form (I.2.313)

Extra syllables:

Whăt cáse stănd Í ĭn? Í mŭst bé thĕ póisŏnĕr (I.2.352)

Weak line endings:

> Ĭ méan thŏu shált – wĕ'll bár thĕe fróm sŭccéssiŏn;
>   (IV.4.426)

Instances from almost every character's speeches might be cited, all contributing to the impression that the rhythmic order with which Shakespeare's audience had become aurally comfortable is threatened repeatedly by subversion and disorder. Some of these poetic characteristics are audible in the late tragedies, especially *Coriolanus* and *Antony and Cleopatra*, and to a lesser extent *King Lear* and *Macbeth*, but by the time *The Winter's Tale* was written the familiar rhythmic foundation is under threat.

It is tempting to conclude simply that the spasmodic language represents the derangement of Leontes' mind.

> Gone already!
> Inch-thick, knee deep, o'er head and ears a forked one!
> Go play, boy, play: thy mother plays, and I
> Play too – but so disgraced a part, whose issue
> Will hiss me to my grave. Contempt and clamour
> Will be my knell. Go play, boy, play. (I.2.185–90)

But such irregular, rhythmically complex passages occur throughout *The Winter's Tale* and the other late works, even in passages not informed by madness.

> Good queen, my lord, good queen, I say good queen;
> And would by combat make her good, so were I
> A man, the worst about you. (II.3.59–61)

Such frequent inversions, hypermetrical lines and conflicts between the sense of the sentence and the requirements of the poetry are typical of the late verse. So unusual and irregular is it that the ageing playwright is sometimes accused of having been nodding, or weary, or careless, or at least unwilling to revise. But the style is so consistently challenging that its difficulty must represent a deliberate choice, not indolence or fatigue. It is significant that those earlier critics who misunderstood the playfulness of the late verse are some of the same ones who complained about these plays' slapdash construction.

WAYS OF READING

The Winter's Tale has generated a wide range of response and evaluation over the past four centuries. Simon Forman, returning from the Globe in May of 1611, seems to have been taken especially with Autolycus, devoting much of his written recollection to the amusing con-games of 'the rogue'. His account of the plot mostly corresponds to the text we have, but he fails to mention the statue scene, which modern audiences find by far the most memorable in the play. Perhaps he went home before the show was over. For some two hundred years after Shakespeare's death *The Winter's Tale* was not much admired: the eighteenth-century poet and editor of Shakespeare, Alexander Pope, doubted that Shakespeare had written very much of it, and William Warburton, in his 1747 edition of the plays, dismissed it as 'a monstrous composition'. Nineteenth-century Romanticism found much to admire in *The Winter's Tale* and the other late plays, reading them as allegories of the author's personal struggle (although the nature of the conflict was never quite clear), and by the middle of the twentieth century

the critic G. Wilson Knight was able to declare confi-
dently that in certain respects Shakespeare produced
'nothing greater' (*The Crown of Life*). More recent critics
have resisted the themes of reconciliation and emphasized
instead Leontes' abuse of his patriarchal role and the crisis
of political authority ('*the King shall live without an heir*').
The multidimensional quality of the play, exceptionally
various even for Shakespeare, has made it hospitable to
many conflicting interpretations.

One persistent point of interest has been the potential
topicality of *The Winter's Tale*. Many readers have sensed
a reflection of the Jacobean political scene, but the potential correspondences are so oblique that sometimes they
are difficult to see at all, or at least to visualize as a coherent
picture. This interpretation rests on the identification of
Leontes with King James: the play is dominated by a king
who holds a very high opinion of his own opinions, who
fathers a son and a daughter, whose son dies in youth,
who makes a politically advantageous marriage for his
daughter, and who silences his wife. Loosely interpreted,
this might be a description of the Scottish King. By 1611
English disappointment with James's rule had begun to
manifest itself, especially in Parliament, and in the face
of this sentiment the King redoubled his efforts to justify
his absolutism. He wrote and spoke loftily about the
paternal role of the monarch, insisting that the tyranny
with which he was sometimes implicitly charged was in
fact his proper, absolute authority. Leontes is conscious
of similar complaints and wishes to 'be cleared | Of being
tyrannous' (III.2.4–5).

The exchanges between Leontes and Mamillius in the
second scene establish concretely a pattern of father–son
relationships that might carry political relevance: just
as, in Archidamus' words to Camillo, 'You have an

unspeakable comfort of your young prince Mamillius'
(I.i.33–4), so the English felt exceptional fondness for
Prince Henry. Neither boy survives. Prince Henry did
not die until 1612, after the play was performed both
publicly and at court. Putting aside Shakespearian clair-
voyance, coincidence seems the most plausible explanation for the parallel. (It is admittedly unlikely, although
not impossible, that Mamillius' death was added after the
death of Prince Henry in an authorial or even non-
authorial revision, and that this is the version printed in
the Folio; such an altered text might have been prepared
for performances surrounding the wedding of Princess
Elizabeth in 1612–13, a political marriage that was some
consolation for the loss of the royal heir.) More specific
correspondences have been proposed, some of them
over-ingenious, but the resemblance between the royal
households of Sicilia and Great Britain remains tanta-
lizing if not entirely satisfying. It seems as if there ought
to be parallels: Shakespeare was the principal dramatist
of the King's Men, nominally the most important of royal
entertainers. Perhaps this inexactitude itself is the answer
to the problem – that the King liked looking at pictures
better than he liked looking in mirrors, and Shakespeare
knew it. But most attempts to read *The Winter's Tale* in
political terms founder as soon as it is staged.

In the theatre the play seems concerned above all with
what used to be called 'universal themes' – good and
evil, families, forgiveness, second chances, the effects of
time (for good and ill), the products of the human imagination (for good and ill), and the magic of the stage. Of
course many of Shakespeare's plays address such topics,
but the dramatist's wider perspective and the professional reorientation apparent in the movement away from
tragedy inflect them with new significance. Nineteenth-

and early-twentieth-century readers identified these themes and interpreted them as proof of a spiritual breakthrough, reading the tragicomic resolutions with a minimum of irony and imputing to the mature artist a transcendental serenity. The phrase that most aptly captures that view is Edward Dowden's description of Shakespeare 'on the heights' (*Shakespere* (1877)). The analysis that follows offers a more practical assessment of those themes, one that credits the centrality of the theatre in that altered vision.

More than any of the other late works, even *The Tempest*, *The Winter's Tale* exhibits the vital role of artifice in the new Shakespearian perspective. In addressing the topic of art directly, the dramatist enters upon a subject of vital interest to early modern Europe: the complex relation of art to nature. The Warwickshire playwright's idealization of nature quickly became a commonplace in the critical tradition: his most celebrated readers over the course of two centuries, notably Ben Jonson, John Milton and Samuel Johnson, recognized and commented on the dominance of that theme. But even those extraordinary readers seem to have undervalued the playwright's conception of art, a misreading perhaps attributable to their own unparalleled learning. Throughout the canon nature is both beneficent and corruptible; art is both sinister and creative. But Shakespeare's redefinition of the problem in this late phase is so sophisticated and subtle that the terms become inextricable from each other. A helpful way of thinking about this intricate relation is to frame it within the larger topic of creativity, one that receives its most forthright expression in the 'flower debate' in Act IV of *The Winter's Tale*.

This exchange between shepherdess (Perdita dressed as a goddess) and king (Polixenes dressed as a wayfarer) adds nothing to the plot: it is one of those moments that literary critics prize and theatre directors often cut. As Perdita welcomes the strangers, she offers them appropriate flowers, and in the course of the courteous exchange she declares her distaste for hybrid plants, 'Which some call Nature's bastards', disdaining them on the grounds that they are unnatural: 'I have heard it said | There is an art which in their piedness shares | With great creating Nature' (IV.4.83, 86–8). Polixenes, taking the contrary position, attributes the grafting of flowers to the permission of nature: 'Nature is made better by no mean | But Nature makes that mean' (IV.4.89–90). He further extols the capacity of art to improve nature, arguing that to 'marry' products of different species improves both the strength and beauty of the purely natural flower:

> You see, sweet maid, we marry
> A gentler scion to the wildest stock,
> And make conceive a bark of baser kind
> By bud of nobler race. This is an art
> Which does mend Nature – change it, rather – but
> The art itself is Nature. (IV.4.92–7)

Polixenes' argument seems indisputable, but while Perdita nominally accepts his logic, she stubbornly retains her aversion to cross-breeding.

The poles of this disagreement are compromised by its context, however, especially by each debater's position on a more immediate kind of marriage. Polixenes, who has endorsed the floral union of low ('bark of baser kind') and high ('bud of nobler race') refuses to permit his high-born son to wed a shepherdess. Contrariwise, Perdita's opposition to such grafting has not prevented her from agreeing, with some misgivings, to marry Prince Florizel. The theme is troubled even further by our awareness that the proposed marriage of Florizel and Perdita is in fact not a crossing of classes, that she is herself a princess. The intricacy and length of the debate help to blur the line between the natural and the artificial.

As soon as Leontes learns of the deaths of Mamillius and Hermione, he awakens to the terrible consequences of his suspicion and, stricken with guilt, commits himself to a life of penance and 'shame perpetual. Once a day I'll visit | The chapel where they lie, and tears shed there | Shall be my recreation' (III.2.236–8). The primary meaning is clear: the penitent declares that the painful consciousness of his crime will serve him as play, that he will take no pleasure except in weeping over the loss of his family and his responsibility for it. But the connotations of the final noun are almost infinitely suggestive. The contrition signified by tears becomes an instrument of re-creation, a means of reconstituting the self. Thus the activity of play, albeit here of a dolorous kind, is identified with health, prayer, renovation and creativity. The stage on which his actors play becomes for Shakespeare explicitly a place of creation. It has always been so, of course, but in this late phase he insists on the therapeutic value of make-believe. The artistic imagination converts the theatrical platform into a playground where the disappointments of the mortal world can at least for a time be remedied.

From the beginning to the end of *The Winter's Tale*, Shakespeare explores the equivocal power of the imagination, its capacity to create and destroy. Leontes' deluded brain produces from nowhere 'Fancies too weak for boys, too green and idle | For girls of nine' (III.2.179–80). His mind polluted with filthy physical images of female

sexuality, he envisages within a few lines a man whose wife
'has been sluiced in's absence, | And his pond fished by
his next neighbour, by | Sir Smile, his neighbour'
(I.2.194–6); 'gates, and those gates opened' (I.2.197); 'No
barricado for a belly' (I.2.204); a 'flax-wench that puts to
| Before her troth-plight' (I.2.277–8). Mamillius, more
innocently, imagines monsters also, the 'sprites and goblins'
with which he hopes to frighten the court ladies in his 'sad
tale . . . for winter' (II.1.25–6). Other forms of fantasy
manifest themselves briefly, such as Antigonus' dream of
a ghostly angelic Hermione (III.3.18–38), or the old
Shepherd's report that 'It was told me I should be rich by
the fairies' (III.3.113–14). Camillo's scheme for getting
Florizel, Perdita, Polixenes and himself back to Sicilia arises
from his imaginative wish for a happy ending – 'Methinks
I see | Leontes opening his free arms and weeping | His
welcomes forth' (IV.4.544–6) – and the resulting inven-
tion is a 'scene' that Florizel and Perdita will 'play',
costumed appropriately and directed by Camillo.

The wily Autolycus – conman, musician, teller of tall
tales, huckster, former servant of the Prince, tease, thief
– introduces the creativity of the petty criminal to the
Bohemian scenes. He enters the play singing, presents
himself as the victim of a robbery in order to pick the
Clown's pocket, sells knick-knacks and ballads to the
country folk (again as a screen for stealing their purses),
and delights in toying with the credulity of the old
Shepherd and his son. Pretending to intimate knowledge
of court news, he frightens the two country fellows with
a fantastic account of how they will be punished for
encouraging the relationship of Perdita and Florizel:

CLOWN Has the old man e'er a son, sir, do you hear, an't like
     you, sir?

AUTOLYCUS He has a son: who shall be flayed alive; then,
  'nointed over with honey, set on the head of a wasp's nest;
  then stand till he be three-quarters and a dram dead; then
  recovered again with aqua-vitae or some other hot infusion;
  then, raw as he is, and in the hottest day prognostication
  proclaims, shall he be set against a brick wall, the sun looking
  with a southward eye upon him, where he is to behold
  him with flies blown to death. But what talk we of these
  traitorly rascals . . . ? (IV.4.777–88)

Such delight in images and stories represents the lighter
side of fantasy: the tall tales by means of which Autolycus
enriches and amuses himself make him a stand-in for the
playwright, who does the same with his audience.

Creativity is also identified with women. Perdita
compares grafted flowers to painted women, recalling
the suspicion of cosmetics Shakespeare expresses most
pointedly in *Hamlet*. By this point, however, his view of
make-up or ornament has changed, as has his representation of women and female sexuality, and in both cases
the altered view is associated with his revised conception
of the theatre. In the late tragedies, female sexuality
seems mostly predatory and fearsome. In *King Lear*, for
example, Goneril and Regan aggressively clamour for
power and for the sexual services of Edmund, now Duke
of Gloucester, a competition that culminates in poisoning
and suicide. The sexual air that attends Lady Macbeth is
ominous: at her first appearance she implores infernal
powers to suppress her humane sensitivity and especially
her femininity ('unsex me here . . .'; I.5.40–48). In *Timon
of Athens* two whores who briefly visit the debased hero
are the only female characters, except for the group of
Amazons – a relevant detail – represented in a masque.
In *Coriolanus* the hero's wife, the dutiful and fruitful

Virgilia, speaks little and is dominated by Volumnia, the gorgon of a mother who famously prefers Hector's bloody forehead to Hecuba's milky breasts (I.3.41–4). In fact, virtuous, healthy females are in peril throughout the tragedies, from Lavinia in *Titus Andronicus* to Brutus' Portia, Ophelia, Desdemona, Cordelia and Lady Macduff.

Many critics who have documented this sense of loathing have also noted that something modified Shakespeare's representation of women at about the time he wrote *Antony and Cleopatra* and *Pericles*. According to C. L. Barber and Richard Wheeler, in their book *The Whole Journey*, for example, the 'fear of femininity' that marks the major tragedies is transformed in the romances into the recovery of a 'benign relationship to feminine presences, accomplished by going through an experience of separation and loss that culminates in reunion'. It may be that the process of staging the story of Antony from Plutarch's *Lives* led to a shift in sympathy. Plutarch presents Cleopatra as the Romans (and, for the most part, their English descendants) saw her: sexually promiscuous, unfaithful, frivolous, inconstant, deceptive – all the attributes the misogynist tradition had assigned to women. Shakespeare's Egyptian queen may be guilty of these traits, but she is also intelligent, eloquent, courageous, and ultimately irresistible. Her characterization is nuanced, and much more positive than Plutarch's image. Significantly, the vociferous opponents of the stage in early modern London attacked theatrical representation for being lascivious, deceptive, frivolous, dishonest – the very faults often attributed to Cleopatra and to strong women in general. It appears that in creating the theatrical persona Shakespeare found himself attracted to Cleopatra and found himself in love once again with the properties of the theatre.

Thus the representation of women changes as Shakespeare moves into his final phase. Historically, romance writers, caught up in the sweep of narrative, tend to use broad strokes in depicting character, and to some degree this technique is true of Shakespeare also: no woman in the romances is as subtly represented as Lady Macbeth or Cleopatra, for example. Still, he extends the possibilities for female action beyond the roles of villainess and victim. The Bawd in *Pericles* and the wicked women in both *Pericles* and *Cymbeline* swagger through their scenes trying to dominate and destroy, but their efforts are comically ineffective, neutralized by the integrity of their intended victims and by the intervention of Providence. In *Pericles* the innocent Marina refuses to be compromised. In *The Winter's Tale* strength and creativity align the three principal women with 'great creating Nature', an identification suggested in Hermione's pregnancy and Perdita's masquerade as Flora in the country festival. Hermione endures Leontes' first accusations with dignity and moral authority, asserting her innocence simply ('You, my lord, | Do but mistake', II.1.80–81), expressing concern for her disturbed husband's feelings ('How will this grieve you', II.1.96), and calmly instructing her gentlewomen not to weep. Publicly arraigned soon after her lying-in, she maintains that dignity by refusing to participate in a show trial:

> Since what I am to say must be but that
> Which contradicts my accusation, and
> The testimony on my part no other
> But what comes from myself, it shall scarce boot me
> To say 'Not guilty' . . . (III.2.21–5)

The innocent Queen professes faith in the forces of time

and Providence to vindicate her and to allow her husband to repent his crime.

Paulina warrants the same connection with natural forces. On her first appearance, entering the prison to rescue the Queen's newborn daughter, she justifies removing the baby on the grounds that 'This child was prisoner to the womb, and is | By law and process of great Nature thence | Freed and enfranchised' (II.2.59–61). This authoritative, eloquent answer is typical: Shakespeare has appropriated the figure of the loquacious female from the misogynist tradition, enlisting her tongue in the service of justice. For example, when Paulina bursts into the royal presence carrying the infant, Leontes summons a series of clichés about shrewish women and henpecked husbands, but the theatrical effect of his insults is entirely ironic, in that he himself is the proper object of censure and the spectator is positioned squarely on her side. At the end of the trial, just after the death of Mamillius and the removal of Hermione, Paulina's tirade against Leontes provides a satisfying emotional release for the audience. Implicit in all her actions and words is a sense of her creativity and moral confidence. In the first scene of the last act, our first sight of Leontes after the passage of sixteen years, Paulina's hectoring of the King by reminding him of his crime helps to prepare for and amplify the joy of the ending. There she acts as a kind of priestess, a benevolent figure with the supernatural ability to animate the replica of Hermione, and thus the conventional image of the witch is upended. Paulina, who has no equivalent in the source, shares a name with the New Testament apostle whose constant theme is the need for faith, what Paul calls 'the substance of things hoped for, the evidence of things not seen' (Hebrews 11:1).

The joy of the reunited family is mitigated by the loss of sixteen years: relatively speaking, Leontes and Hermione are old people in the final scene, Paulina and Camillo even older. The romances quickly disclose that the ageing Shakespeare has become obsessed with the subject of time – its deceptiveness, its inevitability, its constructive powers and negative effects. Repeatedly the events of the drama evoke both the depredations of time and its potential for deliverance, a concern theatrically personified in Time, the Chorus. Such abstractions are relatively rare in Shakespearian drama until the last years, when the nature of his narratives leads him to give visible form to a deity or manifestation of Providence – the goddess Diana in *Pericles*, Jupiter descending on an eagle near the end of *Cymbeline*, the goddesses who perform the masque in *The Tempest*, Queen Katherine and her deathbed vision of angels in *Henry VIII* (known in its own time as *All is True*).

The Winter's Tale offers much discussion of time, beginning with the opening dialogue between Archidamus and Camillo. The two courtiers consider a proposed visit to Bohemia 'this coming summer', the development of the kings' friendship since childhood, and the appeal of the child-prince to the old folks. The opening line of the second scene is Polixenes' announcement of having been a guest in Sicilia for nine months, and he and Hermione converse reflectively about his boyhood days with Leontes. To the Renaissance audience time connoted mortality, the conditions of error and change associated with the Fall, and thus banter about the loss of innocence enters the conversation. The passage of sixteen years, in which Perdita is born and grows to young womanhood, is the dominant temporal fact in *The Winter's Tale*. Other dramatists staged plays with huge

temporal leaps only because such gaps are required by
the story, whereas Shakespeare seems to have chosen his
story *because* its temporal lapse afforded him thematic
advantage. And the source he chose is subtitled *The
Triumph of Time*.

Shakespeare repeatedly invites his audience, in thinking
about the passage of time, to consider the relative claims
of the old and new. A complex instance of this comparison occurs in Time's justification of the leap to Perdita's
young womanhood. Alluding to the ancient doctrine of
the dramatic unities, on which some English writers and
critics insisted, the Chorus reminds the listeners that he
can do as he likes with any rules at all, and certainly with
the rules of drama:

> . . . it is in my power
> To o'erthrow law, and in one self-born hour
> To plant and o'erwhelm custom. Let me pass
> The same I am ere ancient'st order was
> Or what is now received. I witness to
> The times that brought them in; so shall I do
> To th'freshest things now reigning, and make stale
> The glistering of this present, as my tale
> Now seems to it. (IV.1.7–15)

The Chorus takes the long view, cautioning about the
dangers of concentrating too thoroughly on the moment.
'[C]ustom', 'what is now received', 'th'freshest things
now reigning', 'this present' – all these categories are
temporal and therefore relative, impermanent. Implicitly
looking to the age to come, he declares that the latest
style, 'th'freshest things now reigning', will seem as
outmoded as this ridiculous, old-fashioned story seems
at this late date.

Time's remarks may also have subtly indicted members of the play's first audiences. At Blackfriars some of the spectators would have been socially prominent, even aristocratic, a few politically important, and many of them wealthy, with expensive jewellery and clothing. To this London audience the experience of watching an adult company performing in a hall theatre, at night, must have been a novel and socially exciting event. The court performances would have been even more prestigious. In London *circa* 1611, these theatrical patrons would have been among 'th'freshest things now reigning', indisputably fashionable and aware of their fashionable status. To many of them, *The Winter's Tale* must have seemed quaintly old-fashioned, based as it is on a book that people had been reading almost twenty-five years earlier. And furthering that impression of an outdated fiction, Shakespeare, like the anonymous author of the Elizabethan *Mucedorus*, amuses his audience with a bear. But the snickering audience, according to Time, would itself soon be the object of snickers.

So keen is Shakespeare to establish this temporal perspective that he raises it explicitly again, just before the arrival of the Bohemian party in Sicilia (V.1). When a Gentleman announces that the princess accompanying Florizel is 'the most peerless piece of earth, I think, | That e'er the sun shone bright on', Paulina objects on behalf of the dead Queen, and her manner of doing so expands the temporal context:

> O Hermione,
> As every present time doth boast itself
> Above a better gone, so must thy grave
> Give way to what's seen now. (V.1.94-5, 95-8)

In safeguarding Hermione's memory, Paulina comments sardonically on the perils of fashion. Although every generation mistakenly thinks itself more excellent than its predecessor, she insists, the late Queen's beauty is unmatched by the darling of the present.

The generational rivalry underlying such shifts of perspective is counterbalanced by the sense of renewal attendant upon the growth of the young. Time may carve wrinkles in Hermione's brow, but it also replaces her vanished younger self with her teenaged daughter. Sometimes Perdita in the last act is costumed just as her mother had been in the first, and occasionally a single actress will play both mother and daughter (with a double used in the final scene), as Judi Dench did in Trevor Nunn's 1969 production for the Royal Shakespeare Company. Both these devices emphasize time's bene- volence in affording the older generation consolation in the younger. Similarly, the young Bohemian prince stands in for little Mamillius, destroyed by Leontes' cruelty. Of course Florizel's presence in Sicilia at the end of the play, his role as son and son-in-law, is double-edged, reviving the emotional pain of Mamillius' death at the sametime that it offers, if not restitution, at least partial compen- sation. Each human generation is a part of the cycle of natural regeneration, and thus it is apt that Shakespeare invokes the myth of Proserpina and Ceres, the mother who laments the abduction of her daughter, and the return of spring to the suffering earth.

The pattern of familial reunion or reconstruction is yet another token of Shakespeare's shift from tragedy to romance. Whereas tragedy enforces the separation of parents and children – Lear and Cordelia, Macduff and his children, Desdemona and her father – romance reconciles them. In *Pericles* the reunion of Marina and her father is exceptionally moving because it unmistakably reverses the tragic paradigm, restoring to the suffering Pericles what his tragic counterparts wish for but cannot have. Romance also reconciles siblings, who in the tragedies and most of the histories consistently find themselves in opposition. Where Hamlet's uncle Claudius succeeds in murdering his brother, Leontes is unable to kill his 'brother' Polixenes. All the romances, in fact, owe much of their affective power – and in the community of the audience that power is very strong – to such generational consolidation. Time brings about such joy, but it is able to do so thanks to the magic of the theatre.

In order to submit to the magical events of *The Winter's Tale*, as Paulina puts it, 'It is required | You do awake your faith' (V.3.94–5). The need for belief is fundamental to Shakespeare's new emphasis on perspective and point of view. The verb 'believe' derives from Anglo-Saxon roots meaning 'to cherish or hold dear'; thus it is also historically related to the word 'love'. Leontes' suspicion of his wife, the engine that drives the main action, presents the negative side of belief: his giving credence to the product of his diseased imagination. The spectacular conclusion turns on this problem, pointedly so when Paulina declares that her restoration of Hermione defies logic: 'That she is living, | Were it but told you, should be hooted at | Like an old tale' (V.3.115–17). The apparent naivety of all the late plays, their resemblance to fairy tales, keeps the audience engaged with the problem of belief and with the capacity of the theatre to stimulate faith even in the sceptical.

Shakespeare diligently cultivates our confidence in superior knowledge: we pat ourselves on the back for knowing that Perdita is really a princess, that Antigonus is mistaken when he interprets his dream as evidence of Hermione's guilt and Apollo's wishes (III.3.40–45), that Autolycus is manipulating the bumpkins. Foolish credulity is the theme of the episode in which 'the pedlar' describes his merchandise for the country couples.

CLOWN What hast here? Ballads?

MOPSA Pray now, buy some. I love a ballad in print a-life, for then we are sure they are true.

AUTOLYCUS Here's one to a very doleful tune, how a usurer's wife was brought to bed of twenty money-bags at a burden, and how she longed to eat adders' heads and toads carbon-adoed.

MOPSA Is it true, think you?

AUTOLYCUS Very true, and but a month old.

DORCAS Bless me from marrying a usurer!

AUTOLYCUS Here's the midwife's name to't: one Mistress Taleporter, and five or six honest wives that were present. Why should I carry lies abroad? (IV.4.257–69)

Here the spectator smiles knowingly at the gullibility of the ignorant, relishing the trickster's talent and condescension. Yet by the end of the play the same sophisticated spectator will have assented to a story no less impossible than the fictions attested to by Mistress Taleporter. The trickery of the dramatist has something in common with the chicanery of Autolycus, but it is also capable of magic. Perhaps, too, it is related to what might be called divine trickery.

The mysterious events of the final scene depend heavily upon the language of Christianity, especially the vocabulary of forgiveness, redemption, resurrection and new life.

PAULINA   Music, awake her, strike!
   Music
  'Tis time: descend; be stone no more; approach;
  Strike all that look upon with marvel. Come,
  I'll fill your grave up. Stir; nay, come away.
  Bequeath to death your numbness, for from him
  Dear life redeems you. (V.3.98–103)

Accustomed to hearing the Bible read aloud weekly in church, Jacobean audiences would have recognized in Paulina's words the language of the New Testament, particularly the diction of St Paul. (Interestingly, the play's first known performance was in the same year in which the King James translation of the Bible was published.) Supporting the references to resurrection is the allusion to Christ's empty tomb, with its 'stone' rolled away. The noun 'marvel' is also charged with significance: not only does it denote 'a wonderful or astonishing thing' (*Oxford English Dictionary*), deriving etymologically from 'miracle', but also in the period it is interchangeable with 'marble', a telling detail in a scene with a stone statue. Further, viewing the effigy of Hermione with such language in one's ears recalls sacred images, those Catholic icons of saints which the Reformation famously prohibited. Such Christian associations, of which this passage is the most concentrated example, represent a discursive strain common to all the late plays. It is not merely that penance, forgiveness and grace are among the major ideas suggested by the action. What is more pertinent is that the language of the New Testament helps to situate the story in a larger cultural frame, further enlarging the perspective Shakespeare has sought to encourage.

The sense of grace that pervades the final act – some form of the word appears twenty-nine times in the play – may help to clarify the problematic position of Leontes at the conclusion. Certainly he has taken upon himself the burden of guilt and penance, and in the first scene of Act V, at the Sicilian court before the entrance of the Bohemians, the atmosphere of paralysis and loss is overwhelming. Some readers and playgoers have resented the return of Hermione to her husband, feeling that the magnitude of his crime disqualifies him for her restoration. Indeed, the final moments keep such doubts before us: as Hermione descends from her pedestal, she speaks to her daughter, not to her husband. But the stage picture sends a conflicting signal:

POLIXENES   She embraces him.
CAMILLO
     She hangs about his neck. (V.3.111–12)

Leontes gets more than he deserves, but that, of course, is the definition of grace.

The hybridity of *The Winter's Tale* appears also in its final moments, particularly their impact on the spectator. An audience is subject to an exceptionally complicated set of influences and feels an unusually wide range of emotions as Leontes and his reconstructed family sweep from the stage. The gravity of the action, the temporal and geographical scope represented, the juxtaposition of flippancy and reverence in the last two scenes, the wished-for reunions marred by memory of a dead child and the waste of sixteen years – such theatrical effects combine to move, to gratify and to disturb the audience. Paramount among these impressions and responses is the effect of Hermione's return. In the theatre this ending is almost always emotionally wrenching. The First Gentleman in the penultimate scene, describing the reunion of Leontes and Camillo, speaks of them as so intensely moved that 'They looked as they had heard of a world ransomed, or one destroyed' (V.2.14–15). The phrase also captures the audience's sense of wonder at the conclusion. And yet even as we are moved we might recall the play's mockery of those who fall for incredible tales.

Russ McDonald

The Play in Performance

The Winter's Tale contains one of Shakespeare's most intriguing and famous stage directions, '*Exit, pursued by a bear*'. The strange and tragic fate of Antigonus in the middle of Act III, scene 3 is just one of the play's many challenges to live performance. A production of *The Winter's Tale* needs to find ways of balancing the utterly non-naturalistic demands of its narrative with its depiction of the pain and joy of human relationships. In Act V Paulina asks the audience assembled to view Hermione's statue: 'It is required | You do awake your faith' (V.3.94–5). If this same artistic faith which inspires the play's characters can also inspire its readers and its audiences, then *The Winter's Tale* in performance can emerge as one of Shakespeare's most exuberant and resonantly moving achievements; his Sistine Chapel ceiling; his Choral Symphony. These comparisons evoke the highly wrought qualities of the play's tone and the need for any production of it to conjure up a believable yet fairy-tale world; a recognizable yet fantastic political and historical context.

To understand and imagine *The Winter's Tale* in performance is to explore thoroughly its intensely felt articulation of human jealousy (within the context of the dearest of friendships: Leontes, Hermione, Polixenes);

to represent its two totally different yet mutually supporting imaginary social worlds of Leontes' Sicilia and Polixenes' Bohemia; to portray its audacious inter-relationship between the tragic and the comic; to stage a personification of Time; to convince the audience that sixteen years have passed in the middle of the action; and to make convincing not only some of the most opaque and demanding verse in the canon, but also some of the most arrestingly inconsequential prose. And then there is its concluding *coup de théâtre*.

Hermione is heavily pregnant at the beginning, which requires careful movement on the part of the actress (in Adrian Noble's 1992 Royal Shakespeare Company (RSC) production, Samantha Bond, who played Hermione, really was pregnant and required less padding as the run went on). In a *Production Casebook* video, which includes selected scenes from Gregory Doran's 1998/9 RSC pro-duction, Alexandra Gilbreath, who played Hermione, says that the character, being only two weeks before her time, is all 'joy and ripeness' in the opening scene and that the 'ability to endure' all the cruel and extraordinary events is Hermione's strongest character trait. The way in which Hermione's pregnancy is performed will directly affect the audience's response to Leontes' ill-treatment of her.

In Peter Brook's 1951 production at the Phoenix Theatre, London, John Gielgud played Leontes as jealous from the start, but the text does give opportunity for an actor to make a sudden transition. Leontes' jealousy more plausibly begins to reveal itself eighty-seven lines into his first scene when he realizes that Hermione has succeeded where he himself has failed: to persuade his oldest friend and fellow king, Polixenes, to add one week to his already nine-month-long state visit. Polixenes arrived at about the same time that Hermione became pregnant. Leontes' 'At my request he would not' (I.1.87) leads to a moment of close dialogue and seemingly affectionate cross-examination of Hermione (he will cross-examine her again for adultery and on pain of death in Act III, scene 2), before voicing his sinister suspicions – 'Too hot, too hot! | To mingle friendship far is mingling bloods' (I.1.108–109). In some productions, this speech marks the beginning of Leontes' direct relationship with the audience. There is the opportunity for several more such asides. For example, Leontes' speech about 'Sir Smile' (I.2.190–207) can be both humorous and sinister, especially if the actor identifies a man in the theatre holding 'his wife by th'arm' and suggests that the adulterous Sir Smile is sitting next to him. (As well as these extended asides, Leontes has two moments of actual soliloquy: II.3.1–9 and 18–26. Like any soliloquies in Shakespeare, these too can be played as conversations with the audience.) The actor needs to decide whether he is going to find textual motivation for this irrational mood-swing from hospitable state leader to unreasonably suspicious husband, or whether he is simply going to perform the beginning of Leontes' jealousy for its essential narrative value. *Othello* becomes a useful point of comparison. There Shakespeare shows a man being gradually poisoned; here the jealousy seems more innate, already burgeoning from inside Leontes. However, just as a production of *Othello* might choose not to offer explanations for Iago's evil, so too might a production of *The Winter's Tale* decide that Leontes' jealousy need only be accepted as a plot device: the play's title explicitly proclaims its status as fiction, after all.

Leontes' language is as much a challenge for the actor as for the audience. Cicely Berry, a famous voice expert and writer on the subject, appreciates the density of feeling in Leontes' language and finds within it powerful expressions of sexuality. She believes that it is often difficult to determine whether the thought or the word comes first for Shakespeare (see, for example, Leontes' highly internalized and impressionistic speech, I.2.128–46). In Acts IV and V language is more connected with external action and the need to depict the pastoral world of Bohemia. There are the social evocations of Autolycus' comic songs, the responses to nature and love in the speeches of Perdita, Florizel, Camillo, Polixenes and the old Shepherd, and the crucial descriptions of offstage events.

Shakespeare's foil for Leontes is Paulina. She alone dares speak to him with penetrating directness, and to change his thought with her repeated insistence that Hermione is innocent. For a production it would help if Paulina's voice is powerful in a different way from the others which have held the stage before her entrance at the beginning of Act II, scene 2: 'The keeper of the prison, call to him. | Let him have knowledge who I am.' Paulina visits Leontes with 'words as med'cinal as true', as his 'loyal servant', 'physician' and 'obedient counsellor' (II.3.37, 54 and 55). A production will have to decide on the precise social or possibly even blood relationship between Leontes and Paulina. Shakespeare makes this non-specific, but no one else would be allowed to speak to the King of Sicilia as Paulina does.

Hermione's arraignment (III.2), with her powerful speeches of self-vindication (21–53 and 58–75), as well as her direct challenges to Leontes (78–81 and 90–115), presents a gift to any actress. Her costuming and her physical appearance at her trial need particular consideration. Some productions explore the shame of her arriving in her stained birth and prison gown, others take

pains to emphasize her royalty and dress her with careful
and fragile dignity (for example, Declan Donnellan's 1999
production for Moscow's Maly Theatre Company). The
conflict between Hermione and Leontes could almost be
conceded in her favour by her pathetic lines, 'Tell me
what blessings I have here alive | That I should fear
to die' (III.2.106–7), but she goes on to refer herself
to the authority of the Oracle at Delphos. As the court
and the audience share the theatrical tension of the
arrival of the verdict, Hermione is allowed a further call
on the audience's sympathy. This is an opportunity for
the audience to be reminded of Hermione's own royal
lineage and consistent self-possessed dignity:

> The Emperor of Russia was my father.
> O that he were alive, and here beholding
> His daughter's trial! That he did but see
> The flatness of my misery; yet with eyes
> Of pity, not revenge! (III.2.118–22)

The more mystical and quasi-religious the delivery of
the Oracle's pronouncements, the greater will be the sense
of Leontes' profanity against Apollo. Is there the sound
effect of thunder for the lines describing Apollo's anger
(III.2.144–5), perhaps suggesting that the heavens share
in the condemnation of Leontes? And does Paulina yet
know that Hermione is not really dead when she re-enters
after twenty lines to deliver her devastating attack and
challenge to Leontes (III.2.170–230)? Such background
decisions on the part of the director might not be
explicitly performable, but could have an impact on how
the actor playing Paulina delivers her news.

The audience see the generic demands of performance change before their eyes in Act III, scene 3, and the

appearance of the bear itself can serve as the point of
division between tragedy and comedy. The bear can be
absurd, comic, ridiculous and perhaps almost believable
in appearance. These effects can all be achieved to varying
degrees by someone wearing a bear suit as, for example,
in the 1980 BBC television production of the play directed
by Jane Howell. Antigonus' words create space for a
change of effect in the stage lighting: 'The day frowns
more and more . . . I never saw | The heavens so dim
by day' (III.3.53–5), so the non-naturalistic entrance of
the bear might contrast with the more naturalistic use
of shadow, creating a tension between the 'real' and the
artificial. The bear might be more impressionistic and
arise out of an aspect of the stage design itself, or by an
overwhelming effect of shadow and sound. In Terry
Hands's 1986 RSC production, the floor was covered
from the start with an enormous bearskin which rose to
become the bear itself. The bear also introduces the
audience to the world of Bohemia, a pastoral and witty
context where people believe in 'fairy gold' (III.3.119),
and in which there is much song and dance. There
are, for example, Autolycus' songs (IV.3.1–12, 15–22,
121–4; IV.4.220–31, 295–306, 313–21), the dance of the
Shepherds and Shepherdesses (IV.4.167), and the often
sexy dance of the 'satyrs' (IV.4.339). If a production has
decided to make Sicilia appear cold and wintry, then
Bohemia surely demands a world of spring, hope, new
life and regeneration – 'When daffodils begin to peer'
(IV.3.1). In the 1992 RSC production, Richard McCabe
descended from the flies apparently by holding an enormous clutch of colourful balloons for his first entrance
as Autolycus. Crucially, Bohemia is also a community,
whenever the production might be set, which is giving
thanks for and celebrating its economic basis: wool. It is

the weight and value of wool that the Clown is trying
to calculate when he enters lost in thought just before he
is tricked and robbed by Autolycus (IV.3.31–3).

For a production, Bohemia not only means a move
away from the courtly Sicilia to the definitely rustic, but
also to a world sixteen years later. The quality of the
production's make-up will first come under inevitable
scrutiny on the appearance of an older Polixenes and
Camillo in Act IV, scene 2. The effects of ageing need
to be believably sustained throughout the second part,
and will affect all the characters who were initially present
in the Sicilian court.

The figure of Time also presents its challenges to a
director. Time's 32-line speech could be spoken by the
dead Antigonus. Instead of Time's words, Nicholas
Hytner's 2001 Royal National Theatre (RNT) production
had Mamillius speaking Shakespeare's Sonnet 12: 'When
I do count the clock that tells the time'. The whole cast
might enter to perform Time as a chorus of many voices,
both living and dead. Time can also appear as more
overtly abstract and less connected to the production: an
old man or a masked figure with a scythe (for example,
William Squire in Anthony Quayle's 1948 Stratford
production and Robert Eddison in Ronald Eyre's 1981
RSC production). Declan Donnellan's 1999 Russian
production established the onstage presence of an old
woman (played by Tatyana Rasskasova) who swept the
stage between scenes. When, as anticipated, she stepped
forward to perform Time, she threw her hood back and
miraculously revealed herself to be young and beautiful:
in the theatre Time can move backwards as well as
forwards. In its transfer to Stratford-upon-Avon, Matthew
Warchus's 2002 RSC production replaced Time's speech
with the swift flight of a Harris' hawk from the nearby

home of Shakespeare's mother, Mary Arden's House. Time, represented by the hawk, literally flew from the stage over the audience's heads up into the gallery. It was a breathtaking moment. A student production at the Shakespeare Institute in 1996 also cut Time and, since the passage of sixteen years took the production to a 1968 setting, an extract from Simon and Garfunkel's song 'Old Friends/Bookends' was substituted in place of Shakespeare's speech:

> Time it was and what a Time it was, it was
> A time of innocence, a time of confidences.
> Long ago it must be . . . I have a photograph,
> Preserve your memories, they're all that's left you.

Simon Forman, a sixteenth-century astrologer and physician, who saw *The Winter's Tale* at the Globe on 15 May 1611, most remembered the performance of the pedlar Autolycus and deduced from the show the aphorism 'beware of trusting feigned beggars or fawning fellows'. Autolycus, like Falstaff or Feste, revels in inconsequentiality. It would be perfectly possible to tell the story without him, but his presence provides exuberance, comic turns (the pickpocketing of the Clown in Act IV, scene 3, possibly more than once between lines 74 and 115), and puts into circulation many other narratives, not least those contained in the ballads he is talking about and trying to sell (IV.4.260–321). His name literally means 'the lone wolf' and in Bohemia he appears like a wolf in sheep's clothing among sheep-shearers and shepherds. Autolycus criminally exploits the community's gullibility, but at the same time there is the quality of a stand-up comedian about him. More than any other character in the play, Autolycus has the scope for general asides and whole speeches to the audience. There is also much visual humour to be derived from portraying him successfully. It is important to remember that Autolycus is in disguise as the ballad-selling pedlar, so that the Clown does not recognize him as the rogue who picked his pocket (IV.4.250–51), and a production will have to decide how thorough to make the disguise. If Autolycus is not disguised at all, then the Clown will appear to be especially stupid. There is, too, the moment when Autolycus exchanges clothes with Prince Florizel (IV.4.643). Shakespeare's script seems deliberately foreshortened at this point, 'Have you done there?' asks the by-standing Camillo (IV.4.653), which can elicit humorous impromptu aside glances and comments from the actors to the audience. Autolycus' disguise enables him to behave in an exaggeratedly courtly manner later in the same scene when his comments about his own affected behaviour (IV.4.725–33) need to convince the old Shepherd and the Clown that he really is a courtier. By so doing, Shakespeare gives scope to the performance to place the father and the son at an ironic distance from Autolycus' comic and reiterated exploitation. Bohemia, and especially its interactions with Autolycus, can lead an audience to forget where the action of the play started. It seems as if the audience is caught up in a totally different play and the beguilingly comic role of Autolycus helps to disrupt carefully established narrative and dramatic truths.

Shakespeare returns the audience to the sixteen-year-long grief of Leontes and the world of Sicilia for Act V. What has been the impact of such a long period of mourning on Leontes? Do we see him doing ritual penitence like Ian McKellen in John Barton and Trevor Nunn's 1976 RSC production? Jeremy Irons appeared in a wheelchair in Hands's RSC production, as if he had suffered a stroke. How might Leontes' development in grief and Paulina's careful orchestration of it affect their relationship? Just as audiences attending Agatha Christie's *The Mousetrap* are asked not to reveal the play's ending, the final moments of *The Winter's Tale* should be a secret well kept from those who are unfamiliar with it. Paulina's idea to reunite Leontes and Hermione by posing her as a statue which miraculously comes to life is one of the most physically demanding moments for any actor in a Shakespeare play. The pose of the statue could help with the necessity for Hermione to remain perfectly still for a hundred lines (at least five minutes). She might, for instance, appear sitting, Little Mermaid-like, as Clare Skinner did in Hytner's 2001 RNT production, or standing with one arm held out like Anna Calder-Marshall's Hermione in the BBC production (who does not remain quite still enough). Whatever pose is adopted, Shakespeare seems to allow for a degree of imperfection with Paulina's lines, 'No longer shall you gaze on't, lest your fancy | May think anon it moves' (V.3.60–61). The nineteenth-century actress Helena Faucit played Hermione opposite W. C. Macready's Leontes in 1837. She gave her own extended insight and description of the moment (in the form of a letter addressed to Alfred, Lord Tennyson) in her book *On Some of Shakespeare's Female Characters* (1885):

Here, let me say, that I never approached this scene without much inward trepidation. You may imagine how difficult it must be to stand in one position, with a full light thrown upon you, without moving an eyelid for so long a time . . . To her own surprise her heart, so long empty, loveless, and cold, begins to throb again, as she listens to the outpourings of a devotion she had believed to be extinct . . . It was such a comfort to me, as well as true to natural feeling, that Shakespeare gives Hermione no words to say to Leontes, but leaves her to assure him of her joy and forgiveness by look and manner only, as in his arms she feels the old life, so long suspended, come back to her again.

Paulina's call for music (V.3.98) gives great freedom to a composer working on a production to design something which might be gently haunting, gently miraculous: the BBC production used a solitary pan-pipe. In the context of the story, it is as if the music itself is really magical. Here, in its final moments, *The Winter's Tale* shows the effect that forgiveness can have on its whole play-world. And the forgiveness itself has been long suspended by a 'wide gap of time' (V.3.154). Not all directors give the play a rapturous ending. It is crucial, however, that a production complicates the audience's feelings by allowing them to appreciate both Leontes' and Hermione's points of view, both of which are combined in the death of Mamillius and restored in the figure of Perdita. How does Leontes touch Hermione for the line 'O, she's warm!' (V.3.109) – does she reach out to touch him, or is it a moment of tender, mutual physical contact? Some directors might cynically challenge any notion of forgiveness and, since Shakespeare scripts Hermione to speak to Perdita rather than Leontes, play against the text. If the observations of Polixenes and Camillo are cut – 'She embraces him', 'She hangs about his neck' (V.3.111–12) – then a production might lose the sense of a moment so powerful that words need to give way to simple actions and descriptions. In Trevor Nunn's 1969 RSC production Judi Dench performed both Hermione and Perdita (Penny Downie did this also in the 1986 RSC production), but such doubling is probably more suited to film and can make for unnecessary distraction in the final scene (a stunt double was required to play Perdita). The final scene of *The Winter's Tale* requires us all to 'awake [our] faith' and invites us to leave the theatre having worthily become 'precious winners all' (V.3.95 and 131). We have somehow been able to believe in an old and improbable tale and have witnessed the many physical and emotional challenges of its telling. A muted and restrained curtain call will encourage the wonder and emotions inspired in the audience to be reflected back to them. And as we leave the theatre, we might call to mind Paulina's words from a few moments before: 'I like your silence: it the more shows off | Your wonder' (V.3.21–2).

Paul Edmondson

Further Reading

EDITIONS

The Winter's Tale may be read in a range of scholarly and student editions. Of these, Stephen Orgel's Oxford World's Classics edition (1996) offers the complete text of Greene's *Pandosto*, helpful notes and an introduction that takes exception to the category of romance, asserting instead the play's Jacobean origins, generic and political. J. H. P. Pafford's comprehensive Arden edition (1963) exhibits the familiar virtues of that series: a wide-ranging introduction, exhaustive notes and several helpful appendices. Other useful editions, intended mainly for university students, include Frank Kermode's Signet (1963) and Frances E. Dolan's New Pelican (1998).

SOURCES AND INFLUENCES

Robert Greene's *Pandosto* is widely available, most handily in the Oxford World's Classics edition of *The Winter's Tale* (1996). Fitzroy Pyle's *'The Winter's Tale': A Commentary on the Structure* (1969) provides a thoroughgoing analysis of the particulars of Shakespeare's adaptation. More general studies of romance, Elizabethan

fiction and related questions of genre can be found in
Carol Gesner, *Shakespeare and Greek Romance* (1970);
John F. Danby, *Poets on Fortune's Hill* (1952); Stanley
Wells, 'Shakespeare and Romance' in *Later Shakespeare*,
ed. John Russell Brown and Bernard Harris (1966); and
Howard Felperin, *Shakespearean Romance* (1972). Also
significant, especially for its Ovidian emphasis, is E. A.
J. Honigmann's 'Secondary Sources of *The Winter's
Tale*', *Philological Quarterly* 34 (1955).

CRITICAL RESPONSES AND PERFORMANCES

Although Coleridge and others had praised it, *The
Winter's Tale* was relatively neglected by critics until
Edward Dowden's reclassification of the late plays
prompted an enthusiastic reconsideration in *Shakespere,
His Mind and Art* (1875) and *Shakespere* (1877). For much
of the twentieth century inquiry focused chiefly upon the
romantic features of the drama, its resemblance to other
romance fictions, and its mythic affiliations; a convenient
summary of such criticism is available in Philip Edwards,
'Shakespeare's Romances, 1900–1957', *Shakespeare Survey
11* (1958). G. Wilson Knight's 'Great Creating Nature' in
The Crown of Life (1947) set the tone for many subsequent
studies. These include S. L. Bethell, *'The Winter's Tale':
A Study* (1947); Northrop Frye, 'Recognition in *The
Winter's Tale*', reprinted in *Fables of Identity* (1963); Inga-
Stina Ewbank, 'The Triumph of Time in *The Winter's
Tale*', *Review of English Literature* (1964); C. L. Barber,
'"Thou That Beget'st Him That Did Thee Beget":
Transformation in *Pericles* and *The Winter's Tale*',
Shakespeare Survey 22 (1969), the ideas of which are

adapted and developed in C. L. Barber and Richard Wheeler, *The Whole Journey: Shakespeare's Power of Development* (1986); and Charles Frey, *Shakespeare's Vast Romance: A Study of 'The Winter's Tale'* (1980).

Towards the end of the twentieth century, as political criticism gained strength in literary studies generally, *The Winter's Tale* began to be examined from new angles. Neglecting and sometimes even dismissing the romantic strains of the narrative, critics explored its relation to Jacobean discourses of tyranny and monarchy. Among the most judicious of these works is Constance Jordan, *Shakespeare's Monarchies: Ruler and Subject in the Romances* (1997). In *Shakespeare's Last Plays: A New Approach* (1975) Frances Yates identifies important strains of European political philosophy informing the play. Other readers have sought to discern specific topical connections with historical figures and events, although finally such arguments have not been very influential: see David Bergeron, *Shakespeare's Romances and the Royal Family* (1985) and Donna Hamilton, '*The Winter's Tale* and the Language of Union, 1604–10', *Shakespeare Studies* 22 (1993). Feminist critics have responded to the shifting representation of women in the last plays and the special prominence of gender themes in *The Winter's Tale*: see Janet Adelman, *Suffocating Mothers* (1991); Susan Snyder, 'Mamillius and Gender Polarization in *The Winter's Tale*', *Shakespeare Quarterly* 50 (1999); and Lynn Enterline, '"You speak a language that I understand not": The Rhetoric of Animation in *The Winter's Tale*', *Shakespeare Quarterly* 48 (1997).

The difficult verse of the play, characteristic of the late style generally, has lately received welcome notice. See, in addition to the Introduction to Orgel's edition, Anne Barton, 'Leontes and the Spider: Language and

Speaker in Shakespeare's Last Plays' in *Shakespeare's Styles*, ed. Philip Edwards, Inga-Stina Ewbank and G. K. Hunter (1980); Russ McDonald, 'Poetry and Plot in *The Winter's Tale*', *Shakespeare Quarterly* 36 (1985); David Schalkwyk, '"A Lady's 'Verily' is as Good as a Lord's": Women, Word, and Witchcraft in *The Winter's Tale*', *English Literary Renaissance* (1992). Simon Palfrey's *Late Shakespeare: A New World of Words* (1997) attends to the class differences suggested by different patterns of speech.

B. J. Sokol, in *Art and Illusion in 'The Winter's Tale'* (1994), focuses on many of the topics related to creation and imagination, and Stanley Cavell offers a characteristically brilliant treatment of language and idea in 'Recounting Gains, Showing Losses: Reading *The Winter's Tale*' in *Disowning Knowledge in Six Plays of Shakespeare* (2003). T. G. Bishop, *Shakespeare and the Theatre of Wonder* (1996), writes helpfully about the complex theatrical magic of the final scene. Finally, a quirky and stimulating deconstructive essay is Howard Felperin's '"Tongue-tied, our queen?": The Deconstruction of Presence in *The Winter's Tale*' in *Shakespeare and the Question of Theory*, ed. Patricia Parker and Geoffrey Hartmann (1985).

Collections of essays on *The Winter's Tale* and the late plays generally include Brown and Harris's *Later Shakespeare* (mentioned above); *Shakespeare's Romances Reconsidered*, ed. Henry Jacobs and Carol McGinnis Kay (1978); *Critical Essays on 'The Winter's Tale'*, ed. Maurice Hunt (1995); *Shakespeare: The Late Plays*, ed. Kiernan Ryan (1999); *Shakespeare's Late Plays: New Readings*, ed. Jennifer Richards and James Knowles (1999); and *Shakespeare's Romances*, ed. Alison Thorne (2003).

Accounts of the play in performance can be found in Dennis Bartholomeusz, '*The Winter's Tale' in Performance* in *England and America 1611–1976* (1982); Patricia E. Tatspaugh, *The Winter's Tale*, The Arden Shakespeare: Shakespeare at Stratford series (2002); Roger Warren, *Staging Shakespeare's Late Plays* (1990); Stanley Wells (ed.), *Shakespeare in the Theatre: An Anthology of Criticism* (1997).

Available on video are *BBC Shakespeare: 'The Winter's Tale'*, dir. Jane Howell (BBC Worldwide, 1989) and *'The Winter's Tale': A Production Casebook*, dir. Robin Lough (documentary on Gregory Doran's 1998/9 RSC production; Heritage Theatre Ltd, 2002).

THE WINTER'S TALE

The Characters in the Play

LEONTES, King of Sicilia
HERMIONE, his wife
MAMILLIUS, his son
PERDITA, his daughter
CAMILLO
ANTIGONUS
CLEOMENES } Lords at the court of Leontes
DION
PAULINA, wife of Antigonus
EMILIA, a lady attending on Hermione
GAOLER
A MARINER
Other LORDS and GENTLEMEN, LADIES, OFFICERS, and
    SERVANTS at the court of Leontes

POLIXENES, King of Bohemia
FLORIZEL, his son
ARCHIDAMUS, a Bohemian Lord
AUTOLYCUS, a rogue
Old SHEPHERD, reputed father of Perdita
CLOWN, his son
MOPSA
DORCAS } shepherdesses
SERVANT of the old Shepherd

Other shepherds and shepherdesses
Twelve countrymen disguised as satyrs

TIME, as Chorus

ARCHIDAMUS If you shall chance, Camillo, to visit Bohemia, on the like occasion whereon my services are now
  on foot, you shall see, as I have said, great difference betwixt our Bohemia and your Sicilia.

CAMILLO I think this coming summer the King of Sicilia
  means to pay Bohemia the visitation which he justly
  owes him.

ARCHIDAMUS Wherein our entertainment shall shame
  us: we will be justified in our loves. For indeed –

CAMILLO Beseech you –   10

ARCHIDAMUS Verily, I speak it in the freedom of my
  knowledge: we cannot with such magnificence, in so
  rare – I know not what to say. We will give you sleepy
  drinks, that your senses, unintelligent of our insuf-
  ficience, may, though they cannot praise us, as little
  accuse us.

CAMILLO You pay a great deal too dear for what's given
  freely.

ARCHIDAMUS Believe me, I speak as my understanding
  instructs me and as mine honesty puts it to utterance.   20

CAMILLO Sicilia cannot show himself over-kind to Bohemia. They were trained together in their childhoods;
  and there rooted betwixt them then such an affection,

which cannot choose but branch now. Since their more
mature dignities and royal necessities made separation
of their society, their encounters, though not personal,
hath been royally attorneyed with interchange of gifts,
letters, loving embassies: that they have seemed to be
together, though absent; shook hands as over a vast;
30   and embraced, as it were, from the ends of opposed
winds. The heavens continue their loves!

ARCHIDAMUS I think there is not in the world either
malice or matter to alter it. You have an unspeakable
comfort of your young prince Mamillius. It is a gentleman of the greatest promise that ever came into my note.

CAMILLO I very well agree with you in the hopes of him.
It is a gallant child; one that indeed physics the subject,
makes old hearts fresh. They that went on crutches ere
he was born desire yet their life to see him a man.

40 ARCHIDAMUS Would they else be content to die?

CAMILLO Yes – if there were no other excuse why they
should desire to live.

ARCHIDAMUS If the King had no son, they would desire
to live on crutches till he had one.   *Exeunt*

I.2   *Enter Leontes, Hermione, Mamillius, Polixenes,*
             Camillo, and Attendants

POLIXENES
Nine changes of the watery star hath been
The shepherd's note since we have left our throne
Without a burden. Time as long again
Would be filled up, my brother, with our thanks,
And yet we should for perpetuity
Go hence in debt. And therefore, like a cipher
Yet standing in rich place, I multiply
With one 'We thank you' many thousands more
That go before it.

LEONTES   Stay your thanks a while,
And pay them when you part.
POLIXENES   Sir, that's tomorrow.   10
I am questioned by my fears of what may chance
Or breed upon our absence. That may blow
No sneaping winds at home, to make us say
'This is put forth too truly!' Besides, I have stayed
To tire your royalty.
LEONTES   We are tougher, brother,
Than you can put us to't.
POLIXENES   No longer stay.
LEONTES
One sev'n-night longer.
POLIXENES   Very sooth, tomorrow.
LEONTES
We'll part the time between's then; and in that
I'll no gainsaying.
POLIXENES   Press me not, beseech you, so.
There is no tongue that moves, none, none i'th'world,   20
So soon as yours could win me. So it should now,
Were there necessity in your request, although
'Twere needful I denied it. My affairs
Do even drag me homeward; which to hinder
Were, in your love, a whip to me, my stay
To you a charge and trouble. To save both,
Farewell, our brother.
LEONTES   Tongue-tied, our queen? Speak you.
HERMIONE
I had thought, sir, to have held my peace until
You had drawn oaths from him not to stay. You, sir,
Charge him too coldly. Tell him you are sure   30
All in Bohemia's well: this satisfaction
The by-gone day proclaimed. Say this to him,
He's beat from his best ward.
LEONTES   Well said, Hermione.

HERMIONE

To tell he longs to see his son were strong.
But let him say so, then, and let him go;
But let him swear so and he shall not stay:
We'll thwack him hence with distaffs.

Leontes draws apart

Yet of your royal presence I'll adventure
The borrow of a week. When at Bohemia
You take my lord, I'll give him my commission
To let him there a month behind the gest
Prefixed for's parting; yet, good deed, Leontes,
I love thee not a jar o'th'clock behind
What lady she her lord. You'll stay?

POLIXENES   No, madam.

HERMIONE

Nay, but you will!

POLIXENES   I may not, verily.

HERMIONE

Verily!
You put me off with limber vows; but I,
Though you would seek t'unsphere the stars with oaths,
Should yet say, 'Sir, no going.' Verily,
You shall not go. A lady's 'verily' is
As potent as a lord's. Will you go yet?
Force me to keep you as a prisoner,
Not like a guest; so you shall pay your fees
When you depart, and save your thanks. How say you?
My prisoner? Or my guest? By your dread 'verily',
One of them you shall be.

POLIXENES   Your guest, then, madam:
To be your prisoner should import offending;
Which is for me less easy to commit
Than you to punish.

HERMIONE   Not your gaoler, then,

But your kind hostess. Come, I'll question you   60
Of my lord's tricks, and yours, when you were boys.
You were pretty lordings then?

POLIXENES   We were, fair Queen,
Two lads that thought there was no more behind
But such a day tomorrow as today,
And to be boy eternal.

HERMIONE   Was not my lord
The verier wag o'th'two?

POLIXENES
We were as twinned lambs that did frisk i'th'sun,
And bleat the one at th'other. What we changed
Was innocence for innocence: we knew not
The doctrine of ill-doing, nor dreamed   70
That any did. Had we pursued that life,
And our weak spirits ne'er been higher reared
With stronger blood, we should have answered heaven
Boldly 'Not guilty', the imposition cleared
Hereditary ours.

HERMIONE   By this we gather
You have tripped since.

POLIXENES   O my most sacred lady,
Temptations have since then been born to's: for
In those unfledged days was my wife a girl;
Your precious self had then not crossed the eyes
Of my young playfellow.

HERMIONE   Grace to boot!   80
Of this make no conclusion, lest you say
Your queen and I are devils. Yet go on:
Th'offences we have made you do we'll answer,
If you first sinned with us, and that with us
You did continue fault, and that you slipped not
With any but with us.

LEONTES (*approaching*) Is he won yet?

HERMIONE
  He'll stay, my lord.
LEONTES   At my request he would not.
  Hermione, my dearest, thou never spok'st
  To better purpose.
HERMIONE   Never?
LEONTES   Never but once.
HERMIONE
90   What? Have I twice said well? When was't before?
  I prithee tell me. Cram's with praise, and make's
  As fat as tame things. One good deed dying tongueless
  Slaughters a thousand waiting upon that.
  Our praises are our wages. You may ride's
  With one soft kiss a thousand furlongs ere
  With spur we heat an acre. But to th'goal:
  My last good deed was to entreat his stay.
  What was my first? It has an elder sister,
  Or I mistake you. O, would her name were Grace!
100   But once before I spoke to th'purpose? When?
  Nay, let me have't; I long.
LEONTES   Why, that was when
  Three crabbèd months had soured themselves to death
  Ere I could make thee open thy white hand
  And clap thyself my love: then didst thou utter
  'I am yours for ever.'
HERMIONE   'Tis Grace indeed.
  Why, lo you now, I have spoke to th'purpose twice:
  The one for ever earned a royal husband;
  Th'other for some while a friend.
            She gives her hand to Polixenes
LEONTES (*aside*)   Too hot, too hot!
  To mingle friendship far is mingling bloods.
110   I have *tremor cordis* on me: my heart dances,
  But not for joy, not joy. This entertainment

May a free face put on, derive a liberty
From heartiness, from bounty, fertile bosom,
And well become the agent — 't may, I grant.
But to be paddling palms and pinching fingers,
As now they are, and making practised smiles
As in a looking glass; and then to sigh, as 'twere
The mort o'th'deer — O, that is entertainment
My bosom likes not, nor my brows! Mamillius,
Art thou my boy?

MAMILLIUS   Ay, my good lord.

LEONTES   I'fecks!   120
Why, that's my bawcock. What, hast smutched thy nose?
They say it is a copy out of mine. Come, captain,
We must be neat — not neat but cleanly, captain.
And yet the steer, the heifer, and the calf
Are all called neat. Still virginalling
Upon his palm? — How now, you wanton calf!
Art thou my calf?

MAMILLIUS   Yes, if you will, my lord.

LEONTES
Thou want'st a rough pash and the shoots that I have
To be full like me; yet they say we are
Almost as like as eggs. Women say so,   130
That will say anything. But were they false
As o'er-dyed blacks, as wind, as waters, false
As dice are to be wished by one that fixes
No bourn 'twixt his and mine, yet were it true
To say this boy were like me. Come, sir page,
Look on me with your welkin eye. Sweet villain!
Most dear'st! My collop! Can thy dam? May't be?
Affection, thy intention stabs the centre.
Thou dost make possible things not so held,
Communicat'st with dreams — how can this be? —   140
With what's unreal thou coactive art,

And fellow'st nothing. Then 'tis very credent
Thou mayst co-join with something; and thou dost,
And that beyond commission, and I find it,
And that to the infection of my brains
And hardening of my brows.

POLIXENES   What means Sicilia?

HERMIONE
He something seems unsettled.

POLIXENES   How, my lord!
What cheer? How is't with you, best brother?

HERMIONE   You look
As if you held a brow of much distraction.
Are you moved, my lord?

LEONTES   No, in good earnest.
How sometimes Nature will betray its folly,
Its tenderness, and make itself a pastime
To harder bosoms! Looking on the lines
Of my boy's face, methoughts I did recoil
Twenty-three years, and saw myself unbreeched,
In my green velvet coat; my dagger muzzled,
Lest it should bite its master and so prove,
As ornaments oft does, too dangerous.
How like, methought, I then was to this kernel,
This squash, this gentleman. Mine honest friend,
Will you take eggs for money?

MAMILLIUS
No, my lord, I'll fight.

LEONTES
You will? Why, happy man be's dole! My brother,
Are you so fond of your young prince as we
Do seem to be of ours?

POLIXENES   If at home, sir,
He's all my exercise, my mirth, my matter;
Now my sworn friend, and then mine enemy;

My parasite, my soldier, statesman, all.
He makes a July's day short as December,
And with his varying childness cures in me   170
Thoughts that would thick my blood.

LEONTES   So stands this squire
Officed with me. We two will walk, my lord,
And leave you to your graver steps. Hermione,
How thou lov'st us show in our brother's welcome.
Let what is dear in Sicily be cheap.
Next to thyself and my young rover, he's
Apparent to my heart.

HERMIONE   If you would seek us,
We are yours i'th'garden. Shall's attend you there?

LEONTES

To your own bents dispose you: you'll be found,
Be you beneath the sky. (*Aside*) I am angling now,   180
Though you perceive me not how I give line.
Go to, go to!
How she holds up the neb, the bill to him!
And arms her with the boldness of a wife
To her allowing husband!

                              Exeunt Hermione and Polixenes
                    Gone already!
Inch-thick, knee-deep, o'er head and ears a forked one!
Go play, boy, play: thy mother plays, and I
Play too — but so disgraced a part, whose issue
Will hiss me to my grave. Contempt and clamour
Will be my knell. Go play, boy, play. There have been,   190
Or I am much deceived, cuckolds ere now;
And many a man there is, even at this present,
Now, while I speak this, holds his wife by th'arm,
That little thinks she has been sluiced in's absence,
And his pond fished by his next neighbour, by
Sir Smile, his neighbour. Nay, there's comfort in't

Whiles other men have gates, and those gates opened,
As mine, against their will. Should all despair
That have revolted wives, the tenth of mankind
Would hang themselves. Physic for't there's none:
It is a bawdy planet, that will strike
Where 'tis predominant; and 'tis powerful, think it,
From east, west, north, and south. Be it concluded,
No barricado for a belly. Know't:
It will let in and out the enemy
With bag and baggage. Many thousand on's
Have the disease and feel't not. How now, boy?

MAMILLIUS
I am like you, they say.

LEONTES   Why, that's some comfort.
What! Camillo there!

CAMILLO
Ay, my good lord.
                He comes forward

LEONTES
Go play, Mamillius. Thou'rt an honest man.
                                        Exit Mamillius
Camillo, this great sir will yet stay longer.

CAMILLO
You had much ado to make his anchor hold:
When you cast out, it still came home.

LEONTES   Didst note it?

CAMILLO
He would not stay at your petitions, made
His business more material.

LEONTES   Didst perceive it?
(*Aside*) They're here with me already: whispering,
    rounding,
'Sicilia is a so-forth.' 'Tis far gone
When I shall gust it last. – How came 't, Camillo,
That he did stay?

CAMILLO   At the good Queen's entreaty.   220

LEONTES
'At the Queen's' be't. 'Good' should be pertinent;
But, so it is, it is not. Was this taken
By any understanding pate but thine?
For thy conceit is soaking, will draw in
More than the common blocks. Not noted, is't,
But of the finer natures? By some severals
Of headpiece extraordinary? Lower messes
Perchance are to this business purblind? Say.

CAMILLO
Business, my lord? I think most understand
Bohemia stays here longer.

LEONTES   Ha?

CAMILLO   Stays here longer.   230

LEONTES
Ay, but why?

CAMILLO
To satisfy your highness, and the entreaties
Of our most gracious mistress.

LEONTES   Satisfy?
Th'entreaties of your mistress? Satisfy?
Let that suffice. I have trusted thee, Camillo,
With all the nearest things to my heart, as well
My chamber-counsels, wherein, priestlike, thou
Hast cleansed my bosom, I from thee departed
Thy penitent reformed. But we have been
Deceived in thy integrity, deceived   240
In that which seems so.

CAMILLO   Be it forbid, my lord!

LEONTES
To bide upon't: thou art not honest; or
If thou inclin'st that way, thou art a coward,
Which hoxes honesty behind, restraining

From course required. Or else thou must be counted
A servant grafted in my serious trust
And therein negligent, or else a fool
That see'st a game played home, the rich stake drawn,
And tak'st it all for jest.

CAMILLO   My gracious lord,
250 I may be negligent, foolish, and fearful:
In every one of these no man is free,
But that his negligence, his folly, fear,
Among the infinite doings of the world,
Sometime puts forth. In your affairs, my lord,
If ever I were wilful-negligent,
It was my folly; if industriously
I played the fool, it was my negligence,
Not weighing well the end; if ever fearful
To do a thing where I the issue doubted,
260 Whereof the execution did cry out
Against the non-performance, 'twas a fear
Which oft infects the wisest. These, my lord,
Are such allowed infirmities that honesty
Is never free of. But, beseech your grace,
Be plainer with me, let me know my trespass
By its own visage; if I then deny it,
'Tis none of mine.

LEONTES   Ha'not you seen, Camillo —
But that's past doubt, you have, or your eye-glass
Is thicker than a cuckold's horn — or heard —
270 For to a vision so apparent rumour
Cannot be mute — or thought — for cogitation
Resides not in that man that does not think —
My wife is slippery? If thou wilt confess —
Or else be impudently negative
To have nor eyes, nor ears, nor thought — then say
My wife's a hobby-horse, deserves a name

As rank as any flax-wench that puts to
Before her troth-plight: say't and justify't.

CAMILLO
I would not be a stander-by to hear
My sovereign mistress clouded so without   280
My present vengeance taken. 'Shrew my heart,
You never spoke what did become you less
Than this; which to reiterate were sin
As deep as that, though true.

LEONTES   Is whispering nothing?
Is leaning cheek to cheek? Is meeting noses?
Kissing with inside lip? Stopping the career
Of laughter with a sigh? – a note infallible
Of breaking honesty. Horsing foot on foot?
Skulking in corners? Wishing clocks more swift?
Hours minutes? Noon midnight? And all eyes   290
Blind with the pin and web but theirs, theirs only,
That would unseen be wicked – is this nothing?
Why, then the world and all that's in't is nothing;
The covering sky is nothing; Bohemia nothing;
My wife is nothing; nor nothing have these nothings,
If this be nothing.

CAMILLO   Good my lord, be cured
Of this diseased opinion, and betimes,
For 'tis most dangerous.

LEONTES   Say it be, 'tis true.

CAMILLO
No, no, my lord!

LEONTES   It is. You lie, you lie!
I say thou liest, Camillo, and I hate thee,   300
Pronounce thee a gross lout, a mindless slave,
Or else a hovering temporizer, that
Canst with thine eyes at once see good and evil,
Inclining to them both. Were my wife's liver

Infected as her life, she would not live
The running of one glass.

CAMILLO   Who does infect her?

LEONTES

Why, he that wears her like her medal, hanging
About his neck, Bohemia; who, if I
Had servants true about me, that bare eyes
To see alike mine honour as their profits,
Their own particular thrifts, they would do that
Which should undo more doing. Ay, and thou,
His cupbearer – whom I from meaner form
Have benched and reared to worship; who mayst see
Plainly as heaven sees earth and earth sees heaven
How I am galled – mightst bespice a cup
To give mine enemy a lasting wink;
Which draught to me were cordial.

CAMILLO   Sir, my lord,
I could do this, and that with no rash potion,
But with a lingering dram that should not work
Maliciously, like poison: but I cannot
Believe this crack to be in my dread mistress,
So sovereignly being honourable.
I have loved thee –

LEONTES   Make that thy question, and go rot!
Dost think I am so muddy, so unsettled,
To appoint my self in this vexation; sully
The purity and whiteness of my sheets –
Which to preserve is sleep, which being spotted
Is goads, thorns, nettles, tails of wasps;
Give scandal to the blood o'th'Prince, my son –
Who I do think is mine, and love as mine –
Without ripe moving to't? Would I do this?
Could man so blench?

CAMILLO   I must believe you, sir.

I do; and will fetch off Bohemia for't:
Provided that when he's removed your highness
Will take again your queen as yours at first,
Even for your son's sake, and thereby forsealing
The injury of tongues in courts and kingdoms
Known and allied to yours.

LEONTES   Thou dost advise me
Even so as I mine own course have set down.   340
I'll give no blemish to her honour, none.

CAMILLO
My lord,
Go then; and, with a countenance as clear
As friendship wears at feasts, keep with Bohemia
And with your queen. I am his cupbearer.
If from me he have wholesome beverage,
Account me not your servant.

LEONTES   This is all.
Do't and thou hast the one half of my heart;
Do't not, thou split'st thine own.

CAMILLO   I'll do't, my lord.

LEONTES
I will seem friendly, as thou hast advised me.   *Exit*   350

CAMILLO
O miserable lady! But, for me,
What case stand I in? I must be the poisoner
Of good Polixenes, and my ground to do't
Is the obedience to a master – one
Who, in rebellion with himself, will have
All that are his so too. To do this deed,
Promotion follows. If I could find example
Of thousands that had struck anointed kings
And flourished after, I'd not do't; but since
Nor brass, nor stone, nor parchment bears not one,   360
Let villainy itself forswear't. I must

Forsake the court: to do't or no is certain
To me a break-neck. Happy star reign now!
Here comes Bohemia.

Enter Polixenes

POLIXENES   This is strange: methinks
My favour here begins to warp. Not speak?
Good day, Camillo.

CAMILLO   Hail, most royal sir!

POLIXENES
What is the news i'th'court?

CAMILLO   None rare, my lord.

POLIXENES
The King hath on him such a countenance
As he had lost some province, and a region
370 Loved as he loves himself: even now I met him
With customary compliment, when he,
Wafting his eyes to th'contrary, and falling
A lip of much contempt, speeds from me, and
So leaves me to consider what is breeding
That changes thus his manners.

CAMILLO
I dare not know, my lord.

POLIXENES
How, dare not? Do not? Do you know and dare not
Be intelligent to me? 'Tis thereabouts;
For to yourself what you do know you must,
380 And cannot say you dare not. Good Camillo,
Your changed complexions are to me a mirror
Which shows me mine changed too: for I must be
A party in this alteration, finding
Myself thus altered with't.

CAMILLO   There is a sickness
Which puts some of us in distemper, but
I cannot name the disease; and it is caught

Of you, that yet are well.

POLIXENES   How! Caught of me?
Make me not sighted like the basilisk.
I have looked on thousands who have sped the better
By my regard, but killed none so. Camillo,   390
As you are certainly a gentleman, thereto
Clerk-like experienced, which no less adorns
Our gentry than our parents' noble names,
In whose success we are gentle: I beseech you,
If you know aught which does behove my knowledge
Thereof to be informed, imprison't not
In ignorant concealment.

CAMILLO   I may not answer.

POLIXENES
A sickness caught of me, and yet I well?
I must be answered. Dost thou hear, Camillo?
I conjure thee, by all the parts of man   400
Which honour does acknowledge, whereof the least
Is not this suit of mine, that thou declare
What incidency thou dost guess of harm
Is creeping toward me; how far off, how near;
Which way to be prevented, if to be;
If not, how best to bear it.

CAMILLO   Sir, I will tell you,
Since I am charged in honour, and by him
That I think honourable. Therefore mark my counsel,
Which must be ev'n as swiftly followed as
I mean to utter it, or both yourself and me   410
Cry lost, and so good night.

POLIXENES   On, good Camillo.

CAMILLO
I am appointed him to murder you.

POLIXENES
By whom, Camillo?

CAMILLO   By the King.

POLIXENES   For what?

CAMILLO

He thinks, nay, with all confidence he swears,
As he had seen't, or been an instrument
To vice you to't, that you have touched his queen
Forbiddenly.

POLIXENES   O, then my best blood turn
To an infected jelly, and my name
Be yoked with his that did betray the Best!

420 Turn then my freshest reputation to
A savour that may strike the dullest nostril
Where I arrive, and my approach be shunned,
Nay, hated too, worse than the great'st infection
That e'er was heard or read!

CAMILLO   Swear his thought over
By each particular star in heaven and
By all their influences, you may as well
Forbid the sea for to obey the moon
As or by oath remove or counsel shake
The fabric of his folly, whose foundation

430 Is piled upon his faith, and will continue
The standing of his body.

POLIXENES   How should this grow?

CAMILLO

I know not; but I am sure 'tis safer to
Avoid what's grown than question how 'tis born.
If therefore you dare trust my honesty,
That lies enclosèd in this trunk, which you
Shall bear along impawned, away tonight!
Your followers I will whisper to the business,
And will by twos and threes, at several posterns,
Clear them o'th'city. For myself, I'll put

440 My fortunes to your service, which are here

By this discovery lost. Be not uncertain,
For, by the honour of my parents, I
Have uttered truth; which if you seek to prove,
I dare not stand by; nor shall you be safer
Than one condemned by the King's own mouth, thereon
His execution sworn.

POLIXENES   I do believe thee:
I saw his heart in's face. Give me thy hand.
Be pilot to me, and thy places shall
Still neighbour mine. My ships are ready, and
My people did expect my hence departure   450
Two days ago. This jealousy
Is for a precious creature; as she's rare
Must it be great; and as his person's mighty
Must it be violent; and as he does conceive
He is dishonoured by a man which ever
Professed to him, why, his revenges must
In that be made more bitter. Fear o'ershades me.
Good expedition be my friend and comfort
The gracious Queen, part of his theme, but nothing
Of his ill-ta'en suspicion! Come, Camillo,   460
I will respect thee as a father if
Thou bear'st my life off. Hence! Let us avoid.

CAMILLO
It is in mine authority to command
The keys of all the posterns. Please your highness
To take the urgent hour. Come, sir, away.   *Exeunt*

*

II.I   *Enter Hermione, Mamillius, and Ladies*

HERMIONE
    Take the boy to you: he so troubles me,
    'Tis past enduring.

FIRST LADY   Come, my gracious lord,
    Shall I be your playfellow?

MAMILLIUS   No, I'll none of you.

FIRST LADY
    Why, my sweet lord?

MAMILLIUS
    You'll kiss me hard, and speak to me as if
    I were a baby still. – I love you better.

SECOND LADY
    And why so, my lord?

MAMILLIUS   Not for because
    Your brows are blacker; yet black brows, they say,
    Become some women best, so that there be not
10 Too much hair there, but in a semicircle,
    Or a half-moon, made with a pen.

SECOND LADY   Who taught' this?

MAMILLIUS
    I learned it out of women's faces. Pray now,
    What colour are your eyebrows?

FIRST LADY   Blue, my lord.

MAMILLIUS
    Nay, that's a mock. I have seen a lady's nose
    That has been blue, but not her eyebrows.

FIRST LADY   Hark ye:
    The Queen, your mother, rounds apace. We shall
    Present our services to a fine new prince
    One of these days; and then you'd wanton with us,
    If we would have you.

SECOND LADY   She is spread of late
20 Into a goodly bulk. Good time encounter her!

HERMIONE

What wisdom stirs amongst you? Come, sir, now
I am for you again. Pray you, sit by us,
And tell's a tale.

MAMILLIUS   Merry or sad shall't be?

HERMIONE

As merry as you will.

MAMILLIUS

A sad tale's best for winter. I have one
Of sprites and goblins.

HERMIONE   Let's have that, good sir.

Come on, sit down; come on, and do your best
To fright me with your sprites. You're powerful at it.

MAMILLIUS

There was a man –

HERMIONE   Nay, come sit down; then on.

MAMILLIUS

Dwelt by a churchyard – I will tell it softly: 30
Yond crickets shall not hear it.

HERMIONE   Come on, then,
And give't me in mine ear.

Enter Leontes, Antigonus, and Lords

LEONTES

Was he met there? His train? Camillo with him?

LORD

Behind the tuft of pines I met them. Never
Saw I men scour so on their way. I eyed them
Even to their ships.

LEONTES   How blest am I
In my just censure, in my true opinion!
Alack, for lesser knowledge! How accursed
In being so blest! There may be in the cup
A spider steeped, and one may drink, depart,   40
And yet partake no venom, for his knowledge

Is not infected: but if one present
Th'abhorred ingredient to his eye, make known
How he hath drunk, he cracks his gorge, his sides,
With violent hefts. I have drunk, and seen the spider.
Camillo was his help in this, his pander.
There is a plot against my life, my crown.
All's true that is mistrusted. That false villain
Whom I employed was pre-employed by him.
50 He has discovered my design, and I
Remain a pinched thing; yea, a very trick
For them to play at will. How came the posterns
So easily open?

LORD   By his great authority;
Which often hath no less prevailed than so
On your command.

LEONTES   I know't too well.
(*To Hermione*) Give me the boy. I am glad you did not
        nurse him;
Though he does bear some signs of me, yet you
Have too much blood in him.

HERMIONE   What is this? Sport?

LEONTES
Bear the boy hence; he shall not come about her.
60 Away with him, and let her sport herself
With that she's big with: for 'tis Polixenes
Has made thee swell thus.

        Mamillius is led out

HERMIONE   But I'd say he had not,
And I'll be sworn you would believe my saying,
Howe'er you lean to th'nayward.

LEONTES   You, my lords,
Look on her, mark her well: be but about
To say she is a goodly lady and
The justice of your hearts will thereto add,

''Tis pity she's not honest, honourable.'
Praise her but for this her without-door form –
Which, on my faith, deserves high speech – and straight   70
The shrug, the 'hum' or 'ha', these petty brands
That calumny doth use – O, I am out!
That mercy does, for calumny will sear
Virtue itself – these shrugs, these 'hum's and 'ha's,
When you have said she's goodly, come between
Ere you can say she's honest. But be't known,
From him that has most cause to grieve it should be,
She's an adult'ress.

HERMIONE   Should a villain say so,
The most replenished villain in the world,
He were as much more villain. You, my lord,   80
Do but mistake.

LEONTES   You have mistook, my lady,
Polixenes for Leontes. O thou thing
Which I'll not call a creature of thy place,
Lest barbarism, making me the precedent,
Should a like language use to all degrees,
And mannerly distinguishment leave out
Betwixt the prince and beggar. I have said
She's an adult'ress; I have said with whom.
More, she's a traitor, and Camillo is
A fedary with her, and one that knows   90
What she should shame to know herself
But with her most vile principal – that she's
A bed-swerver, even as bad as those
That vulgars give bold'st titles; ay, and privy
To this their late escape.

HERMIONE   No, by my life,
Privy to none of this. How will this grieve you,
When you shall come to clearer knowledge, that
You thus have published me! Gentle my lord,

You scarce can right me throughly then to say
100   You did mistake.

LEONTES   No: if I mistake
In those foundations which I build upon,
The centre is not big enough to bear
A schoolboy's top. Away with her to prison.
He who shall speak for her is afar off guilty
But that he speaks.

HERMIONE   There's some ill planet reigns.
I must be patient till the heavens look
With an aspect more favourable. Good my lords,
I am not prone to weeping, as our sex
Commonly are; the want of which vain dew
110   Perchance shall dry your pities: but I have
That honourable grief lodged here which burns
Worse than tears drown. Beseech you all, my lords,
With thoughts so qualified as your charities
Shall best instruct you measure me; and so
The King's will be performed!

LEONTES   Shall I be heard?

HERMIONE
Who is't that goes with me? Beseech your highness
My women may be with me, for you see
My plight requires it. Do not weep, good fools:
There is no cause. When you shall know your mistress
120   Has deserved prison, then abound in tears
As I come out. This action I now go on
Is for my better grace. Adieu, my lord.
I never wished to see you sorry: now
I trust I shall. My women, come, you have leave.

LEONTES
Go, do our bidding: hence!

                    Exeunt Hermione, guarded, and Ladies

LORD

Beseech your highness, call the Queen again.

ANTIGONUS

Be certain what you do, sir, lest your justice
Prove violence, in the which three great ones suffer:
Yourself, your queen, your son.

LORD   For her, my lord,

I dare my life lay down, and will do't, sir,   130
Please you t'accept it, that the Queen is spotless
I'th'eyes of heaven and to you – I mean
In this which you accuse her.

ANTIGONUS   If it prove

She's otherwise, I'll keep my stables where
I lodge my wife; I'll go in couples with her;
Than when I feel and see her no farther trust her:
For every inch of woman in the world,
Ay, every dram of woman's flesh is false,
If she be.

LEONTES   Hold your peaces.

LORD   Good my lord –

ANTIGONUS

It is for you we speak, not for ourselves.   140
You are abused, and by some putter-on
That will be damned for't. Would I knew the villain!
I would lam-damn him. Be she honour-flawed,
I have three daughters: the eldest is eleven;
The second and the third nine and some five:
If this prove true, they'll pay for't. By mine honour,
I'll geld'em all! Fourteen they shall not see
To bring false generations. They are co-heirs;
And I had rather glib myself than they
Should not produce fair issue.

LEONTES   Cease, no more!   150

You smell this business with a sense as cold

As is a dead man's nose; but I do see't and feel't
As you feel doing thus and see withal
The instruments that feel.

ANTIGONUS   If it be so,
We need no grave to bury honesty:
There's not a grain of it the face to sweeten
Of the whole dungy earth.

LEONTES   What? Lack I credit?

LORD
I had rather you did lack than I, my lord,
Upon this ground; and more it would content me
To have her honour true than your suspicion,
Be blamed for't how you might.

LEONTES   Why, what need we
Commune with you of this, but rather follow
Our forceful instigation? Our prerogative
Calls not your counsels, but our natural goodness
Imparts this; which, if you – or stupefied
Or seeming so in skill – cannot or will not
Relish a truth like us, inform yourselves
We need no more of your advice. The matter,
The loss, the gain, the ord'ring on't, is all
Properly ours.

ANTIGONUS   And I wish, my liege,
You had only in your silent judgement tried it,
Without more overture.

LEONTES   How could that be?
Either thou art most ignorant by age,
Or thou wert born a fool. Camillo's flight,
Added to their familiarity –
Which was as gross as ever touched conjecture
That lacked sight only, naught for approbation
But only seeing, all other circumstances

Made up to th'deed – doth push on this proceeding.
Yet, for a greater confirmation –   180
For in an act of this importance 'twere
Most piteous to be wild – I have dispatched in post
To sacred Delphos, to Apollo's temple,
Cleomenes and Dion, whom you know
Of stuffed sufficiency. Now from the oracle
They will bring all; whose spiritual counsel, had,
Shall stop or spur me. Have I done well?

LORD

Well done, my lord.

LEONTES

Though I am satisfied, and need no more
Than what I know, yet shall the oracle   190
Give rest to th'minds of others, such as he,
Whose ignorant credulity will not
Come up to th'truth. So have we thought it good
From our free person she should be confined,
Lest that the treachery of the two fled hence
Be left her to perform. Come, follow us:
We are to speak in public; for this business
Will raise us all.

ANTIGONUS (*aside*) To laughter, as I take it,
If the good truth were known.   *Exeunt*

                Enter Paulina, a Gentleman, and Attendants   II.2

PAULINA

The keeper of the prison, call to him.
Let him have knowledge who I am.   *Exit Gentleman*
                              Good lady,
No court in Europe is too good for thee:
What dost thou then in prison?

Enter Gentleman with the Gaoler

                                    Now, good sir,
You know me, do you not?
GAOLER   For a worthy lady,
And one who much I honour.
PAULINA   Pray you, then,
Conduct me to the Queen.
GAOLER   I may not, madam:
To the contrary I have express commandment.
PAULINA
Here's ado
To lock up honesty and honour from
Th'access of gentle visitors! Is't lawful, pray you,
To see her women? Any of them? Emilia?
GAOLER
So please you, madam,
To put apart these your attendants, I
Shall bring Emilia forth.
PAULINA   I pray now, call her.
Withdraw yourselves. *Exeunt Gentleman and Attendants*
GAOLER   And, madam,
I must be present at your conference.
PAULINA
Well, be't so, prithee.   *Exit Gaoler*
Here's such ado to make no stain a stain
As passes colouring.
       Enter Gaoler with Emilia
                              Dear gentlewoman,
How fares our gracious lady?
EMILIA
As well as one so great and so forlorn
May hold together. On her frights and griefs –
Which never tender lady hath borne greater –
She is something before her time delivered.

PAULINA
  A boy?
EMILIA   A daughter, and a goodly babe,
    Lusty, and like to live. The Queen receives
    Much comfort in't; says, 'My poor prisoner,
    I am innocent as you.'
PAULINA   I dare be sworn.
    These dangerous, unsafe lunes i'th'King, beshrew them!   30
    He must be told on't, and he shall. The office
    Becomes a woman best. I'll take't upon me.
    If I prove honey-mouthed, let my tongue blister,
    And never to my red-looked anger be
    The trumpet any more. Pray you, Emilia,
    Commend my best obedience to the Queen.
    If she dares trust me with her little babe,
    I'll show't the King, and undertake to be
    Her advocate to th'loud'st. We do not know
    How he may soften at the sight o'th'child: 40
    The silence often of pure innocence
    Persuades when speaking fails.
EMILIA   Most worthy madam,
    Your honour and your goodness is so evident
    That your free undertaking cannot miss
    A thriving issue. There is no lady living
    So meet for this great errand. Please your ladyship
    To visit the next room, I'll presently
    Acquaint the Queen of your most noble offer,
    Who but today hammered of this design,
    But durst not tempt a minister of honour   50
    Lest she should be denied.
PAULINA   Tell her, Emilia,
    I'll use that tongue I have. If wit flow from't
    As boldness from my bosom, let't not be doubted
    I shall do good.

EMILIA   Now be you blest for it!
　I'll to the Queen. Please you come something nearer.

GAOLER
　Madam, if't please the Queen to send the babe,
　I know not what I shall incur to pass it,
　Having no warrant.

PAULINA   You need not fear it, sir.
　This child was prisoner to the womb, and is
60 By law and process of great Nature thence
　Freed and enfranchised; not a party to
　The anger of the King, nor guilty of,
　If any be, the trespass of the Queen.

GAOLER
　I do believe it.

PAULINA
　Do not you fear. Upon mine honour, I
　Will stand betwixt you and danger.   *Exeunt*

II.3   *Enter Leontes*

LEONTES
　Nor night nor day no rest! It is but weakness
　To bear the matter thus, mere weakness. If
　The cause were not in being – part o'th'cause,
　She, th'adult'ress: for the harlot-king
　Is quite beyond mine arm, out of the blank
　And level of my brain, plot-proof; but she
　I can hook to me – say that she were gone,
　Given to the fire, a moiety of my rest
　Might come to me again. Who's there?
　　　Enter Servant

SERVANT   My lord?

LEONTES
　How does the boy?

SERVANT   He took good rest tonight.   10
'Tis hoped his sickness is discharged.

LEONTES
To see his nobleness!
Conceiving the dishonour of his mother,
He straight declined, drooped, took it deeply,
Fastened and fixed the shame on't in himself;
Threw off his spirit, his appetite, his sleep,
And downright languished. Leave me solely. Go,
See how he fares.   *Exit Servant*
                Fie, fie, no thought of him!
The very thought of my revenges that way
Recoil upon me: in himself too mighty,   20
And in his parties, his alliance. Let him be
Until a time may serve; for present vengeance
Take it on her. Camillo and Polixenes
Laugh at me, make their pastime at my sorrow.
They should not laugh if I could reach them, nor
Shall she within my power.
        Enter Paulina, carrying a baby, followed by Anti-
        gonus, Lords, and the Servant, who try to prevent her

LORD   You must not enter.

PAULINA
Nay, rather, good my lords, be second to me.
Fear you his tyrannous passion more, alas,
Than the Queen's life? A gracious, innocent soul,
More free than he is jealous.

ANTIGONUS   That's enough.   30

SERVANT
Madam, he hath not slept tonight, commanded
None should come at him.

PAULINA   Not so hot, good sir.
I come to bring him sleep. 'Tis such as you,
That creep like shadows by him, and do sigh

At each his needless heavings – such as you
Nourish the cause of his awaking. I
Do come with words as med'cinal as true,
Honest as either, to purge him of that humour
That presses him from sleep.

LEONTES   What noise there, ho?

PAULINA

40   No noise, my lord, but needful conference
About some gossips for your highness.

LEONTES   How?
Away with that audacious lady! Antigonus,
I charged thee that she should not come about me.
I knew she would.

ANTIGONUS   I told her so, my lord,
On your displeasure's peril, and on mine,
She should not visit you.

LEONTES   What? Canst not rule her?

PAULINA
From all dishonesty he can. In this –
Unless he take the course that you have done:
Commit me for committing honour – trust it,

50   He shall not rule me.

ANTIGONUS   La you now, you hear.
When she will take the rein, I let her run;
But she'll not stumble.

PAULINA   Good my liege, I come –
And I beseech you hear me, who professes
Myself your loyal servant, your physician,
Your most obedient counsellor; yet that dares
Less appear so in comforting your evils
Than such as most seem yours – I say, I come
From your good queen.

LEONTES   Good queen?

PAULINA

  Good queen, my lord, good queen, I say good queen;

  And would by combat make her good, so were I   60

  A man, the worst about you.

LEONTES   Force her hence.

PAULINA

  Let him that makes but trifles of his eyes

  First hand me. On mine own accord I'll off,

  But first I'll do my errand. The good Queen –

  For she is good – hath brought you forth a daughter:

  Here 'tis; commends it to your blessing.

    She lays down the child

LEONTES   Out!

  A mankind witch! Hence with her, out o'door!

  A most intelligencing bawd!

PAULINA   Not so:

  I am as ignorant in that as you

  In so entitling me; and no less honest   70

  Than you are mad; which is enough, I'll warrant,

  As this world goes, to pass for honest.

LEONTES   Traitors!

  Will you not push her out? Give her the bastard.

  (*To Antigonus*) Thou dotard, thou art woman-tired,

    unroosted

  By thy Dame Partlet here. Take up the bastard!

  Take't up, I say! Give't to thy crone.

PAULINA   For ever

  Unvenerable be thy hands if thou

  Tak'st up the Princess by that forcèd baseness

  Which he has put upon't!

LEONTES   He dreads his wife.

PAULINA

  So I would you did: then 'twere past all doubt   80

  You'd call your children yours.

LEONTES   A nest of traitors!

ANTIGONUS

I am none, by this good light!

PAULINA   Nor I, nor any
But one that's here, and that's himself: for he
The sacred honour of himself, his queen's,
His hopeful son's, his babe's, betrays to slander,
Whose sting is sharper than the sword's; and will not –
For, as the case now stands, it is a curse
He cannot be compelled to't – once remove
The root of his opinion, which is rotten
90   As ever oak or stone was sound.

LEONTES   A callat
Of boundless tongue, who late hath beat her husband,
And now baits me! This brat is none of mine:
It is the issue of Polixenes.
Hence with it, and together with the dam
Commit them to the fire!

PAULINA   It is yours;
And, might we lay th'old proverb to your charge,
So like you, 'tis the worse. Behold, my lords,
Although the print be little, the whole matter
And copy of the father: eye, nose, lip;
100   The trick of 's frown; his forehead; nay, the valley,
The pretty dimples of his chin and cheek; his smiles;
The very mould and frame of hand, nail, finger.
And thou, good goddess Nature, which hast made it
So like to him that got it, if thou hast
The ordering of the mind too, 'mongst all colours
No yellow in't, lest she suspect, as he does,
Her children not her husband's.

LEONTES   A gross hag!
And, losel, thou art worthy to be hanged,
That wilt not stay her tongue.

yellow is colour jealousy

ANTIGONUS   Hang all the husbands
  That cannot do that feat, you'll leave yourself   110
  Hardly one subject.
LEONTES   Once more, take her hence.
PAULINA
  A most unworthy and unnatural lord
  Can do no more.
LEONTES   I'll ha'thee burned.
PAULINA   I care not:
  It is an heretic that makes the fire,
  Not she which burns in't. I'll not call you tyrant;
  But this most cruel usage of your queen –
  Not able to produce more accusation
  Than your own weak-hinged fancy – something savours
  Of tyranny, and will ignoble make you,
  Yea, scandalous to the world.
LEONTES   On your allegiance,   120
  Out of the chamber with her! Were I a tyrant,
  Where were her life? She durst not call me so,
  If she did know me one. Away with her!

    They slowly push her towards the door

PAULINA
  I pray you, do not push me, I'll be gone.
  Look to your babe, my lord; 'tis yours. Jove send her
  A better guiding spirit! What needs these hands?
  You that are thus so tender o'er his follies
  Will never do him good, not one of you.
  So, so. Farewell, we are gone.   *Exit*
LEONTES
  Thou, traitor, hast set on thy wife to this.   130
  My child? Away with't! Even thou, that hast
  A heart so tender o'er it, take it hence
  And see it instantly consumed with fire:
  Even thou, and none but thou. Take it up straight!

Within this hour bring me word 'tis done,
And by good testimony, or I'll seize thy life,
With what thou else call'st thine. If thou refuse,
And wilt encounter with my wrath, say so:
The bastard brains with these my proper hands
140   Shall I dash out. Go, take it to the fire,   *actor changing*
For thou set'st on thy wife.   *convincin*

ANTIGONUS   I did not, sir.
These lords, my noble fellows, if they please,
Can clear me in't.

LORDS   We can. My royal liege,
He is not guilty of her coming hither.

LEONTES
You're liars all.

LORD
Beseech your highness, give us better credit.
We have always truly served you, and beseech'
So to esteem of us; and on our knees we beg,
As recompense of our dear services
150   Past and to come, that you do change this purpose,
Which being so horrible, so bloody, must
Lead on to some foul issue. We all kneel.

LEONTES
I am a feather for each wind that blows.
Shall I live on to see this bastard kneel
And call me father? Better burn it now
Than curse it then. But be it: let it live.
It shall not neither. (*To Antigonus*) You, sir, come you
        hither:
You that have been so tenderly officious
With Lady Margery, your midwife there,
160   To save this bastard's life – for 'tis a bastard,
So sure as this beard's grey – what will you adventure
To save this brat's life?

founelling hospital for abandoned children.
used them as thing should be'
41   THE WINTER'S TALE : II.3

ANTIGONUS   Anything, my lord,
That my ability may undergo,
And nobleness impose — at least thus much:
I'll pawn the little blood which I have left
To save the innocent — anything possible.

LEONTES
It shall be possible. Swear by this sword
Thou wilt perform my bidding.

ANTIGONUS (*his hand upon the hilt*)   Here dealing with
                                            Lord/King. net
                              I will, my lord.   Poor.

LEONTES   out of ordinary.
Mark and perform it, see'st thou? For the fail
Of any point in't shall not only be   170
Death to thyself, but to thy lewd-tongued wife,
Whom for this time we pardon. We enjoin thee,
As thou art liegeman to us, that thou carry —
This female bastard hence, and that thou bear it
To some remote and desert place, quite out
Of our dominions; and that there thou leave it,
Without more mercy, to its own protection
And favour of the climate. As by strange fortune
It came to us, I do in justice charge thee,
On thy soul's peril and thy body's torture,   180
That thou commend it strangely to some place
Where chance may nurse or end it. Take it up.

ANTIGONUS — agreed to do this. Live with ( ) + chapel
I swear to do this, though a present death   agitated
Had been more merciful. Come on, poor babe,
Some powerful spirit instruct the kites and ravens
To be thy nurses! Wolves and bears, they say,   woef-
Casting their savageness aside, have done   bear
Like offices of pity. Sir, be prosperous   romake
In more than this deed does require! And blessing   from
Against this cruelty fight on thy side,   190

element of Mosses — bibl. texts

Poor thing, condemned to loss!   *Exit with the child*
LEONTES   No, I'll not rear
    Another's issue.
        Enter a Servant

SERVANT   Please your highness, posts
    From those you sent to th'oracle are come
    An hour since: Cleomenes and Dion,
    Being well arrived from Delphos, are both landed,
    Hasting to th'court.
LORD   So please you, sir, their speed
    Hath been beyond accompt.
LEONTES   Twenty-three days
    They have been absent. 'Tis good speed; foretells
    The great Apollo suddenly will have
200 The truth of this appear. Prepare you, lords.
    Summon a session, that we may arraign
    Our most disloyal lady: for as she hath
    Been publicly accused, so shall she have
    A just and open trial. While she lives
    My heart will be a burden to me. Leave me,
    And think upon my bidding.   *Exeunt*

*

III.1   *Enter Cleomenes and Dion*
    CLEOMENES
        The climate's delicate, the air most sweet,
        Fertile the isle, the temple much surpassing
        The common praise it bears.
    DION   I shall report,
        For most it caught me, the celestial habits –
        Methinks I so should term them – and the reverence
        Of the grave wearers. O, the sacrifice!

How ceremonious, solemn, and unearthly
It was i'th'off'ring!

CLEOMENES
But of all, the burst
And the ear-deaf'ning voice o'th'oracle,
Kin to Jove's thunder, so surprised my sense
That I was nothing.

DION
If th'event o'th'journey
Prove as successful to the Queen – O, be't so! –
As it hath been to us rare, pleasant, speedy,
The time is worth the use on't.

CLEOMENES
Great Apollo
Turn all to th'best! These proclamations,
So forcing faults upon Hermione,
I little like.

DION
The violent carriage of it
Will clear or end the business. When the oracle,
Thus by Apollo's great divine sealed up,
Shall the contents discover, something rare
Even then will rush to knowledge. Go: fresh horses!
And gracious be the issue. *Exeunt*

Enter Leontes, Lords, and Officers III.2

LEONTES
This sessions, to our great grief we pronounce,
Even pushes 'gainst our heart: the party tried
The daughter of a king, our wife, and one
Of us too much beloved. Let us be cleared
Of being tyrannous, since we so openly
Proceed in justice, which shall have due course,
Even to the guilt or the purgation.
Produce the prisoner.

OFFICER
It is his highness' pleasure that the Queen

10   Appear in person here in court.
        Enter Hermione, guarded, Paulina, and Ladies
        attending
                                              Silence!
LEONTES
        Read the indictment.
OFFICER (*reads*) *Hermione, Queen to the worthy Leontes,*
        King of Sicilia, thou art here accused and arraigned of high
        treason, in committing adultery with Polixenes, King of
        Bohemia, and conspiring with Camillo to take away the
        life of our sovereign lord the King, thy royal husband;
        the pretence whereof being by circumstances partly laid
        open, thou, Hermione, contrary to the faith and allegiance
        of a true subject, didst counsel and aid them, for their
20   *better safety, to fly away by night.*
HERMIONE
        Since what I am to say must be but that
        Which contradicts my accusation, and
        The testimony on my part no other
        But what comes from myself, it shall scarce boot me
        To say 'Not guilty': mine integrity
        Being counted falsehood, shall, as I express it,
        Be so received. But thus: if powers divine
        Behold our human actions – as they do –
        I doubt not then but innocence shall make
30   False accusation blush, and tyranny
        Tremble at patience. You, my lord, best know –
        Who least will seem to do so – my past life
        Hath been as continent, as chaste, as true,
        As I am now unhappy; which is more
        Than history can pattern, though devised
        And played to take spectators. For behold me,
        A fellow of the royal bed, which owe
        A moiety of the throne, a great king's daughter,

The mother to a hopeful prince, here standing
To prate and talk for life and honour 'fore   40
Who please to come and hear. For life, I prize it
As I weigh grief, which I would spare; for honour,
'Tis a derivative from me to mine,
And only that I stand for. I appeal
To your own conscience, sir, before Polixenes
Came to your court, how I was in your grace,
How merited to be so; since he came,
With what encounter so uncurrent I
Have strained t'appear thus: if one jot beyond
The bound of honour, or in act or will   50
That way inclining, hardened be the hearts
Of all that hear me, and my near'st of kin
Cry fie upon my grave!

LEONTES   I ne'er heard yet
That any of these bolder vices wanted
Less impudence to gainsay what they did
Than to perform it first.

HERMIONE   That's true enough,
Though 'tis a saying, sir, not due to me.

LEONTES
You will not own it.

HERMIONE   More than mistress of
Which comes to me in name of fault I must not
At all acknowledge. For Polixenes,   60
With whom I am accused, I do confess
I loved him as in honour he required:
With such a kind of love as might become
A lady like me; with a love even such,
So and no other, as yourself commanded;
Which not to have done I think had been in me
Both disobedience and ingratitude
To you and toward your friend, whose love had spoke

Even since it could speak, from an infant, freely
That it was yours. Now, for conspiracy,
I know not how it tastes, though it be dished
For me to try how. All I know of it
Is that Camillo was an honest man;
And why he left your court the gods themselves,
Wotting no more than I, are ignorant.

LEONTES
You knew of his departure, as you know
What you have underta'en to do in's absence.

HERMIONE
Sir,
You speak a language that I understand not.
My life stands in the level of your dreams,
Which I'll lay down.

LEONTES   Your actions are my dreams.
You had a bastard by Polixenes,
And I but dreamed it. As you were past all shame –
Those of your fact are so – so past all truth;
Which to deny concerns more than avails: for as
Thy brat hath been cast out, like to itself,
No father owning it – which is indeed
More criminal in thee than it – so thou
Shalt feel our justice, in whose easiest passage
Look for no less than death.

HERMIONE   Sir, spare your threats!
The bug which you would fright me with I seek.
To me can life be no commodity:
The crown and comfort of my life, your favour,
I do give lost, for I do feel it gone,
But know not how it went. My second joy,
And first-fruits of my body, from his presence
I am barred, like one infectious. My third comfort,
Starred most unluckily, is from my breast –

The innocent milk in its most innocent mouth –
Haled out to murder. Myself on every post   100
Proclaimed a strumpet; with immodest hatred
The childbed privilege denied, which 'longs
To women of all fashion; lastly, hurried
Here to this place, i'th'open air, before
I have got strength of limit. Now, my liege,
Tell me what blessings I have here alive
That I should fear to die. Therefore proceed.
But yet hear this – mistake me not: no life,
I prize it not a straw; but for mine honour,
Which I would free – if I shall be condemned   110
Upon surmises, all proofs sleeping else
But what your jealousies awake, I tell you
'Tis rigour and not law. Your honours all,
I do refer me to the oracle:
Apollo be my judge!

LORD   This your request
Is altogether just. Therefore bring forth,
And in Apollo's name, his oracle. *Exeunt certain Officers*

HERMIONE
The Emperor of Russia was my father.
O that he were alive, and here beholding
His daughter's trial! That he did but see   120
The flatness of my misery; yet with eyes
Of pity, not revenge!
      Enter Officers, with Cleomenes and Dion

OFFICER
You here shall swear upon this sword of justice
That you, Cleomenes and Dion, have
Been both at Delphos, and from thence have brought
This sealed-up oracle, by the hand delivered
Of great Apollo's priest; and that since then

You have not dared to break the holy seal,
Nor read the secrets in't.

CLEOMENES *and* DION   All this we swear.

LEONTES

130 Break up the seals and read.

OFFICER (*reads*) *Hermione is chaste; Polixenes blameless;*
Camillo a true subject; Leontes a jealous tyrant; his in-
nocent babe truly begotten; and the King shall live without
an heir, if that which is lost be not found.

LORDS

Now blessèd be the great Apollo!

HERMIONE   Praised!

LEONTES

Hast thou read truth?

OFFICER   Ay, my lord, even so
As it is here set down.

LEONTES

There is no truth at all i'th'oracle!
The sessions shall proceed: this is mere falsehood.

    Enter Servant

SERVANT

140 My lord the King, the King!

LEONTES   What is the business?

SERVANT

O sir, I shall be hated to report it:
The Prince your son, with mere conceit and fear
Of the Queen's speed, is gone.

LEONTES   How! Gone?

SERVANT   Is dead.

LEONTES

Apollo's angry, and the heavens themselves
Do strike at my injustice.

    Hermione faints

                              How now there!

PAULINA

   This news is mortal to the Queen: look down
   And see what death is doing.

LEONTES   Take her hence.
   Her heart is but o'ercharged; she will recover.
   I have too much believed mine own suspicion.
   Beseech you, tenderly apply to her   150
   Some remedies for life.

                Exeunt Paulina and Ladies, bearing Hermione
                         Apollo, pardon
   My great profaneness 'gainst thine oracle!
   I'll reconcile me to Polixenes;
   New woo my queen; recall the good Camillo –
   Whom I proclaim a man of truth, of mercy:
   For, being transported by my jealousies
   To bloody thoughts and to revenge, I chose
   Camillo for the minister to poison
   My friend Polixenes; which had been done,
   But that the good mind of Camillo tardied   160
   My swift command, though I with death and with
   Reward did threaten and encourage him,
   Not doing it and being done. He, most humane,
   And filled with honour, to my kingly guest
   Unclasped my practice, quit his fortunes here –
   Which you knew great – and to the hazard
   Of all incertainties himself commended,
   No richer than his honour. How he glisters
   Through my rust! And how his piety
   Does my deeds make the blacker!

      Enter Paulina

PAULINA   Woe the while!   170
   O cut my lace, lest my heart, cracking it,
   Break too!

LORD   What fit is this, good lady?

PAULINA

What studied torments, tyrant, hast for me?
What wheels? Racks? Fires? What flaying? Boiling
In leads or oils? What old or newer torture
Must I receive, whose every word deserves
To taste of thy most worst? Thy tyranny,
Together working with thy jealousies –
Fancies too weak for boys, too green and idle
For girls of nine – O think what they have done,
And then run mad indeed, stark mad! For all
Thy bygone fooleries were but spices of it.
That thou betrayedst Polixenes 'twas nothing:
That did but show thee of a fool inconstant,
And damnable ingrateful. Nor was't much
Thou wouldst have poisoned good Camillo's honour
To have him kill a king – poor trespasses,
More monstrous standing by: whereof I reckon
The casting forth to crows thy baby daughter
To be or none or little, though a devil
Would have shed water out of fire ere done't;
Nor is't directly laid to thee, the death
Of the young Prince, whose honourable thoughts –
Thoughts high for one so tender – cleft the heart
That could conceive a gross and foolish sire
Blemished his gracious dam. This is not, no,
Laid to thy answer. But the last – O lords,
When I have said, cry woe! The Queen, the Queen,
The sweet'st, dear'st creature's dead! And vengeance
    for't
Not dropped down yet.

LORDS   The higher powers forbid!

PAULINA

I say she's dead; I'll swear't. If word nor oath
Prevail not, go and see. If you can bring

Tincture or lustre in her lip, her eye,
Heat outwardly or breath within, I'll serve you
As I would do the gods. But, O thou tyrant,
Do not repent these things, for they are heavier
Than all thy woes can stir. Therefore betake thee
To nothing but despair. A thousand knees,
Ten thousand years together, naked, fasting,
Upon a barren mountain, and still winter   210
In storm perpetual, could not move the gods
To look that way thou wert.

LEONTES   Go on, go on:
Thou canst not speak too much; I have deserved
All tongues to talk their bitt'rest.

LORD   Say no more.
Howe'er the business goes, you have made fault
I'th'boldness of your speech.

PAULINA   I am sorry for't.
All faults I make, when I shall come to know them,
I do repent. Alas, I have showed too much
The rashness of a woman! He is touched
To th'noble heart. What's gone and what's past help   220
Should be past grief. Do not receive affliction
At my petition, I beseech you; rather
Let me be punished, that have minded you
Of what you should forget. Now, good my liege,
Sir, royal sir, forgive a foolish woman.
The love I bore your queen – lo, fool again!
I'll speak of her no more, nor of your children;
I'll not remember you of my own lord,
Who is lost too. Take your patience to you,
And I'll say nothing.

LEONTES   Thou didst speak but well   230
When most the truth; which I receive much better
Than to be pitied of thee. Prithee, bring me

To the dead bodies of my queen and son.
One grave shall be for both: upon them shall
The causes of their death appear, unto
Our shame perpetual. Once a day I'll visit
The chapel where they lie, and tears shed there
Shall be my recreation. So long as nature
Will bear up with this exercise, so long
240   I daily vow to use it. Come,
And lead me to these sorrows.   *Exeunt*

III.3   *Enter Antigonus with the child, and a Mariner*

ANTIGONUS
Thou art perfect, then, our ship hath touched upon
The deserts of Bohemia?
MARINER   Ay, my lord, and fear
We have landed in ill time: the skies look grimly,
And threaten present blusters. In my conscience,
The heavens with that we have in hand are angry
And frown upon's.
ANTIGONUS
Their sacred wills be done! Go, get aboard;
Look to thy bark. I'll not be long before
I call upon thee.
MARINER   Make your best haste, and go not
10   Too far i'th'land: 'tis like to be loud weather.
Besides, this place is famous for the creatures
Of prey that keep upon't.
ANTIGONUS   Go thou away:
I'll follow instantly.
MARINER   I am glad at heart
To be so rid o'th'business.   *Exit*
ANTIGONUS   Come, poor babe.
I have heard, but not believed, the spirits o'th'dead

May walk again: if such thing be, thy mother
Appeared to me last night; for ne'er was dream
So like a waking. To me comes a creature,
Sometimes her head on one side, some another:
I never saw a vessel of like sorrow,   20
So filled and so becoming. In pure white robes,
Like very sanctity, she did approach
My cabin where I lay; thrice bowed before me,
And, gasping to begin some speech, her eyes
Became two spouts; the fury spent, anon
Did this break from her: 'Good Antigonus,
Since fate, against thy better disposition,
Hath made thy person for the thrower-out
Of my poor babe, according to thy oath,
Places remote enough are in Bohemia: 30
There weep, and leave it crying; and for the babe
Is counted lost for ever, Perdita
I prithee call't. For this ungentle business,
Put on thee by my lord, thou ne'er shalt see
Thy wife Paulina more.' And so, with shrieks,
She melted into air. Affrighted much,
I did in time collect myself, and thought
This was so, and no slumber. Dreams are toys:
Yet for this once, yea superstitiously,
I will be squared by this. I do believe   40
Hermione hath suffered death, and that
Apollo would, this being indeed the issue
Of King Polixenes, it should here be laid,
Either for life or death, upon the earth
Of its right father. Blossom, speed thee well!
        He lays down the child, and a scroll
There lie, and there thy character;
        (*he lays down a box*)
                                    there these,

Which may, if fortune please, both breed thee, pretty,
And still rest thine. The storm begins. Poor wretch,
That for thy mother's fault art thus exposed
50   To loss and what may follow! Weep I cannot,
But my heart bleeds; and most accursed am I
To be by oath enjoined to this. Farewell!
The day frowns more and more. Thou'rt like to have
A lullaby too rough: I never saw
The heavens so dim by day. — A savage clamour!
Well may I get aboard! This is the chase.
I am gone for ever!   *Exit, pursued by a bear*
        Enter an old Shepherd
SHEPHERD I would there were no age between ten and
    three-and-twenty, or that youth would sleep out the
60   rest: for there is nothing in the between but getting
    wenches with child, wronging the ancientry, stealing,
    fighting. Hark you now: would any but these boiled
    brains of nineteen and two-and-twenty hunt this
    weather? They have scared away two of my best sheep,
    which I fear the wolf will sooner find than the master. If
    anywhere I have them, 'tis by the seaside, browsing of
    ivy. Good luck, an't be thy will!
        He sees the child
    What have we here? Mercy on's, a barne! A very pretty
    barne. A boy or a child, I wonder? A pretty one, a very
70   pretty one. Sure, some scape. Though I am not bookish,
    yet I can read waiting gentlewoman in the scape: this
    has been some stair-work, some trunk-work, some be-
    hind-door-work. They were warmer that got this than
    the poor thing is here. I'll take it up for pity — yet I'll
    tarry till my son come: he hallowed but even now. Whoa-
    ho-hoa!
        Enter Clown
CLOWN Hilloa, loa!

SHEPHERD What! Art so near? If thou'lt see a thing to
    talk on when thou art dead and rotten, come hither.
    What ail'st thou, man?   80

CLOWN I have seen two such sights, by sea and by land!
    But I am not to say it is a sea, for it is now the sky: be-
    twixt the firmament and it you cannot thrust a bodkin's
    point.

SHEPHERD Why, boy, how is it?

CLOWN I would you did but see how it chafes, how it
    rages, how it takes up the shore – but that's not to the
    point. O, the most piteous cry of the poor souls! Some-
    times to see 'em, and not to see 'em: now the ship boring
    the moon with her mainmast, and anon swallowed with   90
    yeast and froth, as you'd thrust a cork into a hogshead.
    And then for the land-service: to see how the bear tore
    out his shoulder bone, how he cried to me for help, and
    said his name was Antigonus, a nobleman. But to make
    an end of the ship: to see how the sea flap-dragoned it;
    but first, how the poor souls roared, and the sea mocked
    them; and how the poor gentleman roared, and the bear
    mocked him, both roaring louder than the sea or weather.

SHEPHERD Name of mercy, when was this, boy?

CLOWN Now, now! I have not winked since I saw these   100
    sights. The men are not yet cold under water, nor the
    bear half dined on the gentleman; he's at it now.

SHEPHERD Would I had been by, to have helped the old
    man!

CLOWN I would you had been by the ship side, to have
    helped her: there your charity would have lacked
    footing.

SHEPHERD Heavy matters, heavy matters! But look thee
    here, boy. Now bless thyself: thou met'st with things
    dying, I with things new-born. Here's a sight for thee: 110

look thee, a bearing-cloth for a squire's child! Look thee
here!

He points to the box

Take up, take up, boy; open it. So, let's see. It was told
me I should be rich by the fairies. This is some changeling. Open't. What's within, boy?

CLOWN (*opening the box*) You're a made old man. If the
sins of your youth are forgiven you, you're well to live.
Gold! All gold!

SHEPHERD This is fairy gold, boy, and 'twill prove so. Up
with't, keep it close. Home, home, the next way! We are
lucky, boy, and to be so still requires nothing but
secrecy. Let my sheep go! Come, good boy, the next
way home.

CLOWN Go you the next way with your findings. I'll go
see if the bear be gone from the gentleman, and how
much he hath eaten. They are never curst but when
they are hungry. If there be any of him left, I'll bury it.

SHEPHERD That's a good deed. If thou mayst discern by
that which is left of him what he is, fetch me to th'sight
of him.

CLOWN Marry will I; and you shall help to put him
i'th'ground.

SHEPHERD 'Tis a lucky day, boy, and we'll do good deeds
on't.   *Exeunt*

*

IV.1   *Enter Time, the Chorus*

TIME

I that please some, try all; both joy and terror
Of good and bad; that makes and unfolds error,

Now take upon me, in the name of Time,
To use my wings. Impute it not a crime
To me or my swift passage that I slide
O'er sixteen years, and leave the growth untried
Of that wide gap, since it is in my power
To o'erthrow law, and in one self-born hour
To plant and o'erwhelm custom. Let me pass
The same I am ere ancient'st order was   10
Or what is now received. I witness to
The times that brought them in; so shall I do
To th'freshest things now reigning, and make stale
The glistering of this present, as my tale
Now seems to it. Your patience this allowing,
I turn my glass, and give my scene such growing
As you had slept between. Leontes leaving –
Th'effects of his fond jealousies so grieving
That he shuts up himself – imagine me,
Gentle spectators, that I now may be   20
In fair Bohemia; and remember well,
I mentioned a son o'th'King's, which Florizel
I now name to you; and with speed so pace
To speak of Perdita, now grown in grace
Equal with wond'ring. What of her ensues
I list not prophesy; but let Time's news
Be known when 'tis brought forth. A shepherd's
    daughter,
And what to her adheres, which follows after,
Is th'argument of Time. Of this allow,
If ever you have spent time worse ere now;   30
If never, yet that Time himself doth say
He wishes earnestly you never may.   *Exit*

IV.2   *Enter Polixenes and Camillo*

POLIXENES I pray thee, good Camillo, be no more im-
portunate. 'Tis a sickness denying thee anything; a
death to grant this.

CAMILLO It is fifteen years since I saw my country.
Though I have for the most part been aired abroad, I
desire to lay my bones there. Besides, the penitent King,
my master, hath sent for me; to whose feeling sorrows I
might be some allay – or I o'erween to think so – which
is another spur to my departure.

10 POLIXENES As thou lov'st me, Camillo, wipe not out the
rest of thy services by leaving me now. The need I have
of thee thine own goodness hath made. Better not to
have had thee than thus to want thee. Thou, having
made me businesses which none without thee can
sufficiently manage, must either stay to execute them
thyself or take away with thee the very services thou hast
done; which, if I have not enough considered – as too
much I cannot – to be more thankful to thee shall be my
study, and my profit therein the heaping friendships. Of
20 that fatal country, Sicilia, prithee speak no more, whose
very naming punishes me with the remembrance of that
penitent, as thou call'st him, and reconciled king, my
brother; whose loss of his most precious queen and
children are even now to be afresh lamented. Say to me,
when saw'st thou the Prince Florizel, my son? Kings
are no less unhappy, their issue not being gracious, than
they are in losing them when they have approved their
virtues.

CAMILLO Sir, it is three days since I saw the Prince. What
30 his happier affairs may be are to me unknown; but I
have missingly noted he is of late much retired from
court, and is less frequent to his princely exercises than
formerly he hath appeared.

POLIXENES I have considered so much, Camillo, and
with some care; so far that I have eyes under my service
which look upon his removedness, from whom I have
this intelligence: that he is seldom from the house of a
most homely shepherd — a man, they say, that from very
nothing, and beyond the imagination of his neighbours,
is grown into an unspeakable estate.   40

CAMILLO I have heard, sir, of such a man, who hath a
daughter of most rare note; the report of her is extended
more than can be thought to begin from such a cottage.

POLIXENES That's likewise part of my intelligence, but, I
fear, the angle that plucks our son thither. Thou shalt
accompany us to the place, where we will, not appearing
what we are, have some question with the shepherd;
from whose simplicity I think it not uneasy to get the
cause of my son's resort thither. Prithee be my present
partner in this business, and lay aside the thoughts of   50
Sicilia.

CAMILLO I willingly obey your command.

POLIXENES My best Camillo! We must disguise our-
selves.   *Exeunt*

Enter Autolycus, singing   IV.3
AUTOLYCUS
　　When daffodils begin to peer,
　　　　With heigh, the doxy over the dale,
　　Why, then comes in the sweet o'the year,
　　　　For the red blood reigns in the winter's pale.

　　The white sheet bleaching on the hedge,
　　　　With heigh, the sweet birds O, how they sing!
　　Doth set my pugging tooth an edge,
　　　　For a quart of ale is a dish for a king.

The lark, that tirra-lyra chants,
With heigh, with heigh, the thrush and the jay,
Are summer songs for me and my aunts
While we lie tumbling in the hay.

I have served Prince Florizel, and in my time wore
three-pile; but now I am out of service.

But shall I go mourn for that, my dear?
The pale moon shines by night:
And when I wander here and there
I then do most go right.

If tinkers may have leave to live,
And bear the sow-skin budget,
Then my account I well may give,
And in the stocks avouch it.

My traffic is sheets; when the kite builds, look to lesser
linen. My father named me Autolycus, who, being, as I
am, littered under Mercury, was likewise a snapper-up
of unconsidered trifles. With die and drab I purchased
this caparison, and my revenue is the silly cheat. Gallows and knock are too powerful on the highway: beating and hanging are terrors to me. For the life to come, I
sleep out the thought of it. A prize! A prize!
Enter Clown

CLOWN Let me see: every 'leven wether tods, every tod
yields pound and odd shilling; fifteen hundred shorn,
what comes the wool to?

AUTOLYCUS (*aside*) If the springe hold, the cock's mine.

CLOWN I cannot do't without counters. Let me see: what
am I to buy for our sheep-shearing feast? Three pound
of sugar, five pound of currants, rice – what will this

sister of mine do with rice? But my father hath made her
mistress of the feast, and she lays it on. She hath made
me four-and-twenty nosegays for the shearers, three-   40
man-song men all, and very good ones; but they are
most of them means and basses – but one Puritan
amongst them, and he sings psalms to hornpipes. I must
have saffron to colour the warden pies; mace; dates –
none, that's out of my note; nutmegs, seven; a race or
two of ginger, but that I may beg; four pound of prunes,
and as many of raisins o'th'sun.

AUTOLYCUS (*grovelling on the ground*) O that ever I was
born!

CLOWN I'th'name of me!   50

AUTOLYCUS O, help me, help me! Pluck but off these
rags; and then death, death!

CLOWN Alack, poor soul! Thou hast need of more rags
to lay on thee, rather than have these off.

AUTOLYCUS O sir, the loathsomeness of them offend me
more than the stripes I have received, which are mighty
ones and millions.

CLOWN Alas, poor man! A million of beating may come
to a great matter.

AUTOLYCUS I am robbed, sir, and beaten; my money and 60
apparel ta'en from me, and these detestable things put
upon me.

CLOWN What, by a horseman or a footman?

AUTOLYCUS A footman, sweet sir, a footman.

CLOWN Indeed, he should be a footman, by the garments
he has left with thee. If this be a horseman's coat, it hath
seen very hot service. Lend me thy hand, I'll help thee.
Come, lend me thy hand.

   He helps him up

AUTOLYCUS O, good sir, tenderly, O!

CLOWN Alas, poor soul!   70

AUTOLYCUS O, good sir, softly, good sir! I fear, sir, my shoulder-blade is out.

CLOWN How now? Canst stand?

AUTOLYCUS Softly, dear sir; (*he picks his pockets*) good sir, softly. You ha'done me a charitable office.

CLOWN Dost lack any money? I have a little money for thee.

AUTOLYCUS No, good, sweet sir; no, I beseech you, sir. I have a kinsman not past three-quarters of a mile hence, 80 unto whom I was going. I shall there have money, or anything I want. Offer me no money, I pray you: that kills my heart.

CLOWN What manner of fellow was he that robbed you?

AUTOLYCUS A fellow, sir, that I have known to go about with troll-my-dames. I knew him once a servant of the Prince. I cannot tell, good sir, for which of his virtues it was, but he was certainly whipped out of the court.

CLOWN His vices, you would say. There's no virtue whipped out of the court: they cherish it to make it stay 90 there; and yet it will no more but abide.

AUTOLYCUS Vices I would say, sir. I know this man well. He hath been since an ape-bearer; then a process-server, a bailiff; then he compassed a motion of the Prodigal Son, and married a tinker's wife within a mile where my land and living lies; and having flown over many knavish professions, he settled only in rogue. Some call him Autolycus.

CLOWN Out upon him! Prig, for my life, prig! He haunts wakes, fairs, and bear-baitings.

100 AUTOLYCUS Very true, sir; he, sir, he: that's the rogue that put me into this apparel.

CLOWN Not a more cowardly rogue in all Bohemia. If you had but looked big and spit at him, he'd have run.

AUTOLYCUS I must confess to you, sir, I am no fighter. I

am false of heart that way, and that he knew, I warrant
him.

CLOWN How do you now?

AUTOLYCUS Sweet sir, much better than I was: I can
stand and walk. I will even take my leave of you, and
pace softly towards my kinsman's.   110

CLOWN Shall I bring thee on the way?

AUTOLYCUS No, good-faced sir; no, sweet sir.

CLOWN Then fare thee well. I must go buy spices for our
sheep-shearing.

AUTOLYCUS Prosper you, sweet sir!   *Exit Clown*
Your purse is not hot enough to purchase your spice.
I'll be with you at your sheep-shearing too. If I make
not this cheat bring out another, and the shearers prove
sheep, let me be unrolled, and my name put in the book
of virtue! (*Sings*)   120

      Jog on, jog on, the footpath way,
        And merrily hent the stile-a:
      A merry heart goes all the day,
        Your sad tires in a mile-a.   *Exit*

Enter Florizel and Perdita   IV.4

FLORIZEL
These your unusual weeds to each part of you
Does give a life: no shepherdess, but Flora
Peering in April's front. This your sheep-shearing
Is as a meeting of the petty gods,
And you the queen on't.

PERDITA   Sir, my gracious lord,
To chide at your extremes it not becomes me –
O, pardon that I name them: your high self,
The gracious mark o'th'land, you have obscured
With a swain's wearing, and me, poor lowly maid,

10   Most goddess-like pranked up. But that our feasts
      In every mess have folly, and the feeders
      Digest it with accustom, I should blush
      To see you so attired, swoon, I think,
      To show myself a glass.

FLORIZEL   I bless the time
      When my good falcon made her flight across
      Thy father's ground.

PERDITA   Now Jove afford you cause!
      To me the difference forges dread; your greatness
      Hath not been used to fear. Even now I tremble
      To think your father by some accident
20   Should pass this way, as you did. O, the Fates!
      How would he look to see his work, so noble,
      Vilely bound up? What would he say? Or how
      Should I, in these my borrowed flaunts, behold
      The sternness of his presence?

FLORIZEL   Apprehend
      Nothing but jollity. The gods themselves,
      Humbling their deities to love, have taken
      The shapes of beasts upon them: Jupiter
      Became a bull, and bellowed; the green Neptune
      A ram, and bleated; and the fire-robed god,
30   Golden Apollo, a poor, humble swain,
      As I seem now. Their transformations
      Were never for a piece of beauty rarer,
      Nor in a way so chaste, since my desires
      Run not before mine honour, nor my lusts
      Burn hotter than my faith.

PERDITA   O, but sir,
      Your resolution cannot hold when 'tis
      Opposed, as it must be, by th'power of the King.
      One of these two must be necessities,

Which then will speak: that you must change this
    purpose
Or I my life.

FLORIZEL   Thou dearest Perdita,   40
With these forced thoughts, I prithee, darken not
The mirth o'th'feast. Or I'll be thine, my fair,
Or not my father's. For I cannot be
Mine own, nor anything to any, if
I be not thine. To this I am most constant,
Though destiny say no. Be merry, gentle;
Strangle such thoughts as these with anything
That you behold the while. Your guests are coming:
Lift up your countenance as it were the day
Of celebration of that nuptial which   50
We two have sworn shall come.

PERDITA   O lady Fortune,
Stand you auspicious!

FLORIZEL   See, your guests approach.
Address yourself to entertain them sprightly,
And let's be red with mirth.

    Enter Shepherd, with Polixenes and Camillo, dis-
    guised; Clown, Mopsa, Dorcas, and others

SHEPHERD
Fie, daughter! When my old wife lived, upon
This day she was both pantler, butler, cook;
Both dame and servant; welcomed all, served all;
Would sing her song and dance her turn; now here,
At upper end o'th'table, now i'th'middle;
On his shoulder, and his; her face o'fire   60
With labour, and the thing she took to quench it:
She would to each one sip. You are retired,
As if you were a feasted one and not
The hostess of the meeting. Pray you, bid
These unknown friends to's welcome, for it is

A way to make us better friends, more known.
Come, quench your blushes and present yourself
That which you are, Mistress o'th'Feast. Come on,
And bid us welcome to your sheep-shearing,
70   As your good flock shall prosper.

PERDITA (*to Polixenes*)   Sir, welcome.
It is my father's will I should take on me
The hostess-ship o'th'day. (*To Camillo*) You're welcome,
        sir.
Give me those flowers there, Dorcas. Reverend sirs,
For you there's rosemary and rue; these keep
Seeming and savour all the winter long:
Grace and remembrance be to you both,
And welcome to our shearing!

POLIXENES   Shepherdess –
A fair one are you – well you fit our ages
With flowers of winter.

PERDITA   Sir, the year growing ancient,
80   Not yet on summer's death nor on the birth
Of trembling winter, the fairest flowers o'th'season
Are our carnations and streaked gillyvors,
Which some call Nature's bastards; of that kind
Our rustic garden's barren, and I care not
To get slips of them.

POLIXENES   Wherefore, gentle maiden,
Do you neglect them?

PERDITA   For I have heard it said
There is an art which in their piedness shares
With great creating Nature.

POLIXENES   Say there be;
Yet Nature is made better by no mean
90   But Nature makes that mean; so over that art
Which you say adds to Nature is an art
That Nature makes. You see, sweet maid, we marry

A gentler scion to the wildest stock,
And make conceive a bark of baser kind
By bud of nobler race. This is an art
Which does mend Nature – change it, rather – but
The art itself is Nature.

PERDITA   So it is.

POLIXENES
Then make your garden rich in gillyvors,
And do not call them bastards.

PERDITA   I'll not put
The dibble in earth to set one slip of them: 100
No more than, were I painted, I would wish
This youth should say 'twere well, and only therefore
Desire to breed by me. Here's flowers for you:
Hot lavender, mints, savory, marjoram;
The marigold, that goes to bed with' sun
And with him rises weeping; these are flowers
Of middle summer, and I think they are given
To men of middle age. Y'are very welcome.

CAMILLO
I should leave grazing, were I of your flock,
And only live by gazing.

PERDITA   Out, alas!   110
You'd be so lean that blasts of January
Would blow you through and through. (*To Florizel*)
      Now, my fair'st friend,
I would I had some flowers o'th'spring, that might
Become your time of day – (*to the Shepherdesses*) and
      yours, and yours,
That wear upon your virgin branches yet
Your maidenheads growing. O Proserpina,
For the flowers now that, frighted, thou let'st fall
From Dis's wagon! Daffodils,
That come before the swallow dares, and take

120   The winds of March with beauty; violets, dim,
      But sweeter than the lids of Juno's eyes
      Or Cytherea's breath; pale primroses,
      That die unmarried ere they can behold
      Bright Phoebus in his strength – a malady
      Most incident to maids; bold oxlips and
      The crown imperial; lilies of all kinds,
      The flower-de-luce being one: O, these I lack
      To make you garlands of, and my sweet friend
      To strew him o'er and o'er!

FLORIZEL   What, like a corse?
PERDITA
130   No, like a bank for Love to lie and play on,
      Not like a corse; or if, not to be buried,
      But quick and in mine arms. Come, take your flowers.
      Methinks I play as I have seen them do
      In Whitsun pastorals: sure this robe of mine
      Does change my disposition.

FLORIZEL   What you do
      Still betters what is done. When you speak, sweet,
      I'd have you do it ever; when you sing,
      I'd have you buy and sell so, so give alms,
      Pray so, and, for the ord'ring your affairs,
140   To sing them too; when you do dance, I wish you
      A wave o'th'sea, that you might ever do
      Nothing but that – move still, still so,
      And own no other function. Each your doing,
      So singular in each particular,
      Crowns what you are doing in the present deeds,
      That all your acts are queens.

PERDITA   O Doricles,
      Your praises are too large. But that your youth
      And the true blood which peeps fairly through't
      Do plainly give you out an unstained shepherd,

With wisdom I might fear, my Doricles,   150
You wooed me the false way.

FLORIZEL   I think you have
As little skill to fear as I have purpose
To put you to't. But come, our dance, I pray.
Your hand, my Perdita: so turtles pair,
That never mean to part.

PERDITA   I'll swear for 'em.

POLIXENES
This is the prettiest low-born lass that ever
Ran on the greensward: nothing she does or seems
But smacks of something greater than herself,
Too noble for this place.

CAMILLO   He tells her something
That makes her blood look out. Good sooth, she is   160
The queen of curds and cream.

CLOWN Come on, strike up!

DORCAS Mopsa must be your mistress. Marry, garlic to
mend her kissing with!

MOPSA Now, in good time!

CLOWN Not a word, a word: we stand upon our manners.
Come, strike up!

Music. A dance of Shepherds and Shepherdesses

POLIXENES
Pray, good shepherd, what fair swain is this
Which dances with your daughter?

SHEPHERD
They call him Doricles, and boasts himself   170
To have a worthy feeding; but I have it
Upon his own report and I believe it:
He looks like sooth. He says he loves my daughter.
I think so too; for never gazed the moon
Upon the water as he'll stand and read,
As 'twere, my daughter's eyes; and, to be plain,

I think there is not half a kiss to choose
Who loves another best.

POLIXENES   She dances featly.

SHEPHERD

So she does anything – though I report it,
180   That should be silent. If young Doricles
Do light upon her, she shall bring him that
Which he not dreams of.

Enter Servant

SERVANT O master, if you did but hear the pedlar at the
door, you would never dance again after a tabor and
pipe; no, the bagpipe could not move you. He sings
several tunes faster than you'll tell money; he utters
them as he had eaten ballads and all men's ears grew to
his tunes.

CLOWN He could never come better; he shall come in. I
190   love a ballad but even too well, if it be doleful matter
merrily set down; or a very pleasant thing indeed, and
sung lamentably.

SERVANT He hath songs for man or woman, of all sizes:
no milliner can so fit his customers with gloves. He has
the prettiest love-songs for maids; so without bawdry,
which is strange; with such delicate burdens of dildos
and fadings, jump her and thump her; and where some
stretch-mouthed rascal would, as it were, mean mischief, and break a foul gap into the matter, he makes the
200   maid to answer, 'Whoop, do me no harm, good man';
puts him off, slights him, with 'Whoop, do me no harm,
good man.'

POLIXENES This is a brave fellow.

CLOWN Believe me, thou talk'st of an admirable conceited
fellow. Has he any unbraided wares?

SERVANT He hath ribbons of all the colours i'th'rainbow;
points more than all the lawyers in Bohemia can

learnedly handle, though they come to him by th'gross;
inkles, caddisses, cambrics, lawns. Why, he sings 'em
over as they were gods or goddesses; you would think a 210
smock were a she-angel, he so chants to the sleevehand
and the work about the square on't.

CLOWN Prithee bring him in, and let him approach singing.

PERDITA Forewarn him that he use no scurrilous words
in's tunes.   *Exit Servant*

CLOWN You have of these pedlars that have more in them
than you'd think, sister.

PERDITA Ay, good brother, or go about to think.

 Enter Autolycus, singing

AUTOLYCUS

 Lawn as white as driven snow;   220
 Cypress black as e'er was crow;
 Gloves as sweet as damask roses;
 Masks for faces, and for noses;
 Bugle-bracelet, necklace-amber;
 Perfume for a lady's chamber;
 Golden coifs and stomachers
 For my lads to give their dears;
 Pins and poking-sticks of steel;
 What maids lack from head to heel
 Come buy of me, come, come buy, come buy; 230
 Buy, lads, or else your lasses cry: Come buy.

CLOWN If I were not in love with Mopsa, thou shouldst
take no money of me; but being enthralled as I am, it
will also be the bondage of certain ribbons and gloves.

MOPSA I was promised them against the feast, but they
come not too late now.

DORCAS He hath promised you more than that, or there
be liars.

MOPSA He hath paid you all he promised you; may be he

240   has paid you more, which will shame you to give him
again.

CLOWN Is there no manners left among maids? Will they
wear their plackets where they should bear their faces?
Is there not milking-time, when you are going to bed, or
kiln-hole, to whistle of these secrets, but you must be
tittle-tattling before all our guests? 'Tis well they are
whisp'ring. Clamor your tongues, and not a word more.

MOPSA I have done. Come, you promised me a tawdry-
lace and a pair of sweet gloves.

250 CLOWN Have I not told thee how I was cozened by the
way and lost all my money?

AUTOLYCUS And indeed, sir, there are cozeners abroad:
therefore it behoves men to be wary.

CLOWN Fear not thou, man; thou shalt lose nothing here.

AUTOLYCUS I hope so, sir, for I have about me many
parcels of charge.

CLOWN What hast here? Ballads?

MOPSA Pray now, buy some. I love a ballad in print a-life,
for then we are sure they are true.

260 AUTOLYCUS Here's one to a very doleful tune, how a
usurer's wife was brought to bed of twenty money-bags
at a burden, and how she longed to eat adders' heads
and toads carbonadoed.

MOPSA Is it true, think you?

AUTOLYCUS Very true, and but a month old.

DORCAS Bless me from marrying a usurer!

AUTOLYCUS Here's the midwife's name to't: one Mistress
Taleporter, and five or six honest wives that were present. Why should I carry lies abroad?

270 MOPSA Pray you now, buy it.

CLOWN Come on, lay it by, and let's first see more ballads; we'll buy the other things anon.

AUTOLYCUS Here's another ballad, of a fish that appeared

upon the coast on Wednesday the fourscore of April,
forty thousand fathom above water, and sung this ballad
against the hard hearts of maids. It was thought she was
a woman, and was turned into a cold fish for she would
not exchange flesh with one that loved her. The ballad
is very pitiful, and as true.

DORCAS Is it true too, think you?   280

AUTOLYCUS Five justices' hands at it, and witnesses more
than my pack will hold.

CLOWN Lay it by too. Another.

AUTOLYCUS This is a merry ballad, but a very pretty one.

MOPSA Let's have some merry ones.

AUTOLYCUS Why, this is a passing merry one, and goes
to the tune of 'Two maids wooing a man'. There's
scarce a maid westward but she sings it; 'tis in request, I
can tell you.

MOPSA We can both sing it. If thou'lt bear a part, thou   290
shalt hear; 'tis in three parts.

DORCAS We had the tune on't a month ago.

AUTOLYCUS I can bear my part: you must know 'tis my
occupation. Have at it with you.

     They sing

AUTOLYCUS   Get you hence, for I must go.
              Where it fits not you to know.

DORCAS   Whither?

MOPSA   O whither?

DORCAS   Whither?

MOPSA   It becomes thy oath full well
              Thou to me thy secrets tell.

DORCAS   Me too; let me go thither.   300

MOPSA   Or thou go'st to th'grange or mill.

DORCAS   If to either, thou dost ill.

AUTOLYCUS   Neither.

DORCAS   What, neither?

AUTOLYCUS	Neither.
DORCAS	Thou hast sworn my love to be.
MOPSA	Thou hast sworn it more to me.
	Then whither go'st? Say, whither?

CLOWN We'll have this song out anon by ourselves: my
father and the gentlemen are in sad talk, and we'll not
trouble them. Come, bring away thy pack after me.
310 Wenches, I'll buy for you both. Pedlar, let's have the
first choice. Follow me, girls.

Exit with Dorcas and Mopsa

AUTOLYCUS And you shall pay well for 'em.

He follows them, singing
>   Will you buy any tape,
>   Or lace for your cape,
>   My dainty duck, my dear-a?
>   Any silk, any thread,
>   Any toys for your head,
>   Of the new'st and fin'st, fin'st wear-a?
>   Come to the pedlar:
320 >   Money's a meddler
>   That doth utter all men's ware-a.   *Exit*

Enter Servant

SERVANT Master, there is three carters, three shepherds,
three neat-herds, three swine-herds, that have made
themselves all men of hair: they call themselves
Saltiers, and they have a dance which the wenches say
is a gallimaufry of gambols, because they are not in't;
but they themselves are o'th'mind, if it be not too rough
for some that know little but bowling it will please
plentifully.
330 SHEPHERD Away! We'll none on't: here has been too
much homely foolery already. I know, sir, we weary you.

POLIXENES You weary those that refresh us. Pray, let's
see these four threes of herdsmen.

SERVANT One three of them, by their own report, sir,
hath danced before the King; and not the worst of the
three but jumps twelve foot and a half by th'square.

SHEPHERD Leave your prating. Since these good men are
pleased, let them come in; but quickly now.

SERVANT Why, they stay at door, sir.

He lets in the herdsmen, who perform their satyrs'
dance and depart

POLIXENES (*to Shepherd*)

O, father, you'll know more of that hereafter.   340
(*To Camillo*) Is it not too far gone? 'Tis time to part them.
He's simple and tells much. (*To Florizel*) How now, fair
    shepherd!
Your heart is full of something that does take
Your mind from feasting. Sooth, when I was young
And handed love as you do, I was wont
To load my she with knacks. I would have ransacked
The pedlar's silken treasury, and have poured it
To her acceptance: you have let him go
And nothing marted with him. If your lass
Interpretation should abuse and call this   350
Your lack of love or bounty, you were straited
For a reply, at least if you make a care
Of happy holding her.

FLORIZEL   Old sir, I know
She prizes not such trifles as these are:
The gifts she looks from me are packed and locked
Up in my heart, which I have given already,
But not delivered. O, hear me breathe my life
Before this ancient sir, whom, it should seem,
Hath sometime loved! I take thy hand, this hand
As soft as dove's down and as white as it,   360

Or Ethiopian's tooth, or the fanned snow that's bolted
By th'northern blasts twice o'er –

POLIXENES   What follows this?
How prettily the young swain seems to wash
The hand was fair before! I have put you out.
But to your protestation: let me hear
What you profess.

FLORIZEL   Do, and be witness to't.

POLIXENES
And this my neighbour too?

FLORIZEL   And he, and more
Than he, and men; the earth, the heavens, and all:
That were I crowned the most imperial monarch,
370   Thereof most worthy, were I the fairest youth
That ever made eye swerve, had force and knowledge
More than was ever man's, I would not prize them
Without her love; for her employ them all;
Commend them and condemn them to her service
Or to their own perdition.

POLIXENES   Fairly offered.

CAMILLO
This shows a sound affection.

SHEPHERD   But, my daughter,
Say you the like to him?

PERDITA   I cannot speak
So well, nothing so well; no, nor mean better.
By th'pattern of mine own thoughts I cut out
380   The purity of his.

SHEPHERD   Take hands, a bargain!
And, friends unknown, you shall bear witness to't.
I give my daughter to him, and will make
Her portion equal his.

FLORIZEL   O, that must be
I'th'virtue of your daughter. One being dead,

I shall have more than you can dream of yet;
Enough then for your wonder. But come on:
Contract us 'fore these witnesses.

SHEPHERD   Come, your hand;
And, daughter, yours.

POLIXENES   Soft, swain, awhile, beseech you.
Have you a father?

FLORIZEL   I have; but what of him?

POLIXENES
Knows he of this?

FLORIZEL   He neither does nor shall.   390

POLIXENES
Methinks a father
Is at the nuptial of his son a guest
That best becomes the table. Pray you once more,
Is not your father grown incapable
Of reasonable affairs? Is he not stupid
With age and altering rheums? Can he speak? Hear?
Know man from man? Dispute his own estate?
Lies he not bed-rid? And again does nothing
But what he did being childish?

FLORIZEL   No, good sir:
He has his health, and ampler strength indeed   400
Than most have of his age.

POLIXENES   By my white beard,
You offer him, if this be so, a wrong
Something unfilial. Reason my son
Should choose himself a wife, but as good reason
The father, all whose joy is nothing else
But fair posterity, should hold some counsel
In such a business.

FLORIZEL   I yield all this;
But for some other reasons, my grave sir,
Which 'tis not fit you know, I not acquaint

410   My father of this business.

POLIXENES   Let him know't.

FLORIZEL
He shall not.

POLIXENES   Prithee, let him.

FLORIZEL   No, he must not.

SHEPHERD
Let him, my son: he shall not need to grieve
At knowing of thy choice.

FLORIZEL   Come, come, he must not.
Mark our contract.

POLIXENES (*removing his disguise*) Mark your divorce,
       young sir,
Whom son I dare not call: thou art too base
To be acknowledged. Thou a sceptre's heir,
That thus affects a sheep-hook? – Thou, old traitor,
I am sorry that by hanging thee I can
But shorten thy life one week. – And thou, fresh piece
420 Of excellent witchcraft, who of force must know
The royal fool thou cop'st with –

SHEPHERD   O, my heart!

POLIXENES
I'll have thy beauty scratched with briers and made
More homely than thy state. – For thee, fond boy,
If I may ever know thou dost but sigh
That thou no more shalt see this knack – as never
I mean thou shalt – we'll bar thee from succession;
Not hold thee of our blood, no, not our kin,
Far than Deucalion off. Mark thou my words!
Follow us to the court. – Thou, churl, for this time,
430 Though full of our displeasure, yet we free thee
From the dead blow of it. – And you, enchantment,
Worthy enough a herdsman – yea, him too,
That makes himself, but for our honour therein,

Unworthy thee – if ever henceforth thou
These rural latches to his entrance open,
Or hoop his body more with thy embraces,
I will devise a death as cruel for thee
As thou art tender to't.   *Exit*

PERDITA   Even here undone!
  I was not much afeard; for once or twice
  I was about to speak and tell him plainly,   440
  The selfsame sun that shines upon his court
  Hides not his visage from our cottage, but
  Looks on alike. (*To Florizel*) Will't please you, sir, be
    gone?
  I told you what would come of this. Beseech you,
  Of your own state take care. This dream of mine –
  Being now awake, I'll queen it no inch farther,
  But milk my ewes, and weep.

CAMILLO   Why, how now, father!
  Speak ere thou die'st.

SHEPHERD   I cannot speak nor think,
  Nor dare to know that which I know. (*To Florizel*) O sir!
  You have undone a man of fourscore three,   450
  That thought to fill his grave in quiet, yea,
  To die upon the bed my father died,
  To lie close by his honest bones; but now
  Some hangman must put on my shroud and lay me
  Where no priest shovels in dust. (*To Perdita*) O cursed
    wretch,
  That knew'st this was the Prince and wouldst adventure
  To mingle faith with him! Undone, undone!
  If I might die within this hour, I have lived
  To die when I desire.   *Exit*

FLORIZEL   Why look you so upon me?
  I am but sorry, not afeard; delayed,   460
  But nothing altered: what I was I am;

More straining on for plucking back, not following
My leash unwillingly.

CAMILLO   Gracious my lord,
You know your father's temper. At this time
He will allow no speech – which I do guess
You do not purpose to him – and as hardly
Will he endure your sight as yet, I fear.
Then till the fury of his highness settle
Come not before him.

FLORIZEL   I not purpose it.
I think Camillo?

CAMILLO   Even he, my lord.

PERDITA
How often have I told you 'twould be thus!
How often said my dignity would last
But till 'twere known!

FLORIZEL   It cannot fail but by
The violation of my faith; and then
Let Nature crush the sides o'th'earth together
And mar the seeds within! Lift up thy looks.
From my succession wipe me, father, I
Am heir to my affection.

CAMILLO   Be advised.

FLORIZEL
I am, and by my fancy. If my reason
Will thereto be obedient, I have reason;
If not, my senses, better pleased with madness,
Do bid it welcome.

CAMILLO   This is desperate, sir.

FLORIZEL
So call it, but it does fulfil my vow:
I needs must think it honesty. Camillo,
Not for Bohemia, nor the pomp that may
Be thereat gleaned; for all the sun sees or

The close earth wombs or the profound seas hides
In unknown fathoms, will I break my oath
To this my fair beloved. Therefore, I pray you,
As you've e'er been my father's honoured friend,   490
When he shall miss me – as, in faith, I mean not
To see him any more – cast your good counsels
Upon his passion. Let myself and Fortune
Tug for the time to come. This you may know,
And so deliver: I am put to sea
With her who here I cannot hold on shore;
And most opportune to our need I have
A vessel rides fast by, but not prepared
For this design. What course I mean to hold
Shall nothing benefit your knowledge, nor   500
Concern me the reporting.

CAMILLO   O my lord,
I would your spirit were easier for advice,
Or stronger for your need.

FLORIZEL   Hark, Perdita –
(to Camillo) I'll hear you by and by.
    He draws Perdita aside

CAMILLO   He's irremovable,
Resolved for flight. Now were I happy if
His going I could frame to serve my turn,
Save him from danger, do him love and honour,
Purchase the sight again of dear Sicilia
And that unhappy king my master, whom
I so much thirst to see.

FLORIZEL   Now, good Camillo,   510
I am so fraught with curious business that
I leave out ceremony.

CAMILLO   Sir, I think
You have heard of my poor services i'th'love
That I have borne your father?

FLORIZEL   Very nobly
  Have you deserved: it is my father's music
  To speak your deeds, not little of his care
  To have them recompensed as thought on.
CAMILLO   Well, my lord,
  If you may please to think I love the King,
  And through him what's nearest to him, which is
520 Your gracious self, embrace but my direction.
  If your more ponderous and settled project
  May suffer alteration, on mine honour,
  I'll point you where you shall have such receiving
  As shall become your highness: where you may
  Enjoy your mistress, from the whom, I see,
  There's no disjunction to be made but by –
  As heavens forfend! – your ruin; marry her;
  And, with my best endeavours in your absence,
  Your discontenting father strive to qualify,
530 And bring him up to liking.
FLORIZEL   How, Camillo,
  May this, almost a miracle, be done?
  That I may call thee something more than man,
  And after that trust to thee.
CAMILLO   Have you thought on
  A place whereto you'll go?
FLORIZEL   Not any yet:
  But as th'unthought-on accident is guilty
  To what we wildly do, so we profess
  Ourselves to be the slaves of chance, and flies
  Of every wind that blows.
CAMILLO   Then list to me.
  This follows, if you will not change your purpose
540 But undergo this flight: make for Sicilia,
  And there present yourself and your fair princess –
  For so I see she must be – 'fore Leontes.

She shall be habited as it becomes
The partner of your bed. Methinks I see
Leontes opening his free arms and weeping
His welcomes forth; asks thee, the son, forgiveness
As 'twere i'th'father's person; kisses the hands
Of your fresh princess; o'er and o'er divides him
'Twixt his unkindness and his kindness: th'one
He chides to hell and bids the other grow   550
Faster than thought or time.

FLORIZEL   Worthy Camillo,
What colour for my visitation shall I
Hold up before him?

CAMILLO   Sent by the King your father
To greet him and to give him comforts. Sir,
The manner of your bearing towards him, with
What you, as from your father, shall deliver –
Things known betwixt us three – I'll write you down,
The which shall point you forth at every sitting
What you must say: that he shall not perceive
But that you have your father's bosom there   560
And speak his very heart.

FLORIZEL   I am bound to you.
There is some sap in this.

CAMILLO   A course more promising
Than a wild dedication of yourselves
To unpathed waters, undreamed shores, most certain
To miseries enough: no hope to help you,
But as you shake off one to take another;
Nothing so certain as your anchors, who
Do their best office if they can but stay you
Where you'll be loath to be. Besides, you know
Prosperity's the very bond of love,   570
Whose fresh complexion and whose heart together
Affliction alters.

PERDITA   One of these is true:
I think affliction may subdue the cheek,
But not take in the mind.

CAMILLO   Yea? Say you so?
There shall not at your father's house these seven years
Be born another such.

FLORIZEL   My good Camillo,
She is as forward of her breeding as
She is i'th'rear' our birth.

CAMILLO   I cannot say 'tis pity
She lacks instructions, for she seems a mistress
580 To most that teach.

PERDITA   Your pardon, sir; for this
I'll blush you thanks.

FLORIZEL   My prettiest Perdita!
But O, the thorns we stand upon! Camillo –
Preserver of my father, now of me,
The medicine of our house – how shall we do?
We are not furnished like Bohemia's son,
Nor shall appear in Sicilia.

CAMILLO   My lord,
Fear none of this. I think you know my fortunes
Do all lie there. It shall be so my care
To have you royally appointed as if
590 The scene you play were mine. For instance, sir,
That you may know you shall not want, one word.
        They talk aside
        Enter Autolycus

AUTOLYCUS Ha, ha, what a fool Honesty is! And Trust,
his sworn brother, a very simple gentleman! I have sold
all my trumpery: not a counterfeit stone, not a ribbon,
glass, pomander, brooch, table-book, ballad, knife, tape,
glove, shoe-tie, bracelet, horn-ring, to keep my pack
from fasting. They throng who should buy first, as if my

trinkets had been hallowed and brought a benediction to
the buyer; by which means I saw whose purse was best
in picture; and what I saw, to my good use I re-   600
membered. My clown, who wants but something to be a
reasonable man, grew so in love with the wenches' song
that he would not stir his pettitoes till he had both tune
and words; which so drew the rest of the herd to me
that all their other senses stuck in ears: you might have
pinched a placket, it was senseless; 'twas nothing to
geld a codpiece of a purse; I would have filed keys off
that hung in chains. No hearing, no feeling, but my sir's
song, and admiring the nothing of it. So that in this time
of lethargy I picked and cut most of their festival   610
purses; and had not the old man come in with a hubbub
against his daughter and the King's son and scared my
choughs from the chaff, I had not left a purse alive in
the whole army.

Camillo, Florizel, and Perdita come forward

CAMILLO
   Nay, but my letters, by this means being there
   So soon as you arrive, shall clear that doubt.

FLORIZEL
   And those that you'll procure from King Leontes –

CAMILLO
   Shall satisfy your father.

PERDITA   Happy be you!
   All that you speak shows fair.

CAMILLO (*seeing Autolycus*)   Who have we here?
   We'll make an instrument of this, omit   620
   Nothing may give us aid.

AUTOLYCUS (*aside*) If they have overheard me now –
   why, hanging.

CAMILLO How now, good fellow! Why shak'st thou so?
   Fear not, man: here's no harm intended to thee.

AUTOLYCUS I am a poor fellow, sir.

CAMILLO Why, be so still: here's nobody will steal that
from thee. Yet for the outside of thy poverty we must
make an exchange; therefore discase thee instantly –
thou must think there's a necessity in't – and change
garments with this gentleman. Though the pennyworth
on his side be the worst, yet hold thee, there's some
boot.

He gives him money

AUTOLYCUS I am a poor fellow, sir. (*Aside*) I know ye
well enough.

CAMILLO Nay, prithee, dispatch. The gentleman is half
flayed already.

AUTOLYCUS Are you in earnest, sir? (*Aside*) I smell the
trick on't.

FLORIZEL Dispatch, I prithee.

AUTOLYCUS Indeed, I have had earnest, but I cannot
with conscience take it.

CAMILLO Unbuckle, unbuckle.

Florizel and Autolycus exchange garments

Fortunate mistress – let my prophecy
Come home to ye! – you must retire yourself
Into some covert; take your sweetheart's hat
And pluck it o'er your brows, muffle your face,
Dismantle you, and, as you can, disliken
The truth of your own seeming, that you may –
For I do fear eyes over – to shipboard
Get undescried.

PERDITA   I see the play so lies
That I must bear a part.

CAMILLO   No remedy.
Have you done there?

FLORIZEL   Should I now meet my father,
He would not call me son.

CAMILLO   Nay, you shall have no hat.
    He gives the hat to Perdita
    Come, lady, come. Farewell, my friend.
AUTOLYCUS   Adieu, sir.
FLORIZEL
    O Perdita, what have we twain forgot!
    Pray you, a word.
CAMILLO (*aside*)
    What I do next shall be to tell the King
    Of this escape and whither they are bound;
    Wherein my hope is I shall so prevail   660
    To force him after: in whose company
    I shall re-view Sicilia, for whose sight
    I have a woman's longing.
FLORIZEL   Fortune speed us!
    Thus we set on, Camillo, to th'seaside.
CAMILLO
    The swifter speed the better.
                    Exeunt Florizel, Perdita, and Camillo
AUTOLYCUS I understand the business, I hear it. To have
    an open ear, a quick eye, and a nimble hand is necessary
    for a cutpurse; a good nose is requisite also, to smell out
    work for th'other senses. I see this is the time that the
    unjust man doth thrive. What an exchange had this been   670
    without boot! What a boot is here, with this exchange!
    Sure, the gods do this year connive at us, and we may do
    anything extempore. The Prince himself is about a piece
    of iniquity — stealing away from his father, with his clog
    at his heels. If I thought it were a piece of honesty to
    acquaint the King withal, I would not do't. I hold it the
    more knavery to conceal it; and therein am I constant to
    my profession.
        Enter Clown and Shepherd
    Aside, aside! Here is more matter for a hot brain. Every

680 lane's end, every shop, church, session, hanging, yields
     a careful man work.

CLOWN See, see, what a man you are now! There is no
     other way but to tell the King she's a changeling and
     none of your flesh and blood.

SHEPHERD Nay, but hear me.

CLOWN Nay, but hear me.

SHEPHERD Go to, then.

CLOWN She being none of your flesh and blood, your
     flesh and blood has not offended the King; and so your
690 flesh and blood is not to be punished by him. Show
     those things you found about her, those secret things,
     all but what she has with her. This being done, let the
     law go whistle, I warrant you.

SHEPHERD I will tell the King all, every word – yea, and
     his son's pranks too; who, I may say, is no honest man,
     neither to his father nor to me, to go about to make me
     the King's brother-in-law.

CLOWN Indeed, brother-in-law was the farthest off you
     could have been to him; and then your blood had been
700 the dearer by I know not how much an ounce.

AUTOLYCUS (*aside*) Very wisely, puppies!

SHEPHERD Well, let us to the King. There is that in this
     fardel will make him scratch his beard.

AUTOLYCUS (*aside*) I know not what impediment this
     complaint may be to the flight of my master.

CLOWN Pray heartily he be at palace.

AUTOLYCUS (*aside*) Though I am not naturally honest, I
     am so sometimes by chance. Let me pocket up my
     pedlar's excrement.

          He takes off his false beard

710 How now, rustics! Whither are you bound?

SHEPHERD To th'palace, an it like your worship.

AUTOLYCUS Your affairs there, what, with whom, the condition of that fardel, the place of your dwelling, your names, your ages, of what having, breeding, and anything that is fitting to be known, discover.

CLOWN We are but plain fellows, sir.

AUTOLYCUS A lie: you are rough and hairy. Let me have no lying: it becomes none but tradesmen, and they often give us soldiers the lie; but we pay them for it with stamped coin, not stabbing steel; therefore they do not give us the lie.   720

CLOWN Your worship had like to have given us one, if you had not taken yourself with the manner.

SHEPHERD Are you a courtier, an't like you, sir?

AUTOLYCUS Whether it like me or no, I am a courtier. Seest thou not the air of the court in these enfoldings? Hath not my gait in it the measure of the court? Receives not thy nose court-odour from me? Reflect I not on thy baseness court-contempt? Think'st thou, for that I insinuate, to toaze from thee thy business, I am   730 therefore no courtier? I am courtier cap-à-pie; and one that will either push on or pluck back thy business there; whereupon I command thee to open thy affair.

SHEPHERD My business, sir, is to the King.

AUTOLYCUS What advocate hast thou to him?

SHEPHERD I know not, an't like you.

CLOWN Advocate's the court-word for a pheasant: say you have none.

SHEPHERD None, sir; I have no pheasant, cock nor hen.

AUTOLYCUS

How blessed are we that are not simple men!   740
Yet Nature might have made me as these are:
Therefore I'll not disdain.

CLOWN (aside to Shepherd) This cannot be but a great courtier.

SHEPHERD His garments are rich, but he wears them not handsomely.

CLOWN He seems to be the more noble in being fantastical. A great man, I'll warrant. I know by the picking on's teeth.

750 AUTOLYCUS The fardel there, what's i'th'fardel? Wherefore that box?

SHEPHERD Sir, there lies such secrets in this fardel and box, which none must know but the King; and which he shall know within this hour, if I may come to th'speech of him.

AUTOLYCUS Age, thou hast lost thy labour.

SHEPHERD Why, sir?

AUTOLYCUS The King is not at the palace; he is gone aboard a new ship, to purge melancholy and air himself: for, if thou be'st capable of things serious, thou
760 must know the King is full of grief.

SHEPHERD So 'tis said, sir: about his son, that should have married a shepherd's daughter.

AUTOLYCUS If that shepherd be not in handfast, let him fly: the curses he shall have, the tortures he shall feel, will break the back of man, the heart of monster.

CLOWN Think you so, sir?

AUTOLYCUS Not he alone shall suffer what wit can make heavy and vengeance bitter; but those that are germane
770 to him, though removed fifty times, shall all come under the hangman – which, though it be great pity, yet it is necessary. An old sheep-whistling rogue, a ram-tender, to offer to have his daughter come into grace? Some say he shall be stoned; but that death is too soft for him, say I. Draw our throne into a sheep-cote? All deaths are too few, the sharpest too easy.

CLOWN Has the old man e'er a son, sir, do you hear, an't like you, sir?

AUTOLYCUS He has a son: who shall be flayed alive; then, 'nointed over with honey, set on the head of a 780 wasp's nest; then stand till he be three-quarters and a dram dead; then recovered again with aqua-vitae or some other hot infusion; then, raw as he is, and in the hottest day prognostication proclaims, shall he be set against a brick wall, the sun looking with a southward eye upon him, where he is to behold him with flies blown to death. But what talk we of these traitorly rascals, whose miseries are to be smiled at, their offences being so capital? Tell me, for you seem to be honest, plain men, what you have to the King. Being something 790 gently considered, I'll bring you where he is aboard, tender your persons to his presence, whisper him in your behalfs; and if it be in man besides the King to effect your suits, here is man shall do it.

CLOWN He seems to be of great authority. Close with him, give him gold; and though authority be a stubborn bear, yet he is oft led by the nose with gold. Show the inside of your purse to the outside of his hand, and no more ado. Remember, stoned, and flayed alive!

SHEPHERD An't please you, sir, to undertake the business 800 for us, here is that gold I have. I'll make it as much more, and leave this young man in pawn till I bring it you.

AUTOLYCUS After I have done what I promised?

SHEPHERD Ay, sir.

AUTOLYCUS Well, give me the moiety. (*To the Clown*) Are you a party in this business?

CLOWN In some sort, sir: but though my case be a pitiful one, I hope I shall not be flayed out of it.

AUTOLYCUS O, that's the case of the shepherd's son. 810 Hang him, he'll be made an example.

CLOWN (*aside to Shepherd*) Comfort, good comfort! We

must to the King and show our strange sights. He must
know 'tis none of your daughter, nor my sister; we are
gone else. (*To Autolycus*) Sir, I will give you as much as
this old man does, when the business is performed; and
remain, as he says, your pawn till it be brought you.

AUTOLYCUS I will trust you. Walk before toward the seaside; go on the right hand: I will but look upon the
820   hedge, and follow you.

CLOWN (*aside to Shepherd*) We are blest in this man, as I
may say, even blest.

SHEPHERD Let's before, as he bids us. He was provided
to do us good.   *Exeunt Shepherd and Clown*

AUTOLYCUS If I had a mind to be honest, I see Fortune
would not suffer me: she drops booties in my mouth. I
am courted now with a double occasion: gold, and a
means to do the Prince my master good; which who
knows how that may turn back to my advancement? I
830   will bring these two moles, these blind ones, aboard
him. If he think it fit to shore them again, and that the
complaint they have to the King concerns him nothing,
let him call me rogue for being so far officious; for I am
proof against that title, and what shame else belongs
to't. To him will I present them: there may be matter
in it.   *Exit*

*

V.1   *Enter Leontes, Cleomenes, Dion, Paulina, and others*
CLEOMENES
    Sir, you have done enough, and have performed
    A saint-like sorrow. No fault could you make
    Which you have not redeemed; indeed, paid down
    More penitence than done trespass. At the last,

Do as the heavens have done, forget your evil;
With them forgive yourself.

LEONTES   Whilst I remember
Her and her virtues, I cannot forget
My blemishes in them, and so still think of
The wrong I did myself: which was so much
That heirless it hath made my kingdom and   10
Destroyed the sweet'st companion that e'er man
Bred his hopes out of.

PAULINA   True, too true, my lord.
If one by one you wedded all the world,
Or from the all that are took something good
To make a perfect woman, she you killed
Would be unparalleled.

LEONTES   I think so. Killed!
She I killed! I did so; but thou strik'st me
Sorely to say I did. It is as bitter
Upon thy tongue as in my thought. Now, good now,
Say so but seldom.

CLEOMENES   Not at all, good lady.   20
You might have spoken a thousand things that would
Have done the time more benefit and graced
Your kindness better.

PAULINA   You are one of those
Would have him wed again.

DION   If you would not so,
You pity not the state, nor the remembrance
Of his most sovereign name; consider little
What dangers by his highness' fail of issue
May drop upon his kingdom and devour
Incertain lookers-on. What were more holy
Than to rejoice the former queen is well?   30
What holier than, for royalty's repair,
For present comfort and for future good,

To bless the bed of majesty again
With a sweet fellow to't?

PAULINA   There is none worthy,
Respecting her that's gone. Besides the gods
Will have fulfilled their secret purposes:
For has not the divine Apollo said,
Is't not the tenor of his oracle,
That King Leontes shall not have an heir
40 Till his lost child be found? Which that it shall
Is all as monstrous to our human reason
As my Antigonus to break his grave
And come again to me; who, on my life,
Did perish with the infant. 'Tis your counsel
My lord should to the heavens be contrary,
Oppose against their wills. (*To Leontes*) Care not for
    issue.
The crown will find an heir. Great Alexander
Left his to th'worthiest; so his successor
Was like to be the best.

LEONTES   Good Paulina,
50 Who hast the memory of Hermione,
I know, in honour, O that ever I
Had squared me to thy counsel! Then even now
I might have looked upon my queen's full eyes,
Have taken treasure from her lips –

PAULINA   And left them
More rich for what they yielded.

LEONTES   Thou speak'st truth.
No more such wives, therefore no wife: one worse,
And better used, would make her sainted spirit
Again possess her corpse, and on this stage,
Where we offenders move, appear soul-vexed,
60 And begin, 'Why to me?'

PAULINA   Had she such power,

She had just cause.

LEONTES   She had, and would incense me
To murder her I married.

PAULINA   I should so.
Were I the ghost that walked, I'd bid you mark
Her eye, and tell me for what dull part in't
You chose her; then I'd shriek, that even your ears
Should rift to hear me; and the words that followed
Should be 'Remember mine.'

LEONTES   Stars, stars,
And all eyes else dead coals! Fear thou no wife;
I'll have no wife, Paulina.

PAULINA   Will you swear
Never to marry but by my free leave?   70

LEONTES
Never, Paulina, so be blest my spirit!

PAULINA
Then, good my lords, bear witness to his oath.

CLEOMENES
You tempt him over-much.

PAULINA   Unless another,
As like Hermione as is her picture,
Affront his eye.

CLEOMENES   Good madam –

PAULINA   I have done.
Yet if my lord will marry – if you will, sir,
No remedy, but you will – give me the office
To choose you a queen: she shall not be so young
As was your former, but she shall be such
As, walked your first queen's ghost, it should take joy   80
To see her in your arms.

LEONTES   My true Paulina,
We shall not marry till thou bid'st us.

PAULINA   That

Shall be when your first queen's again in breath;
Never till then.

Enter a Gentleman

GENTLEMAN
One that gives out himself Prince Florizel,
Son of Polixenes, with his princess – she
The fairest I have yet beheld – desires access
To your high presence.

LEONTES   What with him? He comes not
Like to his father's greatness. His approach
90   So out of circumstance and sudden tells us
'Tis not a visitation framed, but forced
By need and accident. What train?

GENTLEMAN   But few,
And those but mean.

LEONTES   His princess, say you, with him?

GENTLEMAN
Ay, the most peerless piece of earth, I think,
That e'er the sun shone bright on.

PAULINA   O Hermione,
As every present time doth boast itself
Above a better gone, so must thy grave
Give way to what's seen now. (*To the Gentleman*) Sir,
        you yourself
Have said and writ so – but your writing now
100   Is colder than that theme – she had not been,
Nor was not to be, equalled; thus your verse
Flowed with her beauty once. 'Tis shrewdly ebbed
To say you have seen a better.

GENTLEMAN   Pardon, madam.
The one I have almost forgot – your pardon;
The other, when she has obtained your eye
Will have your tongue too. This is a creature,
Would she begin a sect, might quench the zeal

Of all professors else, make proselytes
Of who she but bid follow.

PAULINA   How? Not women!

GENTLEMAN

Women will love her that she is a woman   110
More worth than any man; men that she is
The rarest of all women.

LEONTES   Go, Cleomenes:
Yourself, assisted with your honoured friends,
Bring them to our embracement.

Exeunt Cleomenes and others
                        Still, 'tis strange
He thus should steal upon us.

PAULINA   Had our prince,
Jewel of children, seen this hour, he had paired
Well with this lord: there was not full a month
Between their births.

LEONTES

                        Prithee, no more! Cease! Thou know'st
He dies to me again when talked of. Sure,
When I shall see this gentleman thy speeches   120
Will bring me to consider that which may
Unfurnish me of reason. They are come.

Enter Florizel, Perdita, Cleomenes, and others
Your mother was most true to wedlock, Prince:
For she did print your royal father off,
Conceiving you. Were I but twenty-one,
Your father's image is so hit in you,
His very air, that I should call you brother,
As I did him, and speak of something wildly
By us performed before. Most dearly welcome,
And your fair princess – goddess! O! Alas,   130
I lost a couple that 'twixt heaven and earth
Might thus have stood, begetting wonder, as

You, gracious couple, do. And then I lost –
All mine own folly – the society,
Amity too, of your brave father, whom,
Though bearing misery, I desire my life
Once more to look on him.

FLORIZEL   By his command
Have I here touched Sicilia, and from him
Give you all greetings that a king, at friend,
Can send his brother; and but infirmity,
Which waits upon worn times, hath something seized
His wished ability, he had himself
The lands and waters 'twixt your throne and his
Measured to look upon you, whom he loves –
He bade me say so – more than all the sceptres
And those that bear them living.

LEONTES   O my brother –
Good gentleman – the wrongs I have done thee stir
Afresh within me; and these thy offices,
So rarely kind, are as interpreters
Of my behindhand slackness! – Welcome hither
As is the spring to th'earth! And hath he too
Exposed this paragon to th'fearful usage,
At least ungentle, of the dreadful Neptune
To greet a man not worth her pains, much less
Th'adventure of her person?

FLORIZEL   Good my lord,
She came from Libya.

LEONTES   Where the warlike Smalus,
That noble, honoured lord, is feared and loved?

FLORIZEL
Most royal sir, from thence; from him whose daughter
His tears proclaimed his, parting with her; thence,
A prosperous south wind friendly, we have crossed,
To execute the charge my father gave me

For visiting your highness. My best train
I have from your Sicilian shores dismissed;
Who for Bohemia bend, to signify
Not only my success in Libya, sir,
But my arrival, and my wife's, in safety
Here where we are.

LEONTES   The blessèd gods
Purge all infection from our air whilst you
Do climate here! You have a holy father,
A graceful gentleman, against whose person,   170
So sacred as it is, I have done sin:
For which the heavens, taking angry note,
Have left me issueless; and your father's blessed,
As he from heaven merits it, with you,
Worthy his goodness. What might I have been,
Might I a son and daughter now have looked on,
Such goodly things as you!

    Enter a Lord

LORD   Most noble sir,
That which I shall report will bear no credit,
Were not the proof so nigh. Please you, great sir,
Bohemia greets you from himself by me;   180
Desires you to attach his son, who has –
His dignity and duty both cast off –
Fled from his father, from his hopes, and with
A shepherd's daughter.

LEONTES   Where's Bohemia? Speak.

LORD
Here in your city: I now came from him.
I speak amazèdly, and it becomes
My marvel and my message. To your court
Whiles he was hast'ning – in the chase, it seems,
Of this fair couple – meets he on the way
The father of this seeming lady, and   190

Her brother, having both their country quitted
With this young prince.

FLORIZEL   Camillo has betrayed me;
Whose honour and whose honesty till now
Endured all weathers.

LORD   Lay't so to his charge.
He's with the King your father.

LEONTES   Who? Camillo?

LORD
Camillo, sir; I spake with him; who now
Has these poor men in question. Never saw I
Wretches so quake: they kneel, they kiss the earth;
Forswear themselves as often as they speak;
Bohemia stops his ears, and threatens them
With divers deaths in death.

PERDITA   O my poor father!
The heaven sets spies upon us, will not have
Our contract celebrated.

LEONTES   You are married?

FLORIZEL
We are not, sir, nor are we like to be.
The stars, I see, will kiss the valleys first:
The odds for high and low's alike.

LEONTES   My lord,
Is this the daughter of a king?

FLORIZEL   She is,
When once she is my wife.

LEONTES
That 'once', I see by your good father's speed,
Will come on very slowly. I am sorry,
Most sorry, you have broken from his liking,
Where you were tied in duty; and as sorry
Your choice is not so rich in worth as beauty,
That you might well enjoy her.

FLORIZEL   Dear, look up.
　Though Fortune, visible an enemy,
　Should chase us, with my father, power no jot
　Hath she to change our loves. Beseech you, sir,
　Remember since you owed no more to Time
　Than I do now. With thought of such affections
　Step forth mine advocate: at your request   220
　My father will grant precious things as trifles.

LEONTES
　Would he do so, I'd beg your precious mistress,
　Which he counts but a trifle.

PAULINA   Sir, my liege,
　Your eye hath too much youth in't. Not a month
　'Fore your queen died she was more worth such gazes
　Than what you look on now.

LEONTES   I thought of her
　Even in these looks I made. But your petition
　Is yet unanswered. I will to your father.
　Your honour not o'erthrown by your desires,
　I am friend to them and you; upon which errand   230
　I now go toward him. Therefore follow me,
　And mark what way I make. Come, good my lord.
                                        Exeunt

Enter Autolycus and a Gentleman   V.2

AUTOLYCUS Beseech you, sir, were you present at this
　relation?

FIRST GENTLEMAN I was by at the opening of the fardel,
　heard the old shepherd deliver the manner how he
　found it; whereupon, after a little amazedness, we were
　all commanded out of the chamber. Only this methought
　I heard the shepherd say: he found the child.

AUTOLYCUS I would most gladly know the issue of it.

FIRST GENTLEMAN I make a broken delivery of the
business; but the changes I perceived in the King and
Camillo were very notes of admiration. They seemed
almost, with staring on one another, to tear the cases of
their eyes. There was speech in their dumbness, language in their very gesture. They looked as they had
heard of a world ransomed, or one destroyed. A notable
passion of wonder appeared in them; but the wisest be-
holder that knew no more but seeing could not say if
th'importance were joy or sorrow: but in the extremity
of the one it must needs be.

Enter another Gentleman

Here comes a gentleman that haply knows more. The
news, Rogero?

SECOND GENTLEMAN Nothing but bonfires. The oracle
is fulfilled: the King's daughter is found. Such a deal of
wonder is broken out within this hour that ballad-
makers cannot be able to express it.

Enter a third Gentleman

Here comes the Lady Paulina's steward; he can deliver
you more. How goes it now, sir? This news, which is
called true, is so like an old tale that the verity of it is in
strong suspicion. Has the King found his heir?

THIRD GENTLEMAN Most true, if ever truth were pregnant by circumstance. That which you hear you'll swear
you see, there is such unity in the proofs: the mantle of
Queen Hermione's; her jewel about the neck of it; the
letters of Antigonus found with it, which they know to
be his character; the majesty of the creature in resemblance of the mother; the affection of nobleness which
nature shows above her breeding, and many other
evidences proclaim her with all certainty to be the King's
daughter. Did you see the meeting of the two kings?

SECOND GENTLEMAN No.

THIRD GENTLEMAN Then have you lost a sight which was to be seen, cannot be spoken of. There might you have beheld one joy crown another, so and in such manner that it seemed sorrow wept to take leave of them: for their joy waded in tears. There was casting up of eyes, holding up of hands, with countenance of such distraction that they were to be known by garment, not by favour. Our king, being ready to leap out of himself for joy of his found daughter, as if that joy were now become a loss cries 'O, thy mother, thy mother!'; then   50
asks Bohemia forgiveness; then embraces his son-in-law; then again worries he his daughter with clipping her; now he thanks the old shepherd, which stands by like a weather-bitten conduit of many kings' reigns. I never heard of such another encounter, which lames report to follow it and undoes description to do it.

SECOND GENTLEMAN What, pray you, became of Antigonus, that carried hence the child?

THIRD GENTLEMAN Like an old tale still, which will have matter to rehearse, though credit be asleep and not   60
an ear open: he was torn to pieces with a bear. This avouches the shepherd's son, who has not only his innocence, which seems much, to justify him, but a handkerchief and rings of his that Paulina knows.

FIRST GENTLEMAN What became of his bark and his followers?

THIRD GENTLEMAN Wracked the same instant of their master's death, and in the view of the shepherd: so that all the instruments which aided to expose the child were even then lost when it was found. But O, the noble   70
combat that 'twixt joy and sorrow was fought in Paulina! She had one eye declined for the loss of her husband, another elevated that the oracle was fulfilled. She lifted the Princess from the earth, and so locks her

in embracing as if she would pin her to her heart, that
she might no more be in danger of losing.

FIRST GENTLEMAN The dignity of this act was worth
the audience of kings and princes, for by such was it
acted.

80 THIRD GENTLEMAN One of the prettiest touches of all,
and that which angled for mine eyes – caught the water
though not the fish – was when at the relation of the
Queen's death, with the manner how she came to't
bravely confessed and lamented by the King, how
attentiveness wounded his daughter; till, from one sign
of dolour to another, she did, with an 'Alas!', I would
fain say bleed tears; for I am sure my heart wept blood.
Who was most marble there changed colour; some
swooned, all sorrowed. If all the world could have seen't,
90 the woe had been universal.

FIRST GENTLEMAN Are they returned to the court?

THIRD GENTLEMAN No: the Princess, hearing of her
mother's statue, which is in the keeping of Paulina – a
piece many years in doing and now newly performed by
that rare Italian master, Julio Romano, who, had he
himself eternity and could put breath into his work,
would beguile Nature of her custom, so perfectly he is
her ape: he so near to Hermione hath done Hermione
that they say one would speak to her and stand in hope
100 of answer. Thither with all greediness of affection are
they gone, and there they intend to sup.

SECOND GENTLEMAN I thought she had some great
matter there in hand, for she hath privately, twice or
thrice a day, ever since the death of Hermione, visited
that removed house. Shall we thither, and with our
company piece the rejoicing?

FIRST GENTLEMAN Who would be thence that has the
benefit of access? Every wink of an eye some new grace

will be born. Our absence makes us unthrifty to our
knowledge. Let's along.   *Exeunt Gentlemen*   110
AUTOLYCUS Now, had I not the dash of my former life
in me, would preferment drop on my head. I brought
the old man and his son aboard the Prince; told him I
heard them talk of a fardel and I know not what: but he
at that time overfond of the shepherd's daughter – so he
then took her to be – who began to be much sea-sick,
and himself little better, extremity of weather continuing, this mystery remained undiscovered. But 'tis
all one to me; for had I been the finder-out of this
secret, it would not have relished among my other dis-   120
credits.

     Enter Shepherd and Clown

Here come those I have done good to against my will,
and already appearing in the blossoms of their fortune.
SHEPHERD Come, boy, I am past more children; but thy
sons and daughters will be all gentlemen born.
CLOWN You are well met, sir. You denied to fight with
me this other day because I was no gentleman born.
See you these clothes? Say you see them not and think
me still no gentleman born. You were best say these
robes are not gentlemen born. Give me the lie, do, and   130
try whether I am not now a gentleman born.
AUTOLYCUS I know you are now, sir, a gentleman born.
CLOWN Ay, and have been so any time these four hours.
SHEPHERD And so have I, boy.
CLOWN So you have; but I was a gentleman born before
my father: for the King's son took me by the hand, and
called me brother; and then the two kings called my
father brother; and then the Prince my brother and the
Princess my sister called my father father. And so we
wept; and there was the first gentleman-like tears that   140
ever we shed.

SHEPHERD We may live, son, to shed many more.

CLOWN Ay, or else 'twere hard luck, being in so preposterous estate as we are.

AUTOLYCUS I humbly beseech you, sir, to pardon me all
the faults I have committed to your worship, and to give
me your good report to the Prince my master.

SHEPHERD Prithee, son, do: for we must be gentle, now
we are gentlemen.

150 CLOWN Thou wilt amend thy life?

AUTOLYCUS Ay, an it like your good worship.

CLOWN Give me thy hand. I will swear to the Prince thou
art as honest a true fellow as any is in Bohemia.

SHEPHERD You may say it, but not swear it.

CLOWN Not swear it, now I am a gentleman? Let boors
and franklins say it, I'll swear it.

SHEPHERD How if it be false, son?

CLOWN If it be ne'er so false, a true gentleman may
swear it in the behalf of his friend; and I'll swear to the
160 Prince thou art a tall fellow of thy hands, and that thou
wilt not be drunk; but I know thou art no tall fellow of
thy hands, and that thou wilt be drunk. But I'll swear it,
and I would thou wouldst be a tall fellow of thy hands.

AUTOLYCUS I will prove so, sir, to my power.

CLOWN Ay, by any means prove a tall fellow. If I do not
wonder how thou dar'st venture to be drunk, not being
a tall fellow, trust me not. Hark, the kings and the
princes, our kindred, are going to see the Queen's
picture. Come, follow us: we'll be thy good masters.

                                        Exeunt

Enter Leontes, Polixenes, Florizel, Perdita, Camillo,   V.3
Paulina, Lords, and Attendants

LEONTES
O grave and good Paulina, the great comfort
That I have had of thee!

PAULINA   What, sovereign sir,
I did not well, I meant well. All my services
You have paid home: but that you have vouchsafed,
With your crowned brother and these your contracted
Heirs of your kingdoms, my poor house to visit,
It is a surplus of your grace, which never
My life may last to answer.

LEONTES   O Paulina,
We honour you with trouble. But we came
To see the statue of our queen: your gallery   10
Have we passed through, not without much content
In many singularities; but we saw not
That which my daughter came to look upon,
The statue of her mother.

PAULINA   As she lived peerless,
So her dead likeness I do well believe
Excels whatever yet you looked upon,
Or hand of man hath done; therefore I keep it
Lonely, apart. But here it is: prepare
To see the life as lively mocked as ever
Still sleep mocked death. Behold, and say 'tis well!   20
    Paulina draws a curtain and reveals Hermione, stand-
    ing like a statue
I like your silence: it the more shows off
Your wonder. But yet speak: first you, my liege.
Comes it not something near?

LEONTES   Her natural posture!
Chide me, dear stone, that I may say indeed
Thou art Hermione; or rather, thou art she

In thy not chiding, for she was as tender
As infancy and grace. But yet, Paulina,
Hermione was not so much wrinkled, nothing
So agèd as this seems.

POLIXENES   O, not by much!

PAULINA

30   So much the more our carver's excellence,
Which lets go by some sixteen years and makes her
As she lived now.

LEONTES   As now she might have done,
So much to my good comfort as it is
Now piercing to my soul. O, thus she stood,
Even with such life of majesty – warm life,
As now it coldly stands – when first I wooed her!
I am ashamed. Does not the stone rebuke me
For being more stone than it? O royal piece!
There's magic in thy majesty, which has

40   My evils conjured to remembrance, and
From thy admiring daughter took the spirits,
Standing like stone with thee.

PERDITA   And give me leave,
And do not say 'tis superstition, that
I kneel and then implore her blessing. Lady,
Dear queen, that ended when I but began,
Give me that hand of yours to kiss!

PAULINA   O, patience!
The statue is but newly fixed, the colour's
Not dry.

CAMILLO
My lord, your sorrow was too sore laid on,

50   Which sixteen winters cannot blow away,
So many summers dry. Scarce any joy
Did ever so long live; no sorrow
But killed itself much sooner.

POLIXENES   Dear my brother,
  Let him that was the cause of this have power
  To take off so much grief from you as he
  Will piece up in himself.

PAULINA   Indeed, my lord,
  If I had thought the sight of my poor image
  Would thus have wrought you – for the stone is mine –
  I'd not have showed it.

LEONTES   Do not draw the curtain.

PAULINA
  No longer shall you gaze on't, lest your fancy   60
  May think anon it moves.

LEONTES   Let be, let be!
  Would I were dead but that methinks already –
  What was he that did make it? See, my lord:
  Would you not deem it breathed, and that those veins
  Did verily bear blood?

POLIXENES   Masterly done!
  The very life seems warm upon her lip.

LEONTES
  The fixure of her eye has motion in't
  As we are mocked with art.

PAULINA   I'll draw the curtain.
  My lord's almost so far transported that
  He'll think anon it lives.

LEONTES   O sweet Paulina,   70
  Make me to think so twenty years together!
  No settled senses of the world can match
  The pleasure of that madness. Let't alone.

PAULINA
  I am sorry, sir, I have thus far stirred you; but
  I could afflict you farther.

LEONTES   Do, Paulina:
  For this affliction has a taste as sweet

As any cordial comfort. Still methinks
There is an air comes from her. What fine chisel
Could ever yet cut breath? Let no man mock me,
80   For I will kiss her.
PAULINA   Good my lord, forbear.
The ruddiness upon her lip is wet:
You'll mar it if you kiss it; stain your own
With oily painting. Shall I draw the curtain?
LEONTES
No, not these twenty years.
PERDITA   So long could I
Stand by, a looker-on.
PAULINA   Either forbear,
Quit presently the chapel, or resolve you
For more amazement. If you can behold it,
I'll make the statue move indeed, descend
And take you by the hand: but then you'll think —
90   Which I protest against — I am assisted
By wicked powers.
LEONTES   What you can make her do
I am content to look on; what to speak
I am content to hear; for 'tis as easy
To make her speak as move.
PAULINA   It is required
You do awake your faith. Then all stand still;
Or those that think it is unlawful business
I am about, let them depart.
LEONTES   Proceed.
No foot shall stir.
PAULINA   Music, awake her, strike!
     Music
'Tis time: descend; be stone no more; approach;
100   Strike all that look upon with marvel. Come,
I'll fill your grave up. Stir; nay, come away.

Bequeath to death your numbness, for from him
Dear life redeems you. You perceive she stirs.
 Hermione descends
Start not: her actions shall be holy as
You hear my spell is lawful. (*To Leontes*) Do not shun her
Until you see her die again, for then
You kill her double. Nay, present your hand.
When she was young you wooed her: now, in age,
Is she become the suitor?
LEONTES   O, she's warm!
 If this be magic, let it be an art   110
 Lawful as eating.
POLIXENES   She embraces him.
CAMILLO
 She hangs about his neck.
 If she pertain to life, let her speak too.
POLIXENES
 Ay, and make it manifest where she has lived,
 Or how stol'n from the dead.
PAULINA   That she is living,
 Were it but told you, should be hooted at
 Like an old tale: but it appears she lives,
 Though yet she speak not. Mark a little while.
 (*To Perdita*) Please you to interpose, fair madam; kneel,
 And pray your mother's blessing. Turn, good lady: 120
 Our Perdita is found.
HERMIONE   You gods, look down,
 And from your sacred vials pour your graces
 Upon my daughter's head! Tell me, mine own,
 Where hast thou been preserved? Where lived? How
   found
 Thy father's court? For thou shalt hear that I,
 Knowing by Paulina that the oracle
 Gave hope thou wast in being, have preserved

Myself to see the issue.

PAULINA   There's time enough for that,
    Lest they desire upon this push to trouble
130   Your joys with like relation. Go together,
    You precious winners all; your exultation
    Partake to everyone. I, an old turtle,
    Will wing me to some withered bough, and there
    My mate, that's never to be found again,
    Lament till I am lost.

LEONTES   O peace, Paulina!
    Thou shouldst a husband take by my consent,
    As I by thine a wife. This is a match,
    And made between's by vows. Thou hast found mine –
    But how is to be questioned: for I saw her,
140   As I thought, dead; and have in vain said many
    A prayer upon her grave. I'll not seek far –
    For him, I partly know his mind – to find thee
    An honourable husband. Come, Camillo,
    And take her by the hand; whose worth and honesty
    Is richly noted, and here justified
    By us, a pair of kings. Let's from this place.
    (*To Hermione*) What! Look upon my brother. Both your
          pardons
    That e'er I put between your holy looks
    My ill suspicion. This' your son-in-law,
150   And son unto the King, whom heavens directing,
    Is troth-plight to your daughter. Good Paulina,
    Lead us from hence, where we may leisurely
    Each one demand and answer to his part
    Performed in this wide gap of time since first
    We were dissevered. Hastily lead away.   *Exeunt*

An Account of the Text

The Winter's Tale was published for the first time in 1623, in the collected edition of Shakespeare's plays known as the first Folio (F). All subsequent editions of it derive from this text, which is therefore our only authority for what Shakespeare wrote. Fortunately it is an exceptionally good text, with very few signs of corruption. The copy used by the printer seems to have been a transcript made by Ralph Crane, a professional scribe, who was sometimes employed as copyist by the King's Men, Shakespeare's company. The Folio text of *The Winter's Tale* has all the marks of Crane's transcripts:

1. The lavish use of brackets, apostrophes and hyphens.

2. The full division of the play into acts and scenes. This division has been adopted by most subsequent editors, though some, chiefly in the eighteenth century, have departed from it by leaving F's IV.1 (the chorus-speech of Time) unnumbered, so that their IV.1, IV.2 and IV.3 are F's (and our) IV.2, IV.3 and IV.4.

3. The use of so-called 'massed entries', that is a listing in the scene heading of all the characters appearing in the course of that scene, whether they are present from the beginning or not. For instance, F's scene heading for II.1 reads *Enter Hermione, Mamillius, Ladies: Leontes, Antigonus, Lords*, though Leontes, Antigonus and the Lords do not enter until line 32. But the use of massed entries is not consistent: they are not found in two scenes, IV.3 and V.2, where the entries are given in the normal manner; and sometimes the entrance of characters listed in the massed entry is also marked at its proper place within the scene, though more often it is not.

4. The paucity of stage directions. The few directions which are to be found consist of a bare listing of exits and entrances (with the exceptions listed below). Most of the stage directions in our text are therefore editorial additions.

Whether Crane's transcript was made from Shakespeare's own manuscript ('foul papers') is uncertain. Whatever its derivation, it must have been a legible and clean text, which set the copyist few problems. We know, however, for certain that the company's prompt book of *The Winter's Tale* had got lost by the summer of 1623, and that there was some delay in printing the play at the end of the Comedy section of the Folio. The most cogent and economical hypothesis seems, therefore, that when it was the turn of *The Winter's Tale* to be printed, in the autumn of 1621, the loss of the prompt book was discovered and that Ralph Crane was commissioned to make a transcript from Shakespeare's own manuscript or a clean copy of it.

The Winter's Tale is one of seven plays in the Folio which provide a list of the characters in the play. It is printed at the end of the text and reads as follows:

The Names of the Actors.

Leontes, King of Sicillia.
Mamillus, yong Prince of Sicillia.
Camillo.
Antigonus.   Foure
Cleomines.   *Lords of Sicillia.*
Dion.
Hermione, Queene to Leontes.
Perdita, Daughter to Leontes and Hermione.
Paulina, wife to Antigonus.
Emilia, a Lady.
Polixenes, King of Bohemia.
Florizell, Prince of Bohemia.
Old Shepheard, reputed Father of Perdita.
Clowne, his Sonne.
Autolicus, a Rogue.
Archidamus, a Lord of Bohemia.
Other Lords, and Gentlemen, and Seruants.
Shepheards, and Shephearddesses.

COLLATIONS

1 Emendations

The following is a list of readings in the present text of *The Winter's Tale* which differ significantly from those found in F (F's reading is printed on the right of the square brackets, in the original spelling, except that the 'long s' (ʃ) has been replaced by 's'). Most of these emendations were introduced by eighteenth-century editors. Those marked with an asterisk are discussed in the Commentary. Purely typographical errors in F have not been listed.

I.2

    104 And] A
  *148 What] *Leo.* What
  *208 you, they say] you say
    276 hobby-horse] Holy-Horse
  *337 forsealing] for sealing
377–8 and dare not | Be intelligent to me?] and dare not? | Be intelligent to me,

II.1

  *90 fedary] Federarie
  *143 lam-damn] Land-damne

II.2

    53 let't] le't

II.3

    39 What] Who
  *177 its] it

III.2

  *10 Silence!] *Silence.*
    32 Who] Whom
    99 its] it

III.3

    28 thrower-out] Thower-out
  *116 made] mad

IV.3

  *10 With heigh, with heigh,] *With heigh,*

IV.4

    *12 Digest it with accustom] Digest with a Custome

    *13 swoon] sworne

    160 out] on't

    245 kiln-hole] kill-hole

    308 gentlemen] Gent.

    416 acknowledged] acknowledge

    420 who] whom

    425 shalt see] shalt neuer see

    436 hoop] hope

    464 your] my

  *490 As you've e'er] As you haue euer

    497 our] her

  *546 thee, the son,] thee there Sonne

    577 She is as] She's as

    607 filed keys off] fill'd Keyes of

    637 flayed] fled

  *700 know not] know

  *730 to toaze] at toaze

    739 pheasant, cock nor hen] Pheazant Cock, nor Hen

    742 I'll] I will

V.1

    12 of. PAULINA True, too true,] of, true. *Paul.* Too true

  *59 Where we offenders move, appear soul-vexed,] (Where we Offendors now appeare) Soule-vext,

    61 just cause] iust such cause

    75 CLEOMENES Good madam – PAULINA I have done] *Cleo.* Good Madame, I haue done

V.3

  *18 Lonely] Louely

  *96 Or those] On: those

2 *Stage Directions*

The following is a list of the only stage directions (other than simple exits and entrances) that appear in F. Other stage directions in this edition are editorial additions.

III.2

      0 *Enter Leontes, Lords, Officers: Hermione (as to her Triall) Ladies: Cleomines, Dion*

III.3

    57 *Exit pursued by a Beare*

IV.1

      0 *Enter Time, the Chorus*

IV.3

      0 *Enter Autolicus singing*

IV.4

   167 *Heere a Daunce of Shepheards and Shephearddesses*

   219 *Enter Autolicus singing*

   339 *Heere a Dance of twelue Satyres*

V.3

      0 *Enter Leontes, Polixenes, Florizell, Perdita, Camillo, Paulina: Hermione (like a Statue:) Lords, &c.*

The Songs

There are six songs in *The Winter's Tale*, all of them sung by Autolycus (one as a three-part song with Dorcas and Mopsa). For three of these the earliest settings that have been preserved belong to the mid eighteenth century: those for 'When daffodils begin to peer' (IV.3.1) and 'Will you buy any tape' (IV.4.313) are by William Boyce (*c.* 1759 and 1769); that for 'But shall I go mourn for that, my dear?' (IV.3.15) is by J. F. Lampe (*c.* 1745). For the other three songs earlier settings have come down to us. They are printed below, in transcriptions made for the 1986 edition by Dr F. W. Sternfeld. The tune of 'Jog on, jog on, the footpath way' (IV.3.121) is found first in the second decade of the seventeenth century, arranged in a set of variations by Richard Farnaby, in the Fitzwilliam Virginal Book. The version here given follows the text in Playford's *Musical Companion* (1667), except for two small variants, which have been taken from the Fitzwilliam Virginal Book. The tune of 'Lawn as white as driven snow' (IV.4.220) was printed for the first time in John Wilson's *Cheerful Airs or Ballads* (1659). It is possible that this setting is Wilson's arrangement of the original tune. For 'Get you hence, for I must go' (IV.4.295) two early settings are extant. The first, which is here transcribed, is found in a manuscript (New York Public Library, Drexel 4175) of the first half of the seventeenth century, and has an accompaniment in lyra-viol tablature. The second, found in a manuscript of about 1640, consists of the same melody transposed to another key. Instead of the lyra-viol tablature it has a thoroughbass accompaniment. This setting is incomplete, ending after 'if to either thou dost ill'.

1. 'Jog on, jog on, the footpath way' (IV.3.121)

Jog on, jog on, the foot-path way, And mer-ri-ly hent the stile - a: A mer-ry heart goes all the day, Your sad tires in a mile - a.

2. 'Lawn as white as driven snow' (IV.4.220)

Lawn as____ white as dri - ven____ snow;____

Cy - press black as e'er__ was__ crow; Gloves as sweet as

da - mask ro - ses;__ Masks for fa - ces,__ and__ for no - ses;

Bu - gle - brace - let, neck - lace - am - ber; Per - fume

for __ a ____ la - dy's cham - ber; Gol - den coifs and sto - ma -

- chers For my lads, for my lads to give their dears;

3. 'Get you hence, for I must go' (IV.4.295)

Commentary

The act and scene division is that found in the 1623 Folio (F). Quotations from Robert Greene's *Pandosto* included in the Introduction and Commentary are taken from Stanley Wells's modern-spelling edition of the 1588 text, reprinted in the Oxford World's Classics edition of *The Winter's Tale*, ed. Stephen Orgel.

The Characters in the Play: For the derivation of the names see notes on III.3.32; IV.1.22; IV.3.24; IV.4.54; V.1.156.

I.1

    0 *Enter Camillo and Archidamus*: The scene headings throughout the Folio text are silent about the location of each scene. This can, however, be usually inferred from its opening lines, for, in the absence of naturalistic sets, Shakespeare took pains to inform his audience of the scene's approximate location whenever such knowledge is wanted. However, a precise localization (attempted by many later editors) is often impossible, as well as unnecessary.

    6 *Bohemia*: The King of Bohemia, Polixenes.

    9 *justified in our loves*: Acquitted (of inferior hospitality) by virtue of our warmth or affection; the phrase also glances at the doctrine of salvation by faith rather than works.

11–12 *in the freedom of my knowledge*: As my knowledge gives me the right to do.

    13 *sleepy*: Inducing sleep.

14 *unintelligent*: Unaware.

21–2 *Sicilia . . . Bohemia*: The King of Sicilia . . . the King of Bohemia.

22–4 *They were trained . . . branch now*: The horticultural meaning of *trained* is responsible for the metaphors in the remainder of the sentence.

27 *hath*: An instance of the third-person plural in 'th'.
   attorneyed: Performed by substitutes.

29 *vast*: Wide expanse.

35 *into my note*: Under my notice.

37 *physics the subject*: Acts as a tonic to the nation.

I.2

1–2 *Nine changes of the watery star hath been | The shepherd's note*: The shepherd has observed nine changes of the moon (*watery star*), i.e. nine months have passed.

3 *burden*: Occupant.

3–9 *Time as long . . . before it*: I ought to spend another nine months thanking you, and yet would depart for ever in your debt; and so one final expression of thanks must multiply all those that preceded it, just as a zero at the end of a number multiplies it, though by itself it is without value.

11 *I am questioned by my fears of what may chance*: My fears raise questions in me as to what may be happening.

12–14 *That may blow . . . too truly*: This passage has been much discussed, but its general meaning is clear enough. Though in F *that* is preceded by a comma, it is probably a wish: 'O, that no sneaping winds may blow at home, to make me say "my fears were only too well grounded!".'

13 *sneaping*: Nipping; biting.

16 *Than you can put us to't*: Than to be taxed beyond our strength by you.

17 *sev'n-night*: Week.
   Very sooth: Truly.

18 *between's*: Between us.

19 *I'll no gainsaying*: I will not be refused.

25 *Were, in your love, a whip to me*: Would be a punishment to me, though you acted out of love.

31–2 *this satisfaction | The by-gone day proclaimed*: We heard this good news yesterday.

33 *ward*: Defensive posture (in fencing).

37 *distaffs*: Long rods, used in spinning for winding wool or flax.

37 *Leontes draws apart*: This seems the most probable moment for the withdrawal of Leontes. Up to this point Hermione has been addressing her words to him, speaking of Polixenes in the third person. Now Leontes withdraws and the remainder of the speech is addressed directly to Polixenes. Her *yet, good deed, Leontes, | I love thee not a jar o'th'clock behind | What lady she her lord* would then be spoken to herself, out of his hearing. This hypothesis is supported by the fact that, whenever elsewhere in the play Hermione addresses her husband, she calls him *sir*, *my lord*, *your highness*, but never *Leontes*.

40 *take*: Probably the meaning here is 'receive', rather than 'charm' or 'delight', as some commentators explain it.

41 *let him*: Allow him (to stay).
   gest: A stage of a royal progress, hence the time allotted for such a stage.

42 *for's*: For his.
   good deed: Indeed; in very truth.

43 *jar*: Tick.

44 *What lady she her lord*: Than any lady whatsoever loves her husband.

47 *limber*: Limp; flabby.

53–4 *so you shall pay your fees | When you depart*: Prisoners in Shakespeare's day were liable to pay fees to the gaoler upon being freed.

57 *should import offending*: Should imply that I had committed some offence against you.

62 *pretty lordings*: Charming young princes.

63 *behind*: To follow.

66 *verier wag*: Greater rascal.

68 *changed*: Exchanged.

73 *stronger blood*: The passions of adulthood.

74–5 *the imposition cleared | Hereditary ours*: A latinism: 'assuming the inherited guilt which is imposed upon us (i.e. original sin) to be set aside'. A possible, but much less likely, alternative explanation – favoured by several commentators – makes Polixenes affirm that their boyhood innocence even cleared them of the taint of original sin.

80 *Grace to boot*: Heaven help us!

81 *Of this make no conclusion*: Do not pursue this argument to a logical conclusion.

83–6 *Th'offences . . . but with us*: If you and he have sinned only with your wife and me, then you are safe because we'll take responsibility.

92–3 *One good deed . . . upon that*: The absence of praise for one good deed leads to the destruction of a thousand others which were ready to be performed.

96 *heat an acre*: Race over a single furlong.

99 *Grace*: The primary meaning here is probably that of 'seemliness', 'becomingness', with an intentional pun on the female name.

104 *clap thyself my love*: Offer the handclasp that seals the bargain, as was customary at betrothals.

109 *To mingle friendship far is mingling bloods*: In Aristotelian physiology sexual intercourse was thought of as a mingling of bloods (cf. Donne's *The Progress of the Soul*, stanza L: 'Adam and Eve had mingled bloods').

110 *tremor cordis*: Palpitation of the heart.

112–13 *May a free face put on . . . bosom*: May wear the look of innocence, may derive a freedom from cordiality, from generosity, from abundance of affection.

112 *put on*: Wear (without any suggestion of deceit).

115 *But to be paddling palms and pinching fingers*: That a lady's 'paddling' with the palm of a gentleman's hand could be seen both as an accepted form of polite behaviour and as a sign of lasciviousness is

illustrated by the conversation between Iago and
Roderigo about Desdemona's bearing towards Cassio
(*Othello*, II.1.246–50):

IAGO . . . Didst thou not see her paddle with the palm
   of his hand? Didst not mark that?
RODERIGO Yes, that I did; but that was but courtesy.
IAGO Lechery, by this hand: an index and obscure pro-
   logue to the history of lust and foul thoughts.

115 *paddling*: Fondly fingering.
116 *practised*: Studied.
118 *mort o'th'deer*: This is a hunting phrase, denoting the
    four notes blown to announce the death of the deer.
    The long-drawn breath needed to blow this could
    be compared with a sigh. But it is much more likely
    that the reference is to the dying deer's last sighs,
    possibly with a pun on *deer*.
119 *nor my brows*: Here and at 124–9, 137, 146 and 186
    the reference is to the popular jest that horns grow
    on the forehead of cuckolds.
120 *I'fecks*: A corruption of 'in faith'.
121 *bawcock*: Fine fellow (from French '*beau coq*'; a
    colloquial term of endearment).
123 *not neat but cleanly*: Recollecting that *neat* also means
    'horned cattle', Leontes corrects himself.
125 *virginalling*: Playing with her fingers as if upon the
    virginals, a keyboard instrument.
126 *wanton*: Frisky; frolicsome.
128 *a rough pash and the shoots*: A bull's shaggy head
    and horns.
132 *o'er-dyed blacks*: Probably blacks (mourning garments)
    dyed over in another colour, so that the suggestion
    not only of falseness in the colour of the clothing
    but also of infidelity in their wearer is involved.
134 *bourn*: Boundary.
136 *welkin*: Blue as the sky.
137 *collop*: Slice of meat (hence 'my flesh and blood').
    dam: Mother (part of the cluster of cattle-images

set off by the allusion to the cuckold's horns
at 119).

138–46 *Affection, thy intention stabs the centre . . . of my
brows*: The meaning of these lines, which have been
called 'the obscurest passage in Shakespeare', has
been endlessly discussed. The chief point at issue is
whether Leontes is speaking of his own feelings or
of Hermione's. One group of commentators thinks
that Leontes is analysing the nature of sexual jealousy and that he is saying: 'The feeling of jealousy
is often based on mere figments; all the more reason,
then, that it may also join with something real, as
it does in my case.' But this train of thought lacks
logic and does not link up well with the immediately
preceding words, *Can thy dam? May't be?* Above all
the word *affection* would be oddly chosen to signify
passionate jealousy. Its meaning here seems to be
rather that of 'sexual desire' (as in *The Rape of
Lucrece*, l. 271). To his own question, whether it is
possible that Hermione is an adulteress, Leontes
replies: 'Yes, for sexual desire, in its intensity, stabs
men to their very soul. It makes possible what is
else thought impossible, creating an imaginary world
of wish-fulfilment in dreams. All the more credible
is it then that it will fasten on a real object, and
this it does in Hermione's passion for Polixenes,
which has maddened me and made me a cuckold.'
The logical train of thought is interrupted by *how
can this be?* at 140, which seems to be a return to
the opening question, *Can thy dam? May't be?* In the
very process of being given a reasoned answer,
the question reasserts itself in Leontes' mind.

138 *Affection*: Sexual desire.
   intention: Intensity.
   centre: Soul; heart.

142 *credent*: Credible.

144 *commission*: Warrant.

146 *What means Sicilia*: This is surely an inquiry not
about what Leontes means but about the meaning

of his distracted appearance. There is therefore no
need or warrant for assuming that any part of his
preceding speech is overheard by Hermione and
Polixenes.

147 *something*: Somewhat.

148 *What cheer? How is't with you, best brother*: In all
the Folios this line is given to Leontes. But the phrase
How is't with you, which with Shakespeare always
has the meaning of 'Are you feeling well?', makes
it highly probable that it is spoken by Polixenes.

150 *moved*: Angered.

151 *Nature*: The bonds of affection between parents and
children.

152–3 *a pastime | To harder bosoms*: A diversion for those
less tender-hearted.

154 *methoughts*: A not uncommon variant of 'methought'.
recoil: Go back in memory.

155 *Twenty-three years*: This fixes the age of Leontes in
the first half of the play at around thirty.
unbreeched: Not yet in breeches.

160 *squash*: Unripe pea-pod.

161 *Will you take eggs for money*: A proverbial expression, meaning: 'Will you allow yourself to be fobbed
off with something of little value?'

163 *happy man be's dole*: A common expression, meaning:
'May it be his lot in life to be a happy man!'

165 *If at home*: When I am at home.

166 *all my exercise, my mirth, my matter*: That which
constantly occupies my attention, the subject of my
merry and my serious moments.

171 *thick my blood*: Make me melancholy.

171–2 *So stands this squire | Officed with me*: Just such a
part is played by this boy in my household (alluding
to the services of squires in royal households).

174–5 *How thou lov'st us . . . be cheap*: The double meaning
of these lines is most probably intended by Leontes.

177 *Apparent to my heart*: Heir to my affection.

178 *Shall's attend you there*: Shall we await you there?

179–80 *you'll be found,* | *Be you beneath the sky*: I'll find you wherever you are (with a pun on *found* as 'found out').

182 *Go to, go to*: An interjection expressing remonstrance or disgust.

183 *neb*: Beak; mouth.

185 *To her allowing husband*: Towards her husband, who licenses such behaviour.

186 *forked one*: An allusion to the cuckold's horns.

187–9 *thy mother plays . . . my grave*: Your mother engages in love-play, and I, too, am playing (namely, the role of a husband who simulates amity towards his unfaithful wife and her lover), but a most shameful part, as the result of which I shall be hissed until the end of my days.

189 *Contempt and clamour*: Probably an example of the rhetorical trope known as hendiadys: 'an outcry of contempt'.

194 *sluiced*: This metaphor, derived from the action of drawing off water from a pond or lake by means of a sluice, leads on to those of the pond and the gates in the succeeding lines.

199 *revolted*: Unfaithful.

200 *Physic*: Medical treatment.

201–2 *It is a bawdy planet, that will strike* | *Where 'tis predominant*: It is like a bawdy planet, which will spread ruin whenever it is in the ascendant (the allusion is to the planet Venus). *strike* ('destroy by malign influence') and *predominant* ('in the ascendant') are both technical terms in astrology.

202 *think it*: Be assured of it.

204 *No barricado for a belly*: There is no way of barricading a womb.

    Know't: Be certain of it.

206 *on's*: Of us.

208 *I am like you, they say*: This emendation of F's *I am like you say* is found for the first time in the second Folio (1632). An alternative emendation would be 'I am like you, you say'. But though the omission of a second 'you' would be a more likely

printer's or copyist's error, *they say* seems the more attractive reading and has been adopted by all editors.

210 *He comes forward*: It must be assumed that up to this point Camillo has hovered at the back of the stage but within hearing of the dialogue.

214 *still came home*: Always came back.

217 *They're here with me already*: People are already aware of my situation.

218 *Sicilia is a so-forth*: The King is a so-and-so (avoiding the open use of 'cuckold').

219 *gust*: Taste (hence 'know of ').

222 *so it is*: As things are.
taken: Comprehended.

224 *thy conceit is soaking*: Your faculty of apprehension is quick to absorb.

225 *blocks*: Blockheads.

226 *But of the finer natures*: Except by the keener minds.

227 *Lower messes*: Inferior people (a 'mess' being a group of people who were served together at table).

228 *purblind*: Quite blind.

233 *Satisfy*: Leontes takes the word in its erotic sense.

236–7 *as well | My chamber-counsels*: And also with my intimate confidences.

242 *bide*: Insist.

244 *Which hoxes honesty behind*: Which hamstrings honesty (the unusual metaphor, derived from the laming of cattle by cutting their hamstrings, was probably suggested by the popular derivation of 'coward' from 'cowherd').

245–7 *Or else . . . or else*: Either . . . or.

248 *played home, the rich stake drawn*: Played to the finish, the high stake taken up by the winner (probably with a bawdy quibble on *the rich stake drawn*).

254 *puts forth*: Shows itself.

256 *industriously*: Intentionally (corresponding to *wilful* in the previous clause).

260–61 *Whereof the execution . . . non-performance*: Probably 'the carrying out of which showed how wrong it would have been not to have done it'.

263 *that*: As.

268 *eye-glass*: Lens of the eye.

270 *to a vision so apparent*: About something which can be seen so clearly.

273 *slippery*: Unchaste.

274-5 *Or else be impudently . . . thought*: Otherwise you must boldly deny that you can see, hear and think.

276 *hobby-horse*: Whore.

277 *puts to*: Fornicates; 'puts out'.

278 *troth-plight*: Engagement or marriage.
      justify: Affirm.

281 *present*: Immediate.
      'Shrew: Beshrew.

283-4 *which to reiterate were sin | As deep as that, though true*: Commentators agree in making *As deep as that* refer to Hermione's adultery. But it makes much better sense if we take it to refer to the sin committed by Leontes in unjustly accusing her.

286 *career*: Literally 'short gallop at full speed', hence 'course'.

288 *honesty*: Chastity.
      Horsing foot on foot: Setting one's foot upon that of the other person (this apparently unique use of the word 'horsing' was presumably sparked off by the equestrian metaphor at 286).

291 *pin and web*: Cataract, a disease of the eye.

297 *betimes*: Early; soon.

302 *hovering*: Wavering.

306 *The running of one glass*: The time it takes for the sand in an hourglass to run out.

307 *like her medal*: Like a miniature portrait of herself (worn in a locket around the neck).

309 *bare*: Bore.

311 *thrifts*: Gains.

313 *form*: Rank; quality.

314 *benched and reared to worship*: Given a position of authority and raised to a place of honour.

317 *To give mine enemy a lasting wink*: To close my enemy's eyes for ever.

318 *cordial*: Restorative; reviving.

319 *rash*: Operating quickly.

321 *Maliciously*: Virulently.

322 *crack*: Flaw.
     dread: Esteemed.

323 *So sovereignly being*: Being so supremely.

324 *I have loved thee*: The use of *thee*, unusual in a
     subject towards his sovereign, has led some editors
     to transfer these words to Leontes, or to emend
     them. But Camillo's special role as the King's inti-
     mate and confessor (235–9) sufficiently justifies its
     use.
     Make that thy question, and go rot: 'If you doubt
     that, go to blazes!' This is a reply to Camillo's
     expression of disbelief in Hermione's guilt, not to
     his last words, which Leontes interrupts.

325 *muddy*: Mixed-up.

326 *To appoint my self in this vexation*: Probably 'to
     ordain this affliction for my own self'; the main
     stress is on *self*.

332 *ripe moving to't*: Full justification for it.

333 *blench*: Swerve (from the path of right conduct).

334 *fetch off*: Do away with; kill. Camillo's choice of this
     uncommon expression, and again of *removed* in the
     next line, may be due to his wish to equivocate in
     order to avoid lying to Leontes, for the common
     Shakespearian meaning of 'fetch off' is 'rescue', an
     action which Camillo may be already contemplating.
     The formulation of his promise at 346–7 may
     be due to the same desire to equivocate, Camillo
     declaring thus covertly his resolution to leave the
     service of Leontes.

337 *forsealing*: F's *for sealing* can be made to yield adequate
     sense if taken to mean 'for the sake of sealing', but
     this entails a very awkward and un-Shakespearian
     construction. It seems highly probable that *for* here
     is an intensive prefix, the word meaning 'sealing up
     close'.

339–41 *Thou dost advise me . . . none*: A marked contrast

with Pandosto, who intends from the outset 'as soon
as Egistus was dead to give his wife a sop of the
same sauce, and so be rid of those which were the
cause of his restless sorrow'. In the play it is only
the flight of Polixenes and his conviction that
Hermione was accessary to it and to a plot against
his life that move Leontes to denounce her publicly
and to seek her death. It is one of many ways in
which Shakespeare makes him more sympathetic than
Pandosto.

350 *I will seem friendly, as thou hast advised me*: Leontes
does not, in fact, succeed in dissimulating his feelings.

355–6 *Who, in rebellion . . . too*: Who, being in rebellion
against his true and worthy self, wants all his subjects
to follow him in this.

356 *To do*: If I do. This use of the infinitive in a gerun-
dive sense is common with Shakespeare.

361 *Let villainy itself forswear't*: Even wickedness personified should refuse to do it.

362–3 *certain | To me a break-neck*: My certain ruin.

365 *warp*: Shrink; shrivel.

367 *None rare*: Nothing unusual.

372–3 *Wafting his eyes . . . contempt*: Looking the other
way, and dropping his lip contemptuously.

374 *breeding*: Afoot.

377–80 *How, dare not? . . . And cannot say you dare not*:
How do you mean, dare not? Is it that you *do* not
know? Or can it be that you do know but dare not
communicate your knowledge to *me*? That must be
it: for you cannot be saying that you don't dare to
communicate it to *yourself*.

381 *complexions*: Looks (those of Leontes and Camillo).

382–4 *for I must be . . . altered with't*: For my looks, too,
must have changed, reflecting the altered position in
which I find myself.

383 *party*: Participant.

388 *Make me not sighted like the basilisk*: Do not make
me out to have a gaze like that of the basilisk (a

fabulous reptile, half cock and half serpent, supposed to be able to kill by its look).

392 *Clerk-like experienced*: Proved to be a man of learning.

394 *In whose success we are gentle*: In succession from whom we are noble.

397 *ignorant concealment*: Concealment that keeps one in ignorance.

400–402 *I conjure thee . . . this suit of mine*: I appeal solemnly to you by all the obligations which honourable men recognize, not the least of which is to answer this request of mine.

403 *incidency*: Event liable to happen.

410–11 *or both . . . good night*: Or proclaim both yourself and me as lost, and so farewell for ever.

412 *him*: The man.

416 *vice*: Force; constrain (as by the use of a vice).

419 *his that did betray the Best*: Judas, who betrayed Jesus (*the Best*).

421 *savour*: Stench.

424 *Swear his thought over*: Though you should over-swear (swear the contrary of) his thought.

426 *influences*: A technical term in astrology, designating the emanation from the stars, which was believed to affect all life on earth.

427 *for to*: To.

428 *or . . . or*: Either . . . or.

429–31 *whose foundation . . . of his body*: The foundation of which is firmly erected upon his settled belief, and which will last as long as his life.

431 *How should this grow*: How should this suspicion have arisen?

435 *this trunk*: This body of mine (with a quibble on *trunk* meaning 'chest').

436 *impawned*: As a pledge of my good faith.

438 *posterns*: Back gates in the city walls.

441 *discovery*: Disclosure.

448 *places*: Dignities.

449 *Still*: Always.

456 *Professed*: Made professions of friendship.

458–60 *Good expedition be my friend and comfort | The gracious
Queen, part of his theme, but nothing | Of his ill-ta'en
suspicion*: This passage has been much discussed and
emended. The perplexities are dispelled once we realize
(1) that *expedition* here means not 'hasty departure' but
'the action of expediting': this same hastening which
Polixenes prays to be his friend, since it will convey him
into safety, he also hopes will bring comfort to the Queen
by quickly putting an end to the King's suspicions; (2)
that *nothing | Of his ill-ta'en suspicion* does not mean
that Hermione is not *included* in her husband's wrongly
conceived suspicions, but that she does not deserve them,
though she is part of his *theme* (which here has the
meaning of 'matter for feeling and action').

462 *Hence! Let us avoid*: Away! let us be gone. Many
editors adopt the tamer but quite possible reading
'Thou bear'st my life off hence. Let us avoid'. F
reads *Thou bear'st my life off, hence: Let vs auoid.*

II.1

1–32 *Take the boy . . . in mine ear*: This episode is
developed from a single line in *Pandosto*, telling how
the guards, sent to carry her to prison, 'coming to
the queen's lodging . . . found her playing with her
young son Garinter'.

3 *I'll none of you*: I will have nothing to do with you.

9 *so that*: Provided that.

11 *taught'*: Taught you (the apostrophe, found in F,
shows that, for metrical reasons, a word has been
omitted).

18 *wanton*: Sport; play.

20 *Good time*: A happy issue.

28 *sprites*: Spirits; ghosts. Note the echo of the words
at III.2.91, *The bug which you would fright me with
I seek.*

31 *Yond crickets*: A reference to the merry chatter of
the ladies-in-waiting.

35 *scour*: Hurry along.

37 *censure*: Judgement.

38 *Alack, for lesser knowledge*: O that I knew less!

39-45 *There may be in the cup . . . seen the spider*: The
spider was believed to be venomous and to poison
any liquid in which it was found. The superstition
referred to here is that its poison operated only if
the person consuming the drink was aware of the
spider's presence. The analogy is therefore a precise
one, reminiscent of a metaphysical conceit.

45 *hefts*: Retchings; heavings.

48 *All's true that is mistrusted*: All one's suspicions prove
to be true.

50 *discovered*: Revealed.

51 *pinched*: Various meanings of the word, such as
'tormented', 'reduced to straits' and 'shrunk', may
be involved. This last meaning seems to have led
on to the image in the next clause.

51 *trick*: Toy; plaything.

52 *play*: Play with.

62 *But I'd say*: I should merely have to say.

64 *to th'nayward*: Towards denial.

66 *goodly*: Comely; good-looking.

68 *honest*: Chaste.

69-76 *Praise her but for . . . can say she's honest*: A difficult
speech, complicated by Leontes' emotional instability
and the stops and starts that represent it. He describes
the hesitations and suggestive mutterings that must
come between the lords' statement that she is attractive and their statement that she is chaste.

69 *without-door form*: External appearance.

70 *high speech*: Praise.
   straight: Straight away.

71-2 *petty brands | That calumny doth use*: Little habits
or phrases associated with suspicion.

72 *I am out*: I am wrong.

79 *replenished*: Complete.

82-3 *O thou thing | Which I'll not call a creature of
thy place*: Leontes will not call a person of
Hermione's exalted position by the name she
deserves. *thing* is a multivalent noun, potentially
neutral or euphemistic, as if Leontes doesn't know

what to call her, but also potentially vulgar, referring
to genitalia (male and female); cf. the suggestive
play on *thing* between Iago and Emilia (*Othello*,
III.3.298 ff.).

85 *degrees*: Ranks of society.

90 *fedary*: Confederate. F's *Federarie* is most probably
a misprint, since there is no other recorded use of
that word. Both the requirements of metre and
Shakespeare's usage elsewhere indicate that he wrote
fedary.

92 *But with her most vile principal*: Probably 'even if no
one except Polixenes were to share that knowledge'.
principal: Person directly responsible for a crime.

93 *bed-swerver*: Adulteress.

94 *That vulgars give bold'st titles*: To whom the common
people give the coarsest names.

98 *published*: Publicly denounced.

102 *centre*: The earth (believed to be the centre of the
universe).

104–5 *is afar off guilty | But that he speaks*: Makes himself
in some measure guilty by merely speaking.

107 *aspect*: A technical term in astrology, denoting the
way in which the planets look upon each other; the
accent falls on the second syllable.

109 *want*: Lack.
vain dew: Pointless tears.

111 *honourable*: Honest.

113 *so qualified*: Of such a nature.

118 *good fools*: A term of endearment.

121 *come out*: Leave the prison.
This action I now go on: The word *action* has been
explained by some as meaning 'indictment', which
fits the context but does not work with *go on*; by others
as meaning 'military operation', which works with
go on but does not fit the context (the notion that
Hermione announces that she is undertaking a
campaign for her honour seems highly implausible).
Perhaps the metaphor, like so many in the play, is
theatrical, *action* meaning 'the acting of plays': 'the

part I now have to play'.

122 *my better grace*: My greater credit.

131 *Please you t'accept it*: If you'll accept it.

134–5 *I'll keep my stables where | I lodge my wife*: The thought of this much debated passage, though highly condensed, is plain enough: if the Queen is unchaste, Antigonus is saying, then all other women are mere animals, and I shall treat my wife as such, turning her chamber into stables, where I shall guard her as strictly as one does one's mares.

135 *in couples with her*: Coupled by a leash to her.

138 *dram*: Drop; tiny amount.

141 *putter-on*: Instigator.

143 *lam-damn*: After more than two centuries of debate, commentators are still uncertain of the word's meaning. Of the many proposed emendations – all of them unconvincing – the most grotesque are Farmer's 'I would laudanum him' and Schmidt's 'I would – Lord, damn him!'. In the form 'landam' it has been claimed to be a Gloucestershire dialect-word, meaning 'to abuse with rancour' or 'to damn through the land'; in the form 'lan-dan' it is said to describe a folk-custom in which the name of a slanderer is publicly proclaimed. It seems, however, quite possible that it is a nonce-word, made up by Antigonus from the *damn* of the preceding line and the verb 'to lam' ('to thrash'), and that he is saying 'I would thrash him unmercifully'. If Shakespeare wrote 'lam' as 'lame', it could easily have been misread as 'land', leading to F's spelling *Land-damne*.

145 *The second and the third nine and some five*: The second nine and the third around five.

148 *bring false generations*: Have illegitimate children (in contrast to *fair* ('legitimate') *issue* at 150).
    They are co-heirs: With daughters the law of primogeniture does not operate, so they are joint heirs.

149 *glib*: Geld.

153–4 *As you feel doing thus and see withal | The instruments that feel*: Most commentators think that Leontes at

this point pulls Antigonus' beard or tweaks his nose.
But *doing thus* without a preceding 'my' and the use
of *feel* at 154 suggest that *you* is here used generi-
cally, and that Leontes is striking against a wall or
chair with his fingers, which can then fitly be called
The instruments that feel, without giving to *feel* the
rather forced meaning of 'touch'.

157 *dungy*: Base.

    Lack I credit: Am I not believed?

159 *Upon this ground*: In this matter.

164 *Calls not*: Does not call for.

165–7 *which, if you – or stupefied | Or seeming so in skill
    – cannot or will not | Relish a truth like us*: A loose
    construction, with both *which* and *a truth* as objects
    of *relish*.

165–6 *or stupefied | Or seeming so in skill*: Either grown
    insensible or cunningly pretending to be so.

167 *Relish*: Appreciate.

172 *overture*: Disclosure.

175 *familiarity*: To make the line scan the word must
    here be given six syllables.

176–7 *as gross as ever . . . sight only*: As palpable as surmise
    that lacked only actual sight ever reached to.

177 *approbation*: Proof.

179 *Made up*: Added up.

182 *wild*: Rash.

182–7 *I have dispatched in post . . . Shall stop or spur me*:
    In *Pandosto* the Queen begs her husband 'to send
    six of his noblemen whom he best trusted to the Isle
    of Delphos, there to inquire of the oracle of Apollo
    whether she had committed adultery with Egistus'.
    By making the idea of consulting the oracle originate
    with Leontes, not the Queen, Shakespeare contrived
    to make him much more sympathetic than Pandosto.

182 *in post*: In haste.

183 *Delphos*: The island of Delos, the birthplace of Apollo,
    which also possessed an oracle, was commonly known
    in Shakespeare's day as 'Delphos'. The fact that Delphi,
    with its more famous oracle, was also generally called

'Delphos' led to a frequent confusion of the two.

185 *Of stuffed sufficiency*: Fully qualified for the office.

186 *all*: The whole truth.

had: When received.

191 *such as he*: Referring to Antigonus.

194 *free*: Unguarded; accessible; noble.

195 *the treachery of the two fled hence*: The supposed plan to murder Leontes, mentioned by him at 47 and 89.

198 *raise*: Rouse.

II.2

14 *put apart*: Dismiss.

20 *As passes colouring*: Paulina seems to be playing with two meanings of *colouring*: (1) 'dyeing' ('as exceeds the dyer's art'); (2) 'excusing' ('as passes all excuse').

23 *On*: In consequence of.

24 *Which*: Than which.

30 *lunes*: Mad freaks.

33 *let my tongue blister*: The reference is to the notion that the utterance of falsehood blisters the tongue.

34–5 *to my red-looked anger be | The trumpet*: The trumpeter, on the field of battle, preceded the herald, who was generally dressed in red and often bore angry messages.

39 *advocate to th'loud'st*: Loudest advocate.

44 *free*: Magnanimous.

45 *thriving issue*: Successful outcome.

47 *presently*: At once.

49 *hammered of*: Deliberated upon.

50 *tempt*: Make trial of.

52 *wit*: Words of wisdom or good sense.

57 *to pass it*: By letting it pass.

II.3

0 *Enter Leontes*: Most editors, misled by F's massed entry, *Enter Leontes, Seruants, Paulina, Antigonus, and Lords*, make Leontes enter accompanied by Antigonus, Lords and Servants, who presumably remain in the background while Leontes soliloquizes. But his *Who's there?* (9) and *Leave me solely* (17) indicate that he enters alone and that Antigonus, Lords and Servants

do not come in until 26, when trying to hold back Paulina.

3 *cause*: It is possible that in addition to its modern meaning the word is here also made to carry the obsolete meaning of 'disease'.

4 *harlot*: Lewd (used of either sex in Shakespeare's time).

5–6 *blank* | *And level*: Terms from shooting, *blank* being the white spot in the centre of the target, *level* meaning either the action of aiming or the mark aimed at, here probably the latter.

7 *hook to me*: Get hold of (the metaphor derives from the use of the grappling-hook in sea-fights).

8 *Given to the fire*: Death by fire was the punishment for women found guilty of high treason or of petty treason (the latter consisted in the murder, or connivance at the murder, of husband or master). Leontes believes Hermione to be guilty of both forms of treason (see III.2.13–16).

13 *Conceiving*: Apprehending the significance of.

17 *solely*: Alone.

18 *no thought of him*: Let me not think of him (Polixenes).

27 *be second to*: Support.

30 *free*: Guiltless.

35 *heavings*: Deep groans or sighs.

38 *humour*: State of mind.

39 *presses him from sleep*: Weighs upon him and prevents him from sleeping.

What noise there, ho: These words suggest that the altercation at 26–39 is meant to take place out of the hearing of Leontes.

41 *gossips*: Godparents (who will be needed at the child's baptism).

47 *dishonesty*: Dishonourable actions.

49 *Commit me for committing honour*: Send me to prison for doing what is honourable.

50 *La you now, you hear*: The words, equivalent to our 'There now, you hear how she will talk', are accompanied by some gesture of resignation.

55–7 *yet that dares . . . seem yours*: Yet one who dares to appear less so when it comes to countenancing your crimes than such people as seem most devoted to you.

60 *by combat make her good*: Prove her to be virtuous in a trial by combat (a traditional means of vindicating a lady's honour).

61 *worst*: Weakest.

67 *mankind*: Mannish; virago-like.

68 *intelligencing bawd*: Scheming pimp; sexual go-between.

74 *woman-tired*: Henpecked (from 'tire', a term in falconry, meaning 'to tear a piece of flesh with the beak').

unroosted: Driven from your perch.

75 *Partlet*: The name of the hen in the medieval satire *Reynard the Fox*, hence a traditional name for a hen.

76 *crone*: The context suggests that the word here does not mean 'withered old woman', which would have little pertinence, but is used in its other sense of 'old ewe'. Paulina's loud reproaches, after being compared to the angry clucking of a hen, are now likened to the bleating of an old ewe.

78 *by that forcèd baseness*: Under the name of bastard, which has been thrust upon her (*forcèd* and *put upon* seem to have much the same meaning, being used to reinforce each other).

90 *callat*: Scold.

94–5 *Hence with it . . . to the fire*: This follows *Pandosto*, where Shakespeare read how 'Bellaria was brought to bed of a fair and beautiful daughter, which no sooner Pandosto heard, but he determined that both Bellaria and the young infant should be burnt with fire'.

96 *th'old proverb*: It is found, for instance, in Overbury's character of a Sergeant: 'The devil calls him his white son; he is so like him that he is the worse for it.'

100 *trick*: Characteristic form.

104 *got*: Begot.

106 *No yellow in't*: Let there be no yellow (the colour of jealousy) in it.

106–7 *lest she suspect, as he does,* | *Her children not her husband's*: Malone, one of Shakespeare's eighteenth-century editors, thought that 'In the ardour of composition Shakespeare seems here to have forgotten the difference of sexes'. But his fellow-editor, Steevens, was probably right in claiming that 'The seeming absurdity in the last clause of Paulina's ardent address to Nature was undoubtedly designed, being an extravagance characteristically preferable to languid correctness, and chastised declamation'. It is one of the many comic touches in the scene by means of which Shakespeare mitigates its tragic impact upon the audience.

108 *losel*: Worthless fellow.

114–15 *It is an heretic that makes the fire,* | *Not she which burns in't*: If you burn me, it will be you who make the fire who are the heretic, not I who burn in it (the stress of 114 falls on *makes*). Burning was the extreme punishment for heresy. Paulina wittily applies it to the heresy of lacking faith in Hermione.

126 *A better guiding spirit*: Someone better fitted than you to guide her.

139 *proper*: Own.

147 *beseech'*: The apostrophe, found in F but absent in later Folios, indicates the omission of 'you'.

149 *dear*: Loving.

158 *officious*: The conjunction with *tenderly* suggests that the word has here not its modern meaning but the obsolete one of 'ready to do kind offices'.

159 *Lady Margery*: Since 'margery-prater' was the cant term for a hen, *Lady Margery* may be a variant of *Dame Partlet* (75).

161 *this beard's grey*: The reference is not to his own beard, since in the first part of the play Leontes cannot be much more than thirty, but to that of Antigonus, who is described as an old man (by himself at 165, and by the Shepherd at III.3.103–4). Perhaps Leontes is meant to pull Antigonus' beard, though it would

suffice if he pointed at it.

165 *pawn*: Venture; hazard.

167 *Swear by this sword*: It was customary to swear by a sword, since its handle is in the form of a cross.

169 *see'st thou*: Do you hear?

fail: Non-performance.

171 *lewd-tongued*: Foul-mouthed.

177 *its*: Here and at III.2.99 F prints *it*, the old form of the possessive pronoun, which was just beginning to be replaced by 'its' when *The Winter's Tale* was written (of the ten instances of 'its' in the entire Folio, six come from *The Winter's Tale*).

178 *climate*: Region; clime.

178–82 *As by strange fortune . . . or end it*: The lines paraphrase a passage in *Pandosto*: 'For he found out this device, that seeing, as he thought, it came by Fortune, so he would commit it to the charge of Fortune.'

181 *commend it strangely*: Commit it as a stranger.

189 *In more than this deed does require*: Probably 'to a greater extent than you deserve by this deed'.

191 *loss*: Perdition; destruction.

197 *beyond accompt*: Probably 'beyond explanation', rather than 'beyond any of which we have account; unprecedented' or 'beyond calculation', as it is usually glossed.

199 *suddenly*: Very speedily.

201 *session*: Judicial trial.

III.1

Some commentators have located this scene on Delphos. But since the return of Cleomenes and Dion to Sicily is announced in the previous scene, and they call for fresh horses at 21, its imagined location must be a Sicilian high road, somewhere between the seaport and the court.

1 *delicate*: Delightful.

4 *habits*: Vestments.

11 *event*: Outcome.

14 *is worth the use*: Has been well spent.

17 *carriage*: Conduct; management.

19 *divine*: Priest.

20 *discover*: Reveal.

III.2

Shakespeare has here fused two court scenes in
Pandosto which are separated by several weeks. In
each the Queen is accused in open court and defends
herself eloquently; some of her words are closely
echoed in Hermione's speeches (27–31, 44–6, 113).
In *Pandosto* the King immediately accepts the truth
of the oracle and repents his actions. By making
Leontes blasphemously deny its truth, Shakespeare
is able to punctuate his trial scene with a crescendo
of climaxes, culminating in Paulina's report of the
Queen's death.

1 *sessions*: Trial (a collective plural, as again at 139).

2 *Even pushes 'gainst our heart*: Strikes even at my
heart.

7 *purgation*: Clearing from the suspicion of guilt.

10 *Silence!*: In F this is printed as *Silence.* towards the
right margin, as if it were a stage direction, and
some editors have accepted it as such. But most have
assigned it as an exclamation to the officer, since it
would be a very unusual stage direction but is a
traditional law-court cry. The entry of Hermione may
be supposed to cause some stir in the court, which
must be silenced before the indictment can be read.

17–20 *the pretence whereof . . . by night*: This follows closely
the wording of the indictment in *Pandosto*: 'their
pretence being partly spied, she counselled them to
fly away by night for their better safety.'

17 *pretence*: Purpose; design.

23–4 *testimony . . . from myself*: Since I am the only witness
pleading on my behalf.

27–31 *if powers divine . . . at patience*: This closely follows
the Queen's speech in *Pandosto*: 'If the divine powers
be privy to human actions – as no doubt they are –
I hope my patience shall make Fortune blush, and
my unspotted life shall stain spiteful discredit.'

35 *history*: Story presented on the stage.

35 *pattern*: Match.

36 *take*: Captivate.

37 *owe*: Own.

42 *As I weigh grief, which I would spare*: As I value grief, which I would do without.

43 *a derivative from me to mine*: A heritage from me to my children.

44 *stand*: Make a stand; fight.

44–6 *I appeal . . . in your grace*: Another echo of the Queen's speech in *Pandosto*: 'how I have led my life before Egistus' coming, I appeal, Pandosto, to the gods and to thy conscience.'

45 *conscience*: Inward knowledge.

48–9 *With what . . . t'appear thus*: With what behaviour so out of the ordinary I have transgressed that I should appear thus (in a court of justice). The difficulty of this much debated passage is caused chiefly by a shift in the nature of the appeal: Hermione first begs Leontes to *remember* how, before the arrival of Polixenes, her behaviour merited his love, and next begs him to *make known* how, after the arrival of Polixenes, her behaviour merited his arraignment of her.

54–6 *wanted | Less impudence to gainsay what they did | Than to perform it first*: As often with Shakespeare, an abundance of negatives obscures the meaning. The substitution in our minds of 'possessed' for *wanted* makes the sense clear.

58–9 *More than mistress of | Which comes to me in name of fault*: To be possessor of more than what may be called a fault (the stress is on *fault*). Hermione acknowledges that she may be guilty of faults, but not of the *bolder vices* (54) with which she has been charged.

62 *required*: Deserved.

71 *dished*: Put before me.

75 *Wotting*: If they know.

77 *What you have underta'en to do in's absence*: Namely to murder Leontes.

80 *level*: The mark shot at.

84 *of your fact*: Guilty of your deed.

85 *concerns more than avails*: Is of more importance than
   use to you.

86 *like to itself*: Like the outcast it is.

91 *bug*: Bugbear.

92 *commodity*: Advantage.

98 *Starred most unluckily*: Born under a most unlucky star.

100 *post*: Public notices were exhibited on posts in Shake-
    speare's day.

101 *immodest*: Immoderate; excessive.

102 *'longs*: Belongs.

103 *of all fashion*: Of all sorts.

104 *i'th'open air*: Fresh air was held to be dangerous for
    invalids.

105 *strength of limit*: Strength through resting the
    prescribed period after childbirth.

110 *free*: Clear.

113 *'Tis rigour and not law*: The phrase comes from
    Pandosto, where the Queen declares that 'if she were
    condemned without any further proof, it was rigour
    and not law'.

118 *The Emperor of Russia was my father*: In *Pandosto* it
    is the wife of Egistus (Shakespeare's Polixenes) who
    is daughter of the Emperor of Russia.

121 *flatness*: Absoluteness.

131–4 *Hermione is chaste . . . be not found*: The words
      follow for the most part verbatim those of the oracle
      in *Pandosto*. In the 1607 edition 'live without an
      heir' was changed to 'die without an heir', thereby
      providing our sole piece of evidence that Shakespeare
      used one of the earlier editions of *Pandosto*.

139 *mere*: Complete.

141 *to report*: For reporting.

142–3 *conceit and fear | Of the Queen's speed*: Thinking
      about and worrying over the Queen's fate.

160 *tardied*: Delayed.

161–3 *though I with death . . . being done*: Though I
      threatened him with death if he did not do it and

encouraged him with the promise of reward if he did it.

165 *Unclasped my practice*: Revealed my plot.

166 *Which you knew great – and to the hazard*: In the second Folio this line is made regular by the insertion of *certain* before *hazard*. This unnecessary emendation has been adopted by many later editors.

167 *commended*: Committed.

168 *No richer than his honour*: Taking only his honour with him.

169 *Through*: The word is here pronounced as two syllables, 'tho-rough'; cf. 'Thorough bush, thorough briar' in *A Midsummer Night's Dream*, II.1.3.

170 *Woe the while*: Literally 'woe for the present time!'.

171 *O cut my lace*: Cleopatra (*Antony and Cleopatra*, I.3.71) and Elizabeth (*Richard III*, IV.1.33) make the same demand to express their great agitation.
    lace: The lacing of her corset stays.

175 *In leads or oils*: In cauldrons of molten lead or boiling oil.

179 *idle*: Foolish; senseless.

182 *spices*: Slight tastes; samples.

184 *That did but show thee of a fool inconstant*: Coleridge's paraphrase of this much discussed line, 'show thee, being a fool naturally, to have improved thy folly by inconstancy', seems to come closest to conveying its probable meaning. The nearest parallel to the construction elsewhere in Shakespeare is found in *Henry VI, Part III*, III.3.24–5: 'That Henry, sole possessor of my love, | Is of a king become a banished man . . .'

185–7 *Nor was't much . . . kill a king*: 'How should Paulina know this?' asks Malone. 'No one had charged the King with this crime except himself, while Paulina was absent, attending on Hermione. The poet seems to have forgotten this circumstance.' Either that or he thought that it would go unnoticed in the theatre.

187–8 *poor trespasses . . . standing by*: Paltry crimes, given the immense ones to come.

191 *shed water out of fire*: Shed tears while standing in hellfire.

195 *conceive*: Apprehend that.

198 *said*: Spoken.

203 *Tincture or lustre in her lip, her eye*: Colour in her lip or lustre in her eye.

210 *still*: Always.

221–2 *Do not . . . petition*: Do not give yourself up to affliction because I have urged you to.

223 *minded you*: Put you in mind.

228 *remember*: Remind.

229 *Who is lost too*: Since the trial of Hermione follows quickly upon the departure of Antigonus, there is no reason why Paulina should suppose this. But Shakespeare expected his audience not to notice such inconsistencies.

Take your patience to you: Arm yourself with patience.

238 *recreation*: Diversion; pastime.

239 *exercise*: Both the meaning of 'habitual employment' and that of 'religious observance' would seem to be involved.

240–41 *Come, | And lead me to these sorrows*: F's line division, *Come, and lead me | To these sorrows*, which modern editors have taken over with remarkable unanimity, makes the speech peter out in a very un-Shakespearian way. Several redivisions were attempted by eighteenth-century editors. The most satisfactory, which is here adopted, is the one found in Steevens's editions of 1778 and 1785. The long pause after *Come*, which fills out the line, is an expression of the King's anguish.

III.3

1 *perfect*: Certain.

2 *The deserts of Bohemia*: Since the day in 1619 when Ben Jonson, in conversation with William Drummond, ridiculed Shakespeare for endowing Bohemia with a sea coast, 'where there is no sea near by some 100 miles', a vast deal of ink has been spilt over this howler. Commentators have taken up

four main positions: (1) that Shakespeare could never have been guilty of such an error (hence Sir Thomas Hanmer, one of his eighteenth-century editors, throughout his text changed 'Bohemia' to 'Bythinia', claiming that the former was a printing-house corruption); (2) that no error is involved, since in the late thirteenth and early sixteenth centuries Bohemia actually possessed a bit of sea coast, or since 'Bohemia' is really another name for 'Apulia', on the south-east coast of Italy; (3) that the error was introduced purposely by Shakespeare in order to convey to his audience that this Bohemia is to be found not on the contemporary map of Europe but in the realms of the imagination – that the sea coast of Bohemia was perhaps even a standard joke of the time, like Wigan Pier or the Swiss Navy in our day; (4) that Shakespeare simply took over the error from *Pandosto*, being, like most of his contemporaries, rather vague about the geography of Central Europe. This last seems the most plausible explanation. A writer who, in *The Tempest*, can think of Milan as a seaport, and in *The Two Gentlemen of Verona* can make Valentine sail there from Verona, would not have boggled at a sea coast for the very much less known Bohemia.

4 *present*: Imminent.

  In my conscience: To my mind.

10 *loud*: Rough, stormy.

12 *keep*: Live.

15–18 *I have heard . . . a waking*: Shakespeare leaves us purposely uncertain whether what Antigonus experienced was a dream or an apparition.

20–21 *I never saw a vessel of like sorrow, | So filled and so becoming*: Although this passage has received a great deal of discussion, this has turned chiefly on the appropriateness of the word *becoming*, which has been often, and quite unnecessarily, emended. The one real problem – whether, with most editors, to place a comma after *sorrow* or whether to follow F, which omits the comma – has been ignored. Though both readings make good sense, the one here adopted seems the more satisfactory. The reference is to the intensity of Hermione's sorrow, coupled with the grace with which she bears it. The same metaphor is found in *Julius Caesar* (V.5.13–14): 'Now is that noble vessel full of grief, | That it runs over even at his eyes.'

32 *Perdita*: This name, meaning 'the lost one', follows the precedent of Marina, named thus 'for she was born at sea' (*Pericles*, III.3.13).

35 *shrieks*: The typical cry of a ghost.

38 *toys*: Things of no value or substance.

39 *superstitiously*: The primary meaning seems to be 'punctiliously', but the modern meaning may be also present, producing a kind of pun.

40 *squared*: Ruled; regulated.

46 *thy character*: The written account of you (*the letters of Antigonus* referred to at V.2.33–4).
he lays down a box: Most editors follow Dr Johnson in making Antigonus lay down 'a bundle', misled, it seems, by the *fardel* referred to repeatedly in IV.4.703 ff. But the Shepherd there speaks of *this fardel and box* (IV.4.752–3). The box is clearly the one in which the gold was stored, while the fardel consists of the *bearing-cloth* (III.3.111) and the *mantle* (V.2.32) in which the child was wrapped, if these are not, in fact, one and the same garment.
these: The pieces of gold in the box.

47 *both breed thee . . . thine*: Be enough to pay for your upbringing, pretty one, and still remain yours (because most of it will be unspent).

50 *loss*: The condition of being lost.
Weep I cannot: The words presumably glance back at *There weep, and leave it crying* (31).

53–4 *Thou'rt like . . . rough*: This echoes the Queen's words in *Pandosto*: 'Shalt thou have the whistling winds for thy lullaby . . . ?'

55–6 *A savage clamour!* | *Well may I get aboard! This is the chase*: 'This clamour was the cry of the dogs and hunters; then seeing the bear, he cries, "This is the chase", or, *the animal pursued*', explained Dr Johnson, and most commentators have agreed with him. The Shepherd's reference to a hunt in the lines that follow seems to support this explanation. Yet it is unacceptable for several reasons: (1) if the hunters are in such close pursuit of the bear that their voices can be heard offstage, it does not make sense that they let him devour Antigonus at his leisure, and are never heard of again; (2) the epithet *savage* is far more suited to the growling of the bear than to the cry of the dogs and hunters. The word *clamour* was used of any 'loud vocal noise of beasts and birds' (*Oxford English Dictionary*); (3) *Well may I get aboard!* suggests a threat to Antigonus' life, which fits the bear but not the hunt. *the chase* then means not 'the hunted animal' (a possible meaning of *chase*) but rather 'the hunt'.

57 *Exit, pursued by a bear*: The question whether Shakespeare's company here used a real bear or an actor dressed in a bear's skin has been much debated. There is a good deal of evidence of various kinds that bears in Elizabethan and Jacobean plays and masques were impersonated by actors dressed in bearskins, none that a real bear was ever used, although there were trained bears in London at the time. Shakespeare's evident desire to rob the death of Antigonus of its horror by adding touches of comedy would probably have made him prefer the use of an actor in a bear's skin; see Introduction.

61 *ancientry*: Old folk. He is thinking of himself. In contrast to the shepherd in *Pandosto*, he is depicted as an old man, already sixty-seven when he finds the child (since at IV.4.450 he speaks of himself as *a man of fourscore three*).

62 *Hark you now*: A number of editors take these words to refer to the sound of the hunt offstage and introduce the stage direction *Horns*. More probably they are addressed to the audience, drawing their

attention to what the Shepherd is going to tell them.

62–3 *boiled brains*: Probably 'addle-brained youths', rather than 'hotheads' or 'lunatics', as it is usually explained.

66–7 *by the seaside, browsing of ivy*: This is an echo of *Pandosto*'s 'to see if perchance the sheep was browsing on the sea ivy, whereon they greatly do feed'.

67 *Good luck, an't be thy will*: Send me good luck, if it be thy (God's) will! The reference is to the search for the sheep, not to the finding of the child, as many editors, misled by F's punctuation, *Good-lucke (and't be thy will) what haue we heere?*, think.

68 *barne*: Child (a dialect form, but not confined to the North in Shakespeare's day).

69 *child*: A female infant (a dialect form found predominantly in the West Country).

70 *scape*: Escapade; slip (especially of a sexual nature).

72–3 *some stair-work, some trunk-work, some behind-door-work*: The reference seems to be not, as has been claimed, to the way in which the lover got access to his mistress – by back stairs, by concealment in a trunk, by hiding behind doors – but rather to the places where the furtive copulation took place. 'Work' is used repeatedly by Shakespeare in the sense of 'sexual intercourse'.

75 *hallowed*: Shouted.

81–102 *I have seen two such sights . . . he's at it now*: The Clown's account of the deaths of Antigonus and the mariners is purposely made to sound ridiculous in order to distance them from the audience and so to reduce their horror and pathos. This device of turning horror into comedy is by no means unique with Shakespeare. It is only the way he does it here that is unique. It is done chiefly (1) by making the Clown, anxious to narrate both calamities at the same time, scuttle to and fro between them; (2) by means of the figurative language he employs. The comic effect is achieved by the opposite means from that used in the mock-heroic: there it results from the discrepancy between the trivial events and the grandiose manner in which these are described; here it results from the discrepancy between extraordinary and fearful events and the homely and trivial manner in which these are described.

87 *takes up*: The primary meaning is probably 'swallows up', with the meaning 'rebukes' perhaps also present as a quibble.

89 *boring*: Penetrating.

91 *yeast*: Foam (cf. *Macbeth*, IV.1.52–3, 'though the yesty waves | Confound and swallow navigation up'). *hogshead*: Barrel.

92 *land-service*: Military, as opposed to naval, service (hence Antigonus as opposed to the sailors). The choice of the word was, perhaps, determined by another sense of *service*, 'that which is served up for a meal', and this meaning may be present as a quibble.

95 *flap-dragoned it*: Swallowed it up as one would a flap-dragon (a small object, usually a raisin, which floated in a glass of lighted spirits and had to be swallowed).

106–7 *there your charity would have lacked footing*: This is probably a quibble on two meanings of *footing*: (1) foothold; (2) establishment (of a charitable foundation).

111 *bearing-cloth*: The wrap in which a child was carried to church for baptism.

114–15 *changeling*: Since it was believed that fairies steal beautiful children, leaving their own ugly and misshapen ones in the cradle, *changeling* must here refer to the human child, stolen by the fairies because of its beauty.

116 *made*: F prints *mad*, but the emendation, first made in the eighteenth century by Theobald, is undoubtedly right, and is supported by *Pandosto*, where the shepherd tells his wife that 'if she could hold her peace, they were made for ever'.

117 *well to live*: Well-to-do; prosperous.

120 *close*: Secret (since to make known the possession of fairies' gifts was held to bring misfortune).

next: Nearest.

121 *still*: For ever.

126 *curst*: Savage.

131 *Marry*: Indeed.

IV.1

0 *Enter Time, the Chorus*: Time is here depicted as he traditionally appears in pictures: an old man with wings (4), bearing an hourglass (16). Another of his conventional attributes, the scythe, is not mentioned, and may have been omitted on the stage in order to emphasize his role in the play as revealer rather than as destroyer. The use of Time as chorus bridging the gap between the two parts of the play is analogous to that of Rumour at the opening of *Henry IV, Part II*, and was presumably suggested by the title page of Greene's novella, which reads: 'Pandosto. The Triumph of Time. Wherein is discovered by a pleasant History that although by the means of sinister fortune Truth may be concealed, yet by Time, in spite of fortune, it is most manifestly revealed . . . *Temporis filia veritas* . . .' Many critics have assigned Time's speech to a collaborator, refusing to believe that Shakespeare could have written such lame and bald verse. But it would seem to be purposely lame, bald and garrulous in order to characterize the speaker; and the need for an idiom strongly marked off from the dramatic verse of the play helps to account for the absence of the unmistakable voice of Shakespeare (its closest parallel in style and matter is the Chorus-speech of Gower in *Pericles*, IV.4). See the Introduction for a discussion of its significance.

1 *try*: Test.

1–2 *both joy and terror* | *Of good and bad*: Probably not, as it is commonly explained, 'the joy of the good and the terror of the bad', but rather 'the joy as well as the terror of good and bad alike'. This accords much better not only with the facts of life

but also with the words that follow: by making error,
Time is the joy of the bad and the terror of the
good; by unfolding it, the terror of the bad and the
joy of the good (cf. *The Rape of Lucrece*, l. 995:
'O time, thou tutor both to good and bad').

3 *in the name of*: Under the designation of (he is telling
the slow-witted members of the audience who he is).

6–7 *and leave . . . wide gap*: And leave unexamined what
has happened during that long interval.

7–9 *since it is in my power | To o'erthrow law, and in one
self-born hour | To plant and o'erwhelm custom*: The
law referred to is evidently that established by
Renaissance critics, who, insisting on 'unity of time',
limited the action of a play to one day (in *Hamlet*,
II.2.400, Polonius speaks of 'the law of writ and
the liberty', meaning plays adhering to the rules of
writing laid down by academic critics and plays
which ignored all such rules). Shakespeare wittily
makes Time defend his own most blatant violation
of the rule of unity of time in this play by having
him point out that all such laws and customs are of
no permanent validity. The crime referred to in lines
4–7 is therefore that of violating the rule of the
unity of time, rather than – as the wording suggests –
that of failing to stage the events of the intervening
sixteen years.

8 *one self-born hour*: Probably 'one hour to which I
myself have given birth': all hours were thought of
as the offspring of time.

9–11 *Let me pass | The same I am ere ancient'st order was |
Or what is now received*: This obscure sentence seems
to carry on the thought of the preceding lines: 'Allow
me to pass, who am the same that I was before the
oldest injunctions became established or what is now
accepted as authoritative.' The use of *I am* for 'I
was', though odd, can be defended as appropriate
to Time, who sees himself as standing outside the
flow of events. The use of *witness* for 'witnessed'
(11) may be a parallel case, though here one is

tempted to emend, since F's *witnesse* could easily be
a misreading of *witnessed* in the manuscript.

10 *order*: Injunction.

11 *received*: Accepted as a rule.

16 *I turn my glass*: Time here turns the hourglass which
he carries in his hands, thus marking the commence-
ment of the second half of the play.
scene: Play presented on the stage.

17 *As*: As if.

17–18 *Leontes leaving . . . so grieving*: Leaving Leontes –
who is filled with such grief by the effects of his
foolish jealousies.

22 *I mentioned*: As at 16 (*my scene*), Time and the
playwright are here identified. The suggestion has
been made that this may be due to the circumstance
that, in the first performances of the play, Shakespeare
himself took the part of Time, and that the references to *my scene* and *I mentioned* were inserted
as jests for those members of the audience who
recognized this fact.
Floriƶel: The name seems to have been derived from
Amadis de Grecia, a Spanish continuation of the prose
romance *Amadis de Gaule*. In it a Prince Florisel
disguises himself as a shepherd in order to woo a
beautiful shepherdess, who, unknown to herself, is
really a princess.

25 *Equal with wond'ring*: Probably 'just as much as men's
wonder at it has grown'.

26 *list not*: Do not care to.

28 *what to her adheres*: What belongs to her story.
after: The 'f' was probably silent, so that the word
rhymed with *daughter*.

29 *argument*: Theme.

31 *yet that Time himself doth say*: Yet allow that Time
himself says.

IV.2

4 *fifteen*: This is presumably a slip, since Time (IV.1.6),
Paulina (V.3.31) and Camillo elsewhere (V.3.50) all
speak of sixteen years, following *Pandosto* in this.

5 *been aired abroad*: Lived abroad.

7 *feeling*: Heartfelt.

8 *allay*: Means of abatement.

  I o'erween: I am presumptuous enough.

13 *want*: Lack.

17 *considered*: Requited.

19 *the heaping friendships*: The heaping up of your friendly services.

27 *approved*: Proved.

31 *missingly*: Regretfully.

32 *frequent to*: Addicted to.

35–6 *eyes . . . removedness*: Servants in my employ who are spying on him during his absences from court.

40 *an unspeakable estate*: Astonishing wealth.

42–3 *the report . . . a cottage*: The (favourable) description makes it seem impossible that she could have come from such humble beginnings.

45 *angle*: Fish-hook.

47 *question*: Talk.

IV.3

1 *peer*: Probably 'appear' (as in IV.4.3) rather than 'peep out'.

2 *doxy*: Beggar's wench.

3 *sweet*: Pleasant part.

4 *pale*: Domain; bounds. The choice of the word was no doubt determined by the preceding *red*. Since *pale* also meant 'pallor', both the meaning of 'The red blood reigns in the former domain of winter' and that of 'The red blood reigns in place of the pallor of winter' may be intended to be present.

7 *Doth set my pugging tooth an edge*: Since 'to pug' means 'to pull, tug', the *pugging tooth* presumably refers to a taste for stealing sheets by pulling them off the hedges (*tooth* meaning 'taste', 'liking'). Most editors emend F's *an edge* to *on edge*, but this produces the opposite sense from the one required: that of a revulsion against 'pugging' rather than of a whetting of the appetite for it, which 'to set an edge' must mean here.

8 *For a quart of ale is a dish for a king*: The ale is to be bought with the money received for the stolen sheets.

10 *With heigh, with heigh, the thrush and the jay*: F reads *With heigh, the Thrush and the Iay*. The duplication of *With heigh*, first found in the second Folio, has been adopted by most subsequent editors. Yet the pattern of the other two stanzas suggests that something else has dropped out, perhaps the name of another bird.

11 *aunts*: A cant term for loose women.

14 *three-pile*: The most costly kind of velvet.

15–18 *But shall I . . . go right*: But shall I mourn because I am out of service? On moonlight nights, when I am wandering about (looking for things to steal), I am living the life which is right for me.

19–22 *If tinkers . . . avouch it*: So long as tinkers are allowed to practise their trade, and carry their pigskin tool bag, I shall be well able to account for myself, and, if they put me in the stocks, affirm it (that I am a tinker and no vagabond). Vagabonds and beggars were commonly set in the stocks in Shakespeare's day. Autolycus carries a leather bag (*budget*) with a tinker's tools to escape arrest as a vagabond. It was not uncommon for thieves to pose as tinkers.

23–4 *My traffic . . . lesser linen*: The kite was notorious for stealing small pieces of linen for nest-building. Autolycus specializes in the stealing of sheets, which he then sells.

23 *traffic*: Saleable commodities; merchandise.

24 *Autolycus*: The name is derived from Greek myth, in which Autolycus is the son of Hermes and the grandfather of Odysseus. He is referred to in the *Odyssey* as one 'who excelled all men in thievery and in oaths', and in Ovid's *Metamorphoses* as 'a wily pie, | And such a fellow as in theft and filching had no peer' (Book XI, Golding's translation).

   who: This refers back to *My father*, not to *Autolycus*.

25 *littered under Mercury*: Born when the planet Mercury

was in the ascendant. The god Mercury was the patron of thieves. As the conception of the planets had become fused with that of the gods after whom they were named, the influence of the planet Mercury was believed to promote thievery. Autolycus therefore jestingly attributes his and his father's propensity for stealing to Mercury's ascendancy at their birth.

26–7 *With die and drab I purchased this caparison*: Gaming and whoring brought me to these rags (literally 'Through dice and harlot I procured this apparel').

27 *my revenue is the silly cheat*: Either 'My income consists in humble booty' or 'My income derives from simple trickery'; Autolycus is contrasting his lowly but comparatively safe way of making a living with the risky life of the highwayman.

27–8 *Gallows and knock*: Hanging (the punishment for highway robbery) and hard blows (which the highwayman may receive from his intended victim).

29 *For the life to come*: Probably 'as for the life in the next world', rather than simply 'as for the future'; like Macbeth, who is ready to 'jump the life to come' if he can escape punishment in this world (*Macbeth*, I.7.7), Autolycus refuses to worry about divine punishment in the afterlife.

31 *every 'leven wether tods*: Every eleven sheep yield a tod (28 lb) of wool.

34 *cock*: Woodcock (a proverbially foolish bird).

39–40 *made me*: Made (a now obsolete construction known as the 'ethical dative').

40–41 *three-man-song men*: Singers of secular part-songs for male voices: treble, tenor and bass.

41–3 *but they are most of them means and basses – but one Puritan amongst them, and he sings psalms to hornpipes*: F, followed by most editors, places a semi-colon after *basses*, thus making the Clown remark that there is only one Puritan among them, as if Puritan and treble voice were synonymous, which they were not. Sense is restored by changing the semicolon to a dash, which makes the Clown add: 'except for one Puritan amongst them (who takes the treble part), and he sings psalms even to lively dance-tunes'. The emphasis seems to be on *psalms*, asserting the devoutness of the Puritan, rather than on *hornpipes*, which would assert his cheerfulness.

44 *warden pies*: Pies made with warden pears (a kind of cooking pear).

45 *out of my note*: Not on my list.

47 *o'th'sun*: Sun-dried (as distinct from oven-dried).

50 *I'th'name of me*: Though no other instance of this exclamation has been discovered, there is a close parallel in Sir Andrew's 'Before me' (*Twelfth Night*, II.3.171). The Act of Abuses (1606), which forbade the vain use of the name of God in stage plays, may be accountable for the unusual, and no doubt intentionally comic, form of the exclamation.

55 *offend*: In the second Folio and most subsequent editions this is changed to *offends*. But it is merely one of the several instances in the play of the 'plural by attraction' (as, for example, at IV.2.24 and 30).

63 *a horseman or a footman*: A mounted highwayman or a footpad.

85 *troll-my-dames*: Troll-my-dame is a game, also called 'troll-madam' (from the French '*trou-madame*'), which is played by 'trolling' balls through hoops set on a board. Since 'to troll' also meant 'to stroll', as well as 'to circulate, be passed round', it seems likely that Autolycus is quibbling on the name of the game, alluding in fact to loose women, his *aunts* (11).

90 *no more but abide*: Probably 'make only a brief stay', since an obsolete meaning of *abide* is 'to wait before proceeding further, to pause'; the *Oxford English Dictionary*, however, records no occurrences of this meaning later than the early sixteenth century.

92 *ape-bearer*: Showman who travels about with a performing monkey.
process-server: Sheriff's officer who serves summonses (much the same as *bailiff*).

93–4 *compassed a motion of the Prodigal Son*: Acquired a
puppet-show representing the story of the Prodigal
Son (puppet-shows depicting scenes from the Bible
were common in Shakespeare's day).

95 *living*: Property; estate.

98 *Prig*: Thief.

105 *I am false of heart that way*: My heart fails me in
such matters.

110 *softly*: Slowly.

116 *Your purse is not hot enough to purchase your spice*:
Since 'a cold purse' meant 'an empty purse',
Autolycus is able to quibble on the nature of spices
and the state of the Clown's purse.

118 *cheat*: Rogue's trick.

119 *unrolled*: Struck off the roll (of the fraternity of
rogues).

122 *hent*: Take hold of (in order to leap over).

IV.4

In *Pandosto* there is no sheep-shearing feast, only 'a
meeting of all the farmers' daughters in Sicilia,
whither Fawnia was also bidden as the mistress of
the feast'. It is on her return from this feast that
she and the Prince first set eyes on each other.

1 *weeds*: Garments.

2–3 *no shepherdess . . . front*: The words were suggested
by a passage in *Pandosto*, telling how Fawnia kept
her sheep, 'defending her face from the heat of the
sun with no other veil but with a garland made of
boughs and flowers, which attire became her so
gallantly as she seemed to be the goddess Flora herself
for beauty'. At the feast Perdita is presumably
garlanded and bedecked with flowers, while Florizel,
following the example of the Prince in *Pandosto*, is
dressed as a shepherd swain.

3 *Peering in April's front*: Appearing at the beginning
of April (cf. IV.3.1).

4 *petty*: Minor.

6 *extremes*: Extravagances.

8 *mark o'th'land*: Object of everyone's attention.

9 *wearing*: Garments.

10 *pranked up*: Tricked out; dressed.

But that: Were it not that.

11 *mess*: The sequence of metaphors makes it probable that the meaning here is 'dish' or 'course of dishes', rather than 'a group of persons who were served together at table', which is its meaning at I.2.227.

12 *with accustom*: Editors have retained F's *with a Custome*, explaining it as meaning 'from habit'. But as no parallels to this phrase are to be found, Dover Wilson's suggested emendation *with accustom* has been adopted. 'Accustom', an obsolete word meaning 'habit' or 'habituation', was still in use in the seventeenth century. The fact of a misreading is all the more probable as two further errors of transcription occur within the same two lines in a text which is remarkably free from such errors.

13 *swoon*: This emendation of F's *sworne*, first suggested in the eighteenth century by Theobald, and adopted by the majority of subsequent editors, almost certainly restores the right reading. Those who retain *sworn* usually explain the passage as meaning that Florizel, in putting on a *swain's wearing*, would seem to have sworn to show Perdita as in a mirror what she herself really is (or, alternatively, how she ought to be attired).

14–16 *I bless the time . . . ground*: This was suggested by *Pandosto*, where the first encounter of the lovers is described as taking place when the Prince was hawking.

17 *difference*: Of rank.

21–2 *his work, so noble,* | *Vilely bound up*: The reverse of this metaphor from book-binding is found in Juliet's 'Was ever book containing such vile matter | So fairly bound?' (*Romeo and Juliet*, III.2.83–4). There the binding stands for Romeo's whole exterior, here it stands only for Florizel's garments.

22 *Vilely*: Meanly; wretchedly.

23 *flaunts*: Ostentatious finery.

25–31 *The gods themselves . . . As I seem now*: The passage

is based on some lines in *Pandosto* in which the
Prince soliloquizes: 'And yet, Dorastus, shame not
at thy shepherd's weed. The heavenly gods have
sometime earthly thoughts. Neptune became a ram,
Jupiter a bull, Apollo a shepherd . . .'

32 *piece*: Person. The word was free from any deroga-
tory sense, and is often used by Shakespeare in the
last plays to designate a woman.

33 *in a way so chaste*: Undertaken with so chaste a
purpose.

35 *faith*: Pledge; promise (to marry her).

38–40 *One of these two . . . Or I my life*: Some commentators take *Or I my life* to mean 'or I change my
life' (from joy to grief). But the two necessities are
alternatives, and the sentence apparently contains
a zeugma: 'Either you will have to give up your
resolution to marry me or, should you adhere to it,
I shall lose my life.' That Perdita's fear of forfeiting
her life is not fanciful is shown by the threats of
Polixenes later in the scene.

41 *forced*: Strained; unnatural.

42–3 *Or . . . Or*: Either . . . or.

46 *gentle*: An appellation somewhat like 'dearest'.

47–8 *with anything . . . the while*: By attending to the
present festivities.

54 *Mopsa, Dorcas*: Mopsa is the name of the shepherd's
wife in *Pandosto*, here given to a young shepherdess;
Dorcas is a woman's name in the Bible (Acts 9:36).

56 *pantler*: Servant in charge of the pantry.
butler: Servant in charge of the cellar.

57 *dame*: Mistress (of a household).

60 *On his shoulder*: At his shoulder.

60–62 *her face o'fire* | *With labour, and the thing she took
to quench it:* | *She would to each one sip*: Many recent
editors have followed F's punctuation, *her face o'fire* |
With labour, and the thing she took to quench it | *She
would to each one sip*. This is, no doubt, a possible
reading. But the one resulting from the punctuation
here adopted sounds less awkward and more

Shakespearian: *the thing she took to quench* the fire
had the effect of inflaming it all the more, just as
the wind of the fans, which was meant to cool
Cleopatra's face, 'did seem | To glow the delicate
cheeks which they did cool, | And what they undid
did' (*Antony and Cleopatra*, II.2.208–10).

66 *more known*: Better acquainted.

75 *Seeming and savour*: Appearance and scent.

76 *Grace and remembrance*: In the flower symbolism of
Shakespeare's day rosemary stood for remembrance,
while rue, which was also called 'herb of grace', stood
for sorrow or repentance. Perdita wishes her guests
divine favour and to be remembered after their death.

79–82 *Sir, the year growing ancient . . . gillyvors*: Some
commentators have taken these lines to indicate that
the sheep-shearing feast takes place in the autumn.
But Perdita is not saying that it is *now* autumn, but
that in autumn the fairest flowers of that season are
carnations, etc. Sheep-shearings in Shakespeare's day
normally took place late in June, and that is, no
doubt, the time-setting he imagined for this scene.

82 *gillyvors*: Gillyflowers; clove-scented pinks.

83 *bastards*: Hybrids (the streaks being produced by the
crossing of different varieties of the plant).

86–103 *For I have heard it said . . . breed by me*: The matter
of this debate was familiar to many in Shakespeare's
audience. He makes Perdita uphold the primitivist
point of view, most notably expressed by Montaigne
in his essay 'Of the Cannibals', where he asserts the
superiority of so-called 'savages' to civilized men and,
by analogy, of wild to cultivated fruits. In lines
which shortly precede the passage that Shakespeare
drew on (in John Florio's translation, 1603) for the
description of Gonzalo's ideal commonwealth in *The
Tempest* (II.1.150 ff.), Montaigne uses the word
'bastardized' of cultivated fruits, and declares that
'there is no reason art should gain the point of
honour of our great and puissant mother Nature'.
The argument put forward by Polixenes – that the

art by means of which man improves the products of Nature is itself the creation of Nature – was equally familiar.

89 *mean*: Agency; means.

90 *But*: Unless.

90–92 *so over that art . . . Nature makes*: Polixenes seems to be saying that Nature's creation of the means of her own improvement (through grafting or crossing) is itself an art which is above that of the gardener, since his art is dependent upon it. The emendation of *over* to 'even', though not essential, is tempting, as it gives the speech much greater clarity.

97 *So it is*: It is possible that Perdita is here momentarily thinking of herself in relation to Florizel. But it may be merely polite assent without real conviction. The dramatic irony of the whole debate is heightened if both disputants are oblivious throughout of its apparent relevance to the intended marriage of the young lovers. Behind it lies the further irony that, unknown to them all, the debate possesses in fact no true relevance to their situation, since Perdita is actually as gentle a scion as is Florizel.

101–3 *No more than, were I painted . . . breed by me*: Perdita's analogy is altogether apposite: in the use of cosmetics as in the crossing of plants Nature's handiwork is being sophisticated by man's efforts to improve it. Perdita's distaste for this is all of a piece with her revulsion against being *Most goddess-like pranked up* (10).

103–8 *Here's flowers for you . . . very welcome*: Some commentators believe these lines to be addressed to another group of guests. It seems much more probable that Perdita is trying to make amends for her previous indiscretion (in giving Polixenes and Camillo flowers of winter) by now giving them flowers of summer, thus suggesting that she considers them to be *men of middle age*.

104 *Hot lavender*: Herbs were divided into 'hot' and 'cold' according to their supposed temperatures,

lavender being classed among the 'hot'.

105–6 *The marigold . . . weeping*: The reference is to the heliotropic nature of the flower, which closes its petals when the sun sets and opens them again, wet with dew, when it rises.

105 *with' sun*: The apostrophe, found in F, indicates the omission of the definite article.

116–18 *O Proserpina . . . Dis's wagon*: Shakespeare is here evidently recalling Ovid's account of the rape of Proserpina (*Metamorphoses*, V.398 ff.), possibly in Golding's translation (1567).

118 *Dis's wagon*: Pluto's chariot.

119 *take*: Bewitch; enchant.

121–2 *sweeter than the lids of Juno's eyes | Or Cytherea's breath*: Sweeter to *behold* than the lids of Juno's eyes, sweeter to *smell* than the breath of Venus.

122 *Cytherea*: The stress falls on the third syllable. Venus was called Cytherea after Cythera, the island where she first stepped ashore after her birth in the sea foam.

122–4 *pale primroses . . . his strength*: In contrast with the marigold, which is also called *Sponsus Solis*, the spouse of the sun, the primrose is pictured as dying unmarried, in early spring, before the bridegroom, Phoebus (the sun), has reached manhood.

124–5 *a malady | Most incident to maids*: The difficulty of this phrase springs from the omission of one important link in the chain of analogy between primroses and young girls: the *malady | Most incident to maids*, from which the primrose is imagined as dying, is greensickness (chlorosis, a form of anaemia). The pale or yellowy-green complexion of girls suffering from this ailment corresponds to the colour of the primrose. The analogy is strengthened by the legend, current in Shakespeare's day, that unmarried young girls who died from this malady were turned into primroses.

126 *crown imperial*: The tall orange or yellow fritillary (which had been introduced into England from Constantinople in the 1590s).

127 *flower-de-luce*: Probably the iris, which was not uncommonly classed among the lilies.

129 *What, like a corse*: It was customary to strew flowers upon the bodies of the dead.

130 *Love*: The reference seems to be to Cupid, the god of love, and F's capital 'L' has therefore been retained.

132 *quick*: Alive (the word *corse* in Elizabethan usage could mean a living as well as a dead body).

134 *Whitsun pastorals*: A variety of theatrical entertainments, including Robin Hood plays, were performed at Whitsuntide in Shakespeare's day.

135–6 *What you do | Still betters what is done*: Whatever you do seems always better than what you have done before.

143–6 *Each your doing . . . queens*: Everything you do, so peerless in every point, makes whatever you are doing at the moment seem supreme, so that all your acts are queens

146 *Doricles*: The name which Florizel has assumed in his disguise as a shepherd.

147 *large*: Lavish.

152 *skill*: Cause.

154–5 *so turtles pair, | That never mean to part*: Turtle-doves were believed to remain true to their mates for life. F omits the comma after *pair*, and is followed in this by later editors. But the statement is non-restrictive. Florizel is speaking not of 'those turtles that never mean to part' but of *all* turtles.

155 *I'll swear for 'em*: I'll be sworn they do.

162–7 *Come on, strike up! . . . Come, strike up*: The accident that several of these lines can be read as blank verse has led most editors since the eighteenth century to set the passage out as such, in spite of the fact that in F it is set out as prose and that the Clown, Mopsa and Dorcas speak nowhere else in verse.

163–4 *garlic to mend her kissing with*: Let her take garlic to overcome her bad breath.

165 *in good time*: Here an expression of indignation.

166 *stand upon*: Value; set store by.

170 *and boasts himself*: Probably 'and, they say, he boasts
    himself . . .' is to be understood, setting off what
    others say about Doricles from what he himself has
    told the old Shepherd.

171 *a worthy feeding*: A valuable grazing-ground.

178 *another*: The other.
    featly: Nimbly.

186 *several*: A good many.
    tell: Count.

187 *as*: As though.
    ballads: The reference throughout is to the popular
    broadsheet ballad, written in doggerel verse on some
    sensational topic of the day, and sung to a familiar
    tune.

191 *pleasant*: Merry; funny.

192 *lamentably*: Mournfully.

193 *sizes*: Kinds.

194 *milliner*: Vendor of such articles of apparel as gloves
    and ribbons; haberdasher.

196–7 *with such delicate burdens of dildos and fadings, jump
    her and thump her*: The joke here is that the Servant,
    while claiming Autolycus' songs to be free from
    bawdry, unwittingly reveals them to be full of it.
    The word *dildo* occurs in the refrains of many ballads
    of the period, but often, through its meaning of
    'phallus', with a bawdy connotation. *fading* was the
    name of a dance, and the refrain 'With a fading,
    fading, fading' is found in a ribald popular song of
    Shakespeare's time.

196 *delicate burdens*: Delightful refrains.

197–200 *and where some stretch-mouthed . . . good man*: The
    probable meaning of this much debated and often
    emended passage is that where the wooer in the song
    would interrupt its progress (*break a foul gap into
    the matter*) by means of some bawdy action, the girl
    checks him with her answer.

198 *stretch-mouthed*: Wide-mouthed.

200 *Whoop, do me no harm, good man*: The refrain of a
    ribald ditty of the time.

203 *brave*: Fine.

204 *admirable*: To be wondered at.

   conceited: Witty; ingenious.

205 *unbraided*: Probably 'not soiled or faded'.

207 *points*: Tagged laces for attaching the hose to the
   doublet, lacing a bodice, etc. (with a quibble on
   'legal points').

208 *by th'gross*: In large quantities.

209 *inkles*: Linen tapes.

   caddisses: Worsted tapes used for garters (short for
   'caddis ribbons').

   lawns: Linen fabrics.

211 *sleevehand*: Wristband.

212 *square*: Square piece of material covering the breast.

217 *You have of these pedlars*: There are pedlars.

219 *go about to*: Wish to.

221 *Cypress*: A crape-like fabric.

222 *Gloves as sweet as damask roses*: Gloves were often
   perfumed.

223 *Masks for faces, and for noses*: Masks to protect
   the whole face or the nose only against the sun
   were commonly worn by ladies in Shakespeare's
   day.

224 *Bugle-bracelet*: Bracelet of tube-shaped glass beads,
   usually black.

228 *poking-sticks*: Rods used for stiffening the pleats of
   ruffs.

229–30 *What maids lack from head to heel | Come buy of
   me*: The colon which is found in F after *heel* and which
   subsequent editors have retained (or replaced by a
   full stop or exclamation mark) seems intrusive and
   has therefore been omitted.

233–4 *being enthralled . . . and gloves*: Since I'm tied up in
   knots over Mopsa, so shall *certain ribbons and gloves*
   be tied up in parcels for gifts.

235 *against*: In time for.

240 *paid you more*: Got you with child.

242–3 *Will they wear their plackets where they should bear
   their faces*: The word *placket* was used for petticoats

or the slit in petticoats, and hence also for the geni-
tals. This last is almost certainly its meaning at 606,
and possibly here, though it seems more probable
that the Clown is saying by means of a clothes
metaphor (*placket* = petticoat): 'will they display
openly what they should keep hidden?'

245 *kiln-hole*: Fire-hole of a kiln or oven (a favourite place
for gossiping).

to whistle of: To speak secretly of. Since Shakespeare
nowhere else uses the word in this sense, the emendation 'to whistle off', adopted by many editors,
may be justified ('to whistle off' is a term in falconry,
meaning 'to release').

247 *Clamor your tongues*: There has been a great deal of
discussion of the meaning of *Clamor* ever since, in
the eighteenth century, Warburton suggested that it
was a technical term from bell-ringing: to 'clamor'
or 'clammer' meant to increase the strokes of the
clapper preparatory to stopping altogether. There is
some evidence that this gave rise to the further
meaning 'to proceed from noise to silence'. The
Clown would then be saying 'Put an end to the
tolling of your tongues'. The choice of metaphor
seems certainly very suited to the Clown, unlike the
emendation 'Charm your tongues', which many
editors have preferred.

248–9 *tawdry-lace*: Silk necktie (much worn by women in
Shakespeare's day; so called from St Audrey).

249 *sweet*: Perfumed.

250 *cozened*: Cheated.

256 *parcels of charge*: Items of value.

258 *a-life*: Dearly.

260–79 *Here's one . . . as true*: Shakespeare here provides an
extravagant parody of some of the topics of the
ballads of his time, which dealt in marvels that were
claimed to be strictly true, and were sometimes
attested by witnesses.

262 *at a burden*: At one birth. The word was used by
Shakespeare in this rare sense only once before, in

The Comedy of Errors, V.1.344: 'That bore thee at a burden two fair sons'.

263 *carbonadoed*: Scored across and grilled upon the coals.

266 *Bless*: Guard; keep.

272 *anon*: Shortly; later.

281 *hands*: Signatures.

286 *passing*: Exceedingly.

288 *westward*: In the West Country.

294 *Have at it*: I will attempt it.

295–306 *Get you hence . . . Say, whither*: The words of this song are clearly those of 'Two maids wooing a man', not those of Autolycus' *merry ballad*, which are to be sung to the same tune. When Mopsa says *We can both sing it. If thou'lt bear a part, thou shalt hear* (290–91) she evidently means not only the tune but also the words of 'Two maids wooing a man'. There is therefore no indication that she and Dorcas can read either words or music, as has been claimed for them. Like Autolycus, they sing the song from memory.

295–6 *go. | Where*: F and most subsequent editors omit the stop after *go*, but the wording seems to require its insertion.

301 *Or . . . or*: Either . . . or.

308 *sad*: Serious.

317 *toys*: Trifling ornaments.

320–21 *Money's a . . . ware-a*: Money has a share in everything, putting all men's ware in circulation.

323 *neat-herds*: Cowherds.

323–4 *that have made themselves all men of hair*: By dressing themselves in skins in order to look like satyrs; dances of satyrs were not uncommon in medieval and Renaissance entertainments.

325 *Saltiers*: Jumpers (with the Servant's blunder for *satyrs*).

326 *gallimaufry*: Ridiculous medley.

328 *bowling*: Regarded by the Servant as a gentle, quiet game.

334–5 *One three of them, by their own report, sir, hath danced before the King*: It seems probable that we have here a topical allusion to the performance of Ben Jonson's *The Masque of Oberon* before King James and his court on 1 January 1611. This contained an anti-masque dance of ten or twelve satyrs, described by Jonson as 'an antic dance, full of gesture, and swift motion'. Since the anti-masque dances in court masques were performed by professional actors, it is quite possible that some, if not all, of the actors who performed the satyrs' dance in *The Winter's Tale* had also performed it in *The Masque of Oberon*, and that the Servant's reference was meant to be recognized as pointing to this event, outside the play-world. While it seems probable that the insertion of the satyrs' dance in *The Winter's Tale* is a consequence of its success in *The Masque of Oberon*, this does not help us to fix the date after which the play must have been written, for the dance, with the lines leading up to it (322–39), may well have been inserted at a later date. There are, indeed, a few pointers in the text that this is, in fact, what happened (see Allardyce Nicoll's discussion in *Shakespeare Jahrbuch* XCIV (1958), pp. 56–7).

336 *by th'square*: Precisely.

340 *O, father, you'll know more of that hereafter*: Polixenes has been continuing his *sad talk* (308) with the old Shepherd.

342 *He's simple and tells much*: This plainly refers not to Florizel, as has been claimed, but to the old Shepherd, whom he has been sounding on the subject of the lovers.

345 *handed*: Had to do with.

346 *knacks*: Knick-knacks.

349 *nothing marted*: Made no deal.

350 *Interpretation should abuse*: Should misinterpret.

351 *straited*: At a loss.

352–3 *if you make . . . holding her*: If you are concerned to keep her happy.

355 *looks*: Looks for.

356–7 *which I have given already, | But not delivered*: Florizel is distinguishing between the free gift of his heart and the formal handing over of it, 'delivery' as a legal term being 'the formal transfer of a deed by the grantor'. The attempted marriage contract that follows is to be this 'delivery'.

358 *Before this ancient sir*: The dramatic irony of the scene requires, and the lines that follow make clear, that this refers to Polixenes and not, as some commentators have argued, to Camillo.

whom, it should seem: Shakespeare frequently uses *whom* where we should use 'who'.

361 *bolted*: Sifted.

364 *was*: That was.

371 *force*: Physical strength.

374–5 *Commend them . . . perdition*: Commend them to her service or condemn them to their own complete ruin.

386 *Enough then for your wonder*: Probably 'enough to amaze you even then' (when you know who I am).

387 *Contract us 'fore these witnesses*: There were two kinds of marriage contracts in Shakespeare's time: *per verba de futuro* (in which the couple engaged themselves to become husband and wife at a future date), a contract which could be dissolved for a variety of reasons; and *per verba de praesenti* (in which the couple declared that henceforth they were husband and wife), a contract which constituted a legally binding marriage. Polixenes' interruption makes it impossible to discover which of the two it was to be, though his reference to *nuptial* (392) suggests that Shakespeare thought of it as a *de praesenti* contract.

396 *altering rheums*: Catarrhs which affect his mind.

397 *Dispute his own estate*: Discuss his own affairs.

399 *being childish*: When a child.

403 *Something*: Somewhat.

Reason: It is reasonable that.

417 *affects*: Aims at; aspires to.

420 *of force*: Of necessity.

421 *cop'st with*: Have to do with.

423 *state*: Class; rank.

fond: Foolish.

425 *knack*: Trifle; toy.

428 *Far*: Farther (like 'near', 'far' could also be used for the comparative).

Deucalion: The equivalent in Greek mythology to Noah.

431 *dead*: Deadly; mortal.

432–4 *yea, him too, | That makes himself, but for our honour therein, | Unworthy thee*: Probably Polixenes is using the plural of majesty, *honour* having here the rare meaning of 'exalted position': 'yea, worthy of him too, who makes himself unworthy of thee (by the nature of his actions), if my exalted position were not involved.'

440 *him*: Polixenes.

448 *Speak ere thou die'st*: Neither Camillo nor the Shepherd (453–5) seems to have taken in the King's words of reprieve (429–31).

455 *Where no priest shovels in dust*: Hanged men were buried under the gallows, without a funeral service.

457 *mingle faith*: Join in a pledge (of marriage).

462–3 *More straining on . . . unwillingly*: Florizel sees himself as a hound on a leash, all the more eager to pursue his course for being plucked back, refusing to let himself unwillingly be dragged off by his master.

468 *highness*: Probably 'haughtiness' rather than the title.

470 *I think Camillo*: Perhaps Camillo is just beginning to remove his disguise and becomes therefore recognizable (the convention being that all disguise is impenetrable).

475–6 *Let Nature crush the sides o'th'earth together | And mar the seeds within*: All material substances were believed to be derived from *seeds* (called 'germens' in *Macbeth*, IV.1.58 and *King Lear*, III.2.8). Nature would thus be destroying not only all actual but also all potential life on earth.

478 *affection*: The word had much stronger meanings in Shakespeare's time than it has now. It could signify

'sexual desire', as at I.2.138, or 'passionate love', as here.

479 *fancy*: Love.

490 *As you've e'er been my father's honoured friend*: F reads *As you haue euer bin my Fathers honour'd friend*, which is metrically quite un-Shakespearian; later Folios omitted *honour'd*. The elisions here adopted are a less drastic attempt to restore the metre. It seems far more probable that the scribe or compositor ignored Shakespeare's elisions than that he added an adjective not found in the manuscript.

494 *Tug*: Contend.

497 *opportune*: Stressed on the second syllable.

500–501 *benefit your knowledge . . . reporting*: Profit you to know, nor is it for me to tell.

502 *easier for*: More open to.

504 *irremovable*: Immovable. The word may here, as often with Shakespeare, be used adverbially: 'He's immovably resolved for flight.' F's comma after *irremovable* means little, since commas are found in the oddest places throughout the Folio text of the play (for instance, two lines later F prints a comma after *going*).

510–12 *Now, good Camillo . . . ceremony*: Florizel is apologizing for talking apart to Perdita in Camillo's presence, a breach of courtesy which derives from Shakespeare's need to let Camillo reveal his thoughts to the audience (cf. the note to 656).

511 *curious*: Causing anxiety; worrying.

517 *as thought on*: As fully as they are borne in mind.

520–22 *direction. | If . . . alteration, on . . .*: F punctuates *direction, | If . . . alteration. On . . .* This punctuation is certainly possible, and a number of editors have adopted it. But the two conditional clauses in one sentence are awkward, and the verse as here punctuated (in accord with most editors since Pope) sounds more Shakespearian.

521 *ponderous*: Of great import.

524 *become your highness*: Accord with your high station.

528–9 *And, with my best endeavours . . . qualify*: Commentators

are divided on whether this means 'and where, together
with my best endeavours in your absence, you may strive
to appease your angry father' or 'and with my best
endeavours in your absence *I shall* strive to appease your
angry father'. The syntax strongly suggests that the
former represents Shakespeare's meaning, and the
passage has been punctuated accordingly. The implication seems to be that Florizel could make use of the
power of intercession with Polixenes that Leontes can
command.

529 *discontenting*: Vexed; angry.
      qualify: Appease.

530 *bring him up to liking*: Get him to the point of
      approving.

535–6 *But as th'unthought-on . . . wildly do*: But as the
      unexpected accident (the intervention by Polixenes)
      is responsible for what we rashly are about to do.

545 *free*: Noble; generous.

546 *asks thee, the son, forgiveness*: A number of recent
      editors have adhered to F's *asks thee there Sonne
      forgiuenesse*, punctuating 'asks thee there "Son,
      forgiveness!"' or 'asks thee there, son, forgiveness'.
      This reading seems, however, very forced and
      implausible. The emendation first introduced in
      the third Folio, and accepted by most editors, has
      therefore been adopted.

548 *fresh*: Young and lovely.

548–9 *o'er and o'er divides . . . kindness*: Keeps on talking
      in turn of his (former) wicked behaviour (towards
      Polixenes) and his (present) love (for him and you).

556 *deliver*: Say.

558 *The which . . . sitting*: Which shall indicate to you
      at every meeting.

560 *bosom*: Intimate thoughts.

574 *take in*: Conquer; subdue.

575 *these seven years*: This is a proverbial expression,
      signifying 'for a very long time'.
      seven: Here monosyllabic.

577–8 *She is as forward of her breeding as | She is i'th'rear' our birth*: She is as much above her upbringing as she is below me in birth. The apostrophe after *rear*, taken over from F, indicates that a word ('of') has been omitted.

584 *medicine*: The word could also mean 'physician' (from French '*médecin*'), and this may, but need not, be its meaning here.

586 *appear*: Appear as such.

587 *fortunes*: Possessions; wealth.

589 *royally appointed*: Equipped like royalty.

590 *scene*: Stage performance.

595 *table-book*: A pocket notebook.

597 *fasting*: Being empty.

598 *a benediction*: Blessedness.

599–600 *best in picture*: No parallel usage has been traced, presumably because it is a nonce-use, coined to suggest punningly 'best looking' (because fattest) and hence 'best to pick'.

603 *pettitoes*: Pigs' trotters (but also used jestingly of human feet).

605 *stuck in ears*: Went to their ears; became hearing.

606 *placket*: See note on 242–3.

606–7 *to geld a codpiece of a purse*: To cut off a purse from the bag-like appendage worn in the front of breeches in Shakespeare's day.

608 *my sir's*: The Clown's.

609 *nothing*: Nothingness.

610 *festival*: Brought for the feast (adjective).

621 *Nothing may*: Nothing that may.

623 *hanging*: The punishment in Shakespeare's day for any theft over twelve pence in value.

624–5 *How now . . . to thee*: F sets this out as verse, and is followed by many editors. But it is clearly meant to be prose, the medium in which Camillo talks with Autolycus throughout.

629 *discase*: Undress.

630 *thou must think*: You must realize.

631–2 *Though the pennyworth on his side be the worst*: Though he gets the worst of the exchange.

632–3 *some boot*: Something into the bargain.

637 *flayed*: Skinned (undressed).

641 *earnest*: Money in part payment (the *boot* of 633).
A quibble on the *earnest* of 638.

644 *my prophecy*: The prophecy he just made in calling
her *Fortunate*.

648–9 *Dismantle you . . . seeming*: Remove your outer
garment (presumably the *unusual weeds* referred to at
1), and make yourself as unlike your true appearance
as you can.

650 *eyes over*: Spying eyes (cf. IV.2.35).

656 *what have we twain forgot*: A mere device to get them
out of the way so that Camillo can deliver his aside;
hence we must not ask what it was that they had forgot.

674 *clog*: Encumbrance (an ungallant reference to Perdita).

675–8 *If I thought it were . . . my profession*: The lines have
been much emended, since, as they stand, the argument is somewhat baffling. The illogicality seems
due to excessive compression, which has led to the
omission of one of the links in the chain of reasoning,
to the effect that, since it would be a piece of knavery
towards Florizel to reveal it to the King, he may
do so; but as it is even more knavish to conceal it,
this is what he will do.

678 *profession*: Avowed practice.

679 *hot*: Keen.

683 *changeling*: See note on III.3.114–15.

687 *Go to*: Go on.

692 *all but what she has with her*: This presumably refers
to Hermione's jewel, which Perdita was wearing
round her neck when she was found (see V.2.33),
and which she has, it seems, put on for the feast.

700 *by I know not how much an ounce*: The majority of
editors have adhered to F's reading *by I know how
much an ounce*, claiming that this makes adequate sense
if the Clown's assertion is accompanied by a knowing
wink. But this explanation seems very strained, and
the insertion of 'not', first made by eighteenth-century
editors, fully justified.

705 *my master*: Autolycus had been in Florizel's service (see IV.3.13) and still thinks of him as his master.

709 *excrement*: Outgrowth (here the false beard that Autolycus wears in his pedlar's disguise).

713 *condition*: Nature.

714 *having*: Property.

715 *discover*: Reveal.

717 *A lie: you are rough and hairy*: One of the meanings of *plain* was 'smooth'. Autolycus pretends to understand the word in this sense.

718–21 *it becomes none . . . give us the lie*: Tradesmen give soldiers the lie in the sense of lying to them about their wares. But they are paid for it with good money (*stamped coin*), not with *stabbing steel* (the soldier's retort to being given the lie in the usual sense, that of being accused to his face of lying). Hence tradesmen do not *give* soldiers the lie, they sell it (the stress in the last sentence falls on *give*).

722–3 *Your worship . . . taken yourself with the manner*: This puzzling remark has been variously explained. Most probably the Clown is saying: 'Your worship would have told *us* an untruth (when you claimed that tradesmen often accuse soldiers to their face of lying), had you not caught yourself in the act (and changed your statement).' 'To be taken with the manner' (or 'mainour') is a legal phrase, meaning 'to be caught in the act of doing something unlawful'.

727 *measure*: Stately motion.

730 *insinuate*: The word seems to be here used intransitively, meaning 'make my way in a sinuous or subtle manner'.

to toaʒe: F's *at toaʒe* was changed in subsequent Folios to *or toaʒe*, and this reading has been adopted by most later editors. A more plausible emendation is, however, *to toaʒe*, meaning 'in order to tease' (a metaphor from the carding of wool).

731 *cap-à-pie*: From top to toe.

733 *open*: Disclose.

737 *Advocate's the court-word for a pheasant*: The Clown,
     ignorant of the meaning of Autolycus' *advocate*,
     thinks he and his father need a bribe, i.e. a pheasant.

740–42 *How blessed are we . . . disdain*: As part of his parody
     of the language of the court, Autolycus falls momen-
     tarily into blank verse. Perhaps he purposely rhymes
     men with the *hen* of the preceding line, which also
     happens to be blank verse.

745 *His garments are rich*: Shakespeare had probably
     forgotten that Florizel's garments, which Autolycus
     has put on, are *a swain's wearing* (IV.4.9). See note
     on IV.4.2–3.

747–8 *fantastical*: Eccentric; odd.

748–9 *the picking on's teeth*: The fact that he picks his
     teeth. The use and display of toothpicks (they were
     even worn in the hat) were considered marks of a
     fashionable gentleman in Shakespeare's day.

752–3 *this fardel and box*: The *fardel* consists of the garments
     worn by the infant Perdita when found; the *box*
     contains presumably the remainder of the gold and
     the scroll left with her by Antigonus (see III.3.113–18
     and V.2.33–5).

756–60 *Age, thou hast lost thy labour . . . air himself*: This
     echoes *Pandosto*: "'But', quoth Capnio, "you lose
     your labour in going to the palace, for the King
     means this day to take the air of the sea, and to go
     aboard of a ship that lies in the haven."'

764 *handfast*: Custody; durance.

768 *wit*: Ingenuity.

769 *germane*: Related.

773 *offer*: Dare; presume.

779–87 *He has a son . . . blown to death*: It is usually claimed
     that the description of these tortures is based on
     Boccaccio's story of Bernabò and Zinevra (*Decameron*,
     II.9), which Shakespeare had read for the writing of
     Cymbeline. There the villain is tied to a post in the
     sun, anointed with honey, and killed and devoured to
     the bone by flies, wasps and gadflies. (See *Elizabethan
     Love Stories*, ed. T. J. B. Spencer (1968), pp. 161–75.)

It is possible that Shakespeare was drawing on memo-
ries of this incident, but quite as likely that what
he had in mind were reports of the cruel tortures
inflicted by the Spaniards upon Negroes and American
Indians. 'Drake found a negro who had been sentenced
to be whipped raw, set in the sun, and tortured to
death by mosquitoes. An Indian was smeared with
brimstone, fired, restored to health, anointed with
honey, chained to a tree, "where mosquitoes flocked
about him like motes in the sun and did pitifully
sting him"' (*Shakespeare's England*, ed. Sir Sidney
Lee and C. T. Onions (1916), vol. I, p. 185).

784 *prognostication*: Weather forecast for the year in the
almanac.

786 *he*: The sun.

flies: Any winged insects.

787 *blown*: The few editors who comment on the word
at all explain its meaning as 'filled with eggs' or
'befouled'. But this seems a very improbable way
of killing a man. It is much more likely that its
meaning is 'puffed up, swollen' (through the insects'
stings). Shakespeare used the word 'blow' in the
sense of 'puff up' in *Twelfth Night*, II.5.41–2 ('Look
how imagination blows him') and probably also, in
connection with flies' stings, in *Antony and Cleopatra*,
V.2.59–60 ('and let the waterflies | Blow me into
abhorring').

790 *what you have to the King*: What your business is
with the King.

790–91 *something gently considered*: Rather generously remu-
nerated.

795–6 *Close with him*: Accept his offer.

796 *and though*: Even though.

808–9 *though my case . . . flayed out of it*: The Clown puns on
two meanings of *case*: 'plight' and 'covering' or 'skin'.

815 *gone*: Lost.

819–20 *look upon the hedge*: Relieve myself (a common
euphemism).

826–7 *I am courted now with a double occasion*: I am

wooed (by Fortune) with a twofold opportunity (for gain).

829 *turn back*: Redound.

831 *shore them*: Put them ashore.

832 *concerns him nothing*: Is of no importance to him.

V.I

2 *sorrow*: Mourning.

4 *penitence*: The word's primary meaning seems here to be 'penance'.

8 *in them*: Probably 'in thinking of her virtues'.

19 *good now*: A phrase of entreaty frequently used by Shakespeare.

25 *You pity not . . . remembrance*: You pity not the state, nor give thought to the remembrance (a zeugma).

27 *fail*: Failure.

28–9 *and devour | Incertain lookers-on*: Probably 'and destroy the onlookers, who will not know what to do'.

30 *is well*: The phrase is repeatedly used by Shakespeare to describe the state of the dead.

35 *Respecting*: In comparison with.

36 *Will*: Are determined to.

48 *successor*: The stress falls on the first syllable.

52 *squared me to*: Let myself be ruled by.

59 *Where we offenders move, appear soul-vexed*: F reads *(Where we Offendors now appeare) Soule-vext*. Of the many emendations that have been proposed the one here adopted seems the most Shakespearian and plausible ('move' in the manuscript could easily have been misread as 'now').

60 *Why to me*: Why is this insult offered to me?

61 *incense*: Incite; stir up.

66 *rift*: Split.

67 *mine*: My eyes.

70 *free leave*: Unhesitating permission.

73 *tempt*: Try; put to the test.

75 *Affront*: Confront.

84 *Enter a Gentleman*: F's *Enter a Seruant* has been altered, as it is likely to mislead the modern reader. It is, however, not inaccurate, since a gentleman in

the king's service could be so described.

88 *What with him*: What are those with him? (The question is repeated four lines later in *What train?*)

89 *Like to*: In a manner appropriate to.

90 *out of circumstance*: Without ceremony.

91 *framed*: Designed.

93 *mean*: Of low social status.

97 *so must thy grave*: So must you, now that you are in your grave.

100 *Is colder than that theme*: Is colder than the subject of your verses is (now that she is dead).

100–101 *she had not been, | Nor was not to be, equalled*: Since the eighteenth century, editors have put these words in inverted commas, claiming them to be an extract from the Gentleman's verse. But the tenses prove this to be mistaken (what the Gentleman must have written is 'she has not been, nor is not to be, equalled'), and make clear that Paulina is not quoting his exact words. This edition, therefore, follows F in omitting the inverted commas.

102 *shrewdly ebbed*: Greatly declined (i.e. his changed opinion).

108 *professors*: Those who proclaim their adherence to a religion.

109 *Not women!*: Editors follow F in placing a question mark after *women*. But Paulina is exclaiming, 'This surely does not apply to women!' In Elizabethan punctuation the question mark often stands for an exclamation mark.

113 *assisted with*: Accompanied by.

135 *brave*: Noble.

135–7 *whom . . . look on him*: To look on whom once more I desire to go on living, though my life is one of misery (*him* is redundant).

139 *at friend*: In the way of friendship.

140–42 *and but infirmity . . . ability*: And were it not that infirmity, which attends old age, has to some extent taken prisoner the ability he desires to have.

144 *Measured*: Travelled.

148 *offices*: Kindnesses.

149 *rarely*: Exceptionally.

149–50 *are as . . . slackness*: Make manifest how slack I have been (in my *offices* towards him).

155 *adventure of her person*: Hazard of her life.

156 *Smalus*: Shakespeare seems to have derived this name, like several others in the play, from Plutarch, who, in the *Life of Dion*, speaks of a voyage from Libya to a village in Sicily which is governed by a Carthaginian captain called Synalus. *Smalus* may be the scribe's or compositor's misreading of that name.

158–9 *whose daughter . . . with her*: Whose tears, when he was parting with her, proclaimed her to be his daughter.

160 *friendly*: Being favourable.

164 *Who for Bohemia bend*: And they are now making for Bohemia.

169 *climate here*: Dwell in this country.

170 *graceful*: Full of divine grace.

175–7 *What might I . . . as you*: We have here one of the many touches of dramatic irony in this scene, an irony which is heightened through the Elizabethan usage of 'son' and 'daughter' for 'son-in-law' and 'daughter-in-law' (a usage which forms the basis of Florizel's reply at 207–8).

181 *attach*: Seize; arrest.

182 *His dignity and duty both cast off*: Having thrown off his dignity as a prince and his duty as a son.

186–7 *it becomes | My marvel*: It befits my astonishment.

197 *Has . . . in question*: Is interrogating.

206 *The odds for high and low's alike*: Many different explanations of this line have been given. The most probable meaning is: 'The odds on high and low being united in marriage are similar to those on the stars kissing the valleys.'

213 *worth*: Rank.

215–16 *Though Fortune . . . my father*: Probably 'though Fortune were actually to be seen as an enemy pursuing us, together with my father'.

218–19   *Remember since . . . now*: Remember the days when
you were no older than I am now.

222–3   *Would he do so . . . a trifle*: What in *Pandosto* is a
violent and protracted passion has been reduced by
Shakespeare to a moment of amiable banter.

V.2

2   *relation*: Explanatory narrative.

8   *issue*: Outcome.

9   *broken delivery*: Disjointed account.

11   *notes of admiration*: Marks of wonder (as *notes of
admiration* could also mean 'exclamation marks', a
quibble may be intended).

17   *seeing*: What he saw.

18   *importance*: Import; meaning.

18–19   *the extremity of the one*: The utmost degree of one
or the other.

24–5   *that ballad-makers cannot be able to express it*: See
note to IV.4.260–79.

30–31   *pregnant by circumstance*: Clear through circumstan-
tial evidence.

33–4   *the letters of Antigonus*: What had been written by
Antigonus.

35   *character*: Handwriting.

36   *affection of*: Bent towards.

46   *countenance*: Bearing; demeanour.

48   *favour*: Look; appearance.

52   *worries*: Pesters.
clipping: Embracing.

54   *like a weather-bitten conduit of many kings' reigns*:
Like a weather-worn water-spout which has seen the
reigns of many kings (the tears flowing down the
old Shepherd's face prompt the image of the water-
spout, which, on large medieval buildings, was often
in the form of an old man's head; there may also
be a pun on *reigns*).

56   *undoes description to do it*: Beggars description to
paint it.

60   *rehearse*: Relate; narrate.

62–3 *innocence*: Guilelessness.

72–3 *She had one eye declined . . . fulfilled*: The expression 'to cry (or look down) with one eye and laugh (or look up) with the other', meaning 'to experience a mixture of grief and joy', was proverbial. A version of it is found in Claudius's 'With an auspicious and a dropping eye' (*Hamlet*, I.2.11).

76 *losing*: Being lost.

77 *act*: The primary meaning is evidently 'that which took place' (referring not merely to Paulina's actions but to everything that has been described). But the further, obsolete, meaning of 'performance of part of a play' is also present, and is responsible for the playhouse-metaphors in the rest of the sentence.

86 *dolour*: Grief.

86–7 *would fain*: Am inclined to.

88 *Who was most marble*: Even the most hard-hearted.

93–5 *a piece . . . Julio Romano*: This is Shakespeare's most celebrated anachronism, in a play which is full of similar, if less glaring, anachronisms. The fact that Shakespeare turned Giulio Romano (d. 1546) into a sculptor, when he was widely known only as a painter, may be due either to ignorance (Shakespeare, having heard of him as a famous painter, just assuming that he was also a sculptor) or to learning. For in Vasari's *Lives of . . . Painters* he would have found the following Latin epitaph for Giulio: 'Jupiter saw sculptured and painted statues breathe and earthly buildings made equal to those in heaven by the skill of Giulio Romano.' If Shakespeare had read these lines they may, in fact, have determined his choice of Giulio as the sculptor who so perfectly is Nature's *ape* (98). Yet there is the alternative possibility that Shakespeare thought of Giulio as merely having painted the statue, which had been carved by someone else. In that case *performed* may have not just the meaning of 'carried through to completion' but the more specific one (already, it seems, obsolete by 1611) of 'completed by adding what is wanting'. However, the praise of Giulio as Nature's ape seems far more appropriate if he is thought of as not only the statue's painter but also its sculptor. It is worth noting that Giulio Romano was also notorious in early modern Europe as the creator of a series of pornographic illustrations for the erotic sonnets of Pietro Aretino.

97 *beguile Nature of her custom*: Rob Nature of her trade.

98 *ape*: Imitator.

100 *greediness of affection*: Eager desire.

106 *piece*: Augment; add to.

109–10 *unthrifty to our knowledge*: Wasting the opportunity to increase our knowledge.

120 *relished*: Found acceptance.

125 *gentlemen born*: To be officially accepted as a 'gentleman born' in Shakespeare's day, one had to be descended from three degrees of gentry on both sides.

130 *Give me the lie*: When accused to his face of lying, a gentleman's honour required him to fight (see *As You Like It*, V.4.45 ff.).

143–4 *preposterous*: A malapropism for 'prosperous'.

148 *gentle*: Kind; generous (a characteristic contrast between father and son: where for the Clown the chief marks of the gentleman are his fine clothes and his readiness to fight and swear, for the old Shepherd they are generosity and courtesy).

151 *an it like*: If it please.

155 *Not swear it, now I am a gentleman*: Swearing, like duelling, was held to be the prerogative of gentlemen.

155–6 *boors and franklins*: Peasants and yeomen.

160 *a tall fellow of thy hands*: A valiant fellow in a fight.

164 *I will prove so, sir, to my power*: No doubt Autolycus is secretly making his promise refer to his valiant use of his hands as a cut-purse and pickpocket. We are clearly not meant to think of him as in any way reformed at the end of the play.

169 *picture*: Sculptured figure; effigy.

V.3

1 *grave*: Probably here 'having weight and importance', rather than 'of a dignified and serious demeanour'.

4 *paid home*: Amply repaid.

9 *We honour you with trouble*: Probably 'Our visit, which you call an honour, is really a trouble'.

12 *singularities*: Rarities; curiosities.

18 *Lonely*: Isolated. F's *Louely* has found its defenders, but most editors since the eighteenth century have chosen to emend.

19 *as lively mocked*: As closely counterfeited.

25 *Hermione*: The name, which normally in the play has four syllables, is here and at 28 reduced to three, the 'o' being scarcely sounded.

38 *piece*: Work of art.

41 *admiring*: Filled with wonder.

47 *The statue is but newly fixed*: The colours of the statue have only just been made fast.

49 *sore*: Heavily; thickly (the metaphor here and in the next two lines comes from painting, inspired, no doubt, by the immediately preceding lines).

56 *piece up*: Add to (his own store of grief).

57 *image*: Statue.

58 *wrought*: Moved; affected.

62 *Would I were dead but that methinks already*: May I die if it does not seem to me already (that it moves).

67 *fixure*: An earlier form of 'fixture'.

68 *As*: So that.

72 *No settled senses of the world*: No calm mind in the world.

83 *painting*: Paint.

85 *forbear*: Withdraw.

86 *presently*: Immediately.

96 *Or those*: F's *On: those* has been retained and defended by some editors; but the emendation to *Or those*, generally adopted since the eighteenth century, is almost certainly correct.

100 *look upon*: Look on.

106 *Until*: To the point that.

107 *double*: A second time.

113 *pertain*: Belong; be connected.

125–8 *For thou shalt hear . . . issue*: This is the only

explanation of Hermione's sixteen-year-long seques-
tration that Shakespeare provides, and not a few
readers have felt that he ought to have thought up
a better one. Coleridge declared that 'it seems a
mere indolence of the great bard not to have provided
in the oracular response . . . some ground for
Hermione's seeming death and fifteen years volun-
tary concealment. This might have been easily
effected by some obscure sentence of the oracle, as
for example: "Nor shall he ever recover an heir, if
he have a wife before that recovery."' In fact,
Shakespeare needed only to change one word in the
oracle, making its last sentence read, 'and the King
shall live without a *wife*, if that which is lost be not
found'.

126 *Knowing by Paulina*: Shakespeare appears to have
forgotten that Hermione was present when the oracle
was read.

129 *upon this push*: Probably 'at this moment of stress'.

130 *with like relation*: The meaning seems to be not, as
most commentators claim, 'by telling their stories
too' but rather 'by asking you similarly to tell your
story'.

132 *Partake*: Impart; make known.
    turtle: See note on IV.4.154–5.

135 *till I am lost*: Till I perish.

142 *For*: As for.

144 *whose worth and honesty*: This undoubtedly refers not
to Paulina, as has been claimed, but to Camillo.

145 *richly noted*: Abundantly well known.
    justified: Affirmed.

149 *This' your son-in-law*: The apostrophe, absent in F,
has been inserted to mark the omission of 'is', a
contraction frequently used by Shakespeare and his
contemporaries.

151 *troth-plight*: Betrothed.

Penguin Shakespeare

ALL'S WELL THAT ENDS WELL
WILLIAM SHAKESPEARE

A poor physician's daughter cures the King of France, and in return is promised the hand of any nobleman she wishes. But the man she chooses, the proud young Count of Rosillion, refuses to consummate the forced marriage and flees to Florence. Depicting the triumph of trickery over youthful arrogance, *All's Well that Ends Well* is among Shakespeare's darkest romantic comedies, yet it remains a powerful tribute to the strength of love.

This book includes a general introduction to Shakespeare's life and the Elizabethan theatre, a separate introduction to *All's Well That Ends Well*, a chronology of his works, suggestions for further reading, an essay discussing performance options on both stage and screen, and a commentary.

Edited by Barbara Everett

With an introduction by Janette Dillon

General Editor: Stanley Wells

Penguin Shakespeare

ANTONY AND CLEOPATRA
WILLIAM SHAKESPEARE

A battle-hardened soldier, Antony is one of the three leaders of the
Roman world. But he is also a man in the grip of an all-consuming
passion for the exotic and tempestuous Queen of Egypt. And when
their life of pleasure together is threatened by the encroaching politics
of Rome, the conflict between love and duty has devastating
consequences.

This book includes a general introduction to Shakespeare's life and the
Elizabethan theatre, a separate introduction to *Antony and Cleopatra*,
a chronology of his works, suggestions for further reading, an essay
discussing performance options on both stage and screen, and a
commentary.

Edited by Emrys Jones

With an introduction by René Weis

General Editor: Stanley Wells

PENGUIN SHAKESPEARE

AS YOU LIKE IT
WILLIAM SHAKESPEARE

When Rosalind is banished by her uncle, who has usurped her father's throne, she flees to the Forest of Arden where her exiled father holds court. There, dressed as a boy to avoid discovery, she encounters the man she loves – now a fellow exile – and resolves to remain in disguise to test his feelings for her. A gloriously sunny comedy, *As You Like It* is an exuberant combination of concealed identities and verbal jousting, reconciliations and multiple weddings.

This book includes a general introduction to Shakespeare's life and the Elizabethan theatre, a separate introduction to *As You Like It*, a chronology of his works, suggestions for further reading, an essay discussing performance options on both stage and screen, and a commentary.

Edited by H. J. Oliver

With an introduction by Katherine Duncan-Jones

General Editor: Stanley Wells

Penguin Shakespeare

CYMBELINE
WILLIAM SHAKESPEARE

The King of Britain, enraged by his daughter's disobedience in marrying against his wishes, banishes his new son-in-law. Having fled to Rome, the exiled husband makes a foolish wager with a villain he encounters there – gambling on the fidelity of his abandoned wife. Combining courtly menace and horror, comedy and melodrama, *Cymbeline* is a moving depiction of two young lovers driven apart by deceit and self-doubt.

This book includes a general introduction to Shakespeare's life and the Elizabethan theatre, a separate introduction to *Cymbeline*, a chronology of his works, suggestions for further reading, an essay discussing performance options on both stage and screen, and a commentary.

Edited with an introduction by John Pitcher

General Editor: Stanley Wells

PENGUIN SHAKESPEARE

HAMLET
WILLIAM SHAKESPEARE

A young Prince meets with his father's ghost, who alleges that his own brother, now married to his widow, murdered him. The Prince devises a scheme to test the truth of the ghost's accusation, feigning wild madness while plotting a brutal revenge. But his apparent insanity soon begins to wreak havoc on innocent and guilty alike.

This book includes a general introduction to Shakespeare's life and the Elizabethan theatre, a separate introduction to *Hamlet*, a chronology of his works, suggestions for further reading, an essay discussing performance options on both stage and screen by Paul Prescott, and a commentary.

Edited by T. J. B. Spencer

With an introduction by Alan Sinfield

General Editor: Stanley Wells

Penguin Shakespeare

HENRY IV, PART I
WILLIAM SHAKESPEARE

Prince Hal, the son of King Henry IV, spends his time in idle pleasure with dissolute friends, among them the roguish Sir John Falstaff. But when the kingdom is threatened by rebellious forces, the prince must abandon his reckless ways. Taking arms against a heroic enemy, he begins a great and compelling transformation – from irresponsible reprobate to noble ruler of men.

This book includes a general introduction to Shakespeare's life and the Elizabethan theatre, a separate introduction to *Henry IV, Part I*, a chronology of his works, suggestions for further reading, an essay discussing performance options on both stage and screen, and a commentary.

Edited by: Peter Davison

With an introduction by Charles Edelman

General Editor: Stanley Wells

PENGUIN SHAKESPEARE

HENRY IV, PART II
WILLIAM SHAKESPEARE

Angered by the loss of his son in battle, the Earl of Northumberland supports another rebellion against King Henry IV, bringing the country to the brink of civil war. Sick and weary, the old King sends out his forces, including the unruly Sir John Falstaff, to meet the rebels. But as the conflict grows, he must also confront a more personal problem – how to make his reprobate son Prince Hal aware of the duties he must bear, as heir to the throne.

This book includes a general introduction to Shakespeare's life and the Elizabethan theatre, a separate introduction to *Henry IV, Part II*, a chronology of his works, suggestions for further reading, an essay discussing performance options on both stage and screen, and a commentary.

Edited by Peter Davison

With an introduction by Adrian Poole

General Editor: Stanley Wells

PENGUIN SHAKESPEARE

HENRY VI, PART II
WILLIAM SHAKESPEARE

Henry VI is tricked into marrying Margaret – lover of the Earl of
Suffolk, who hopes to rule the kingdom through her influence. There is
one great obstacle in Suffolk's path, however – the noble Lord
Protector, whom he slyly orders to be murdered. Discovering this
betrayal, Henry banishes Suffolk, but with his Lord Protector gone the
unworldly young King must face his greatest challenge: impending
civil war and the rising threat of the House of York.

This book includes a general introduction to Shakespeare's life and the
Elizabethan theatre, a separate introduction to *Henry VI, Part II*, a
chronology of his works, suggestions for further reading, an essay
discussing performance options on both stage and screen by Rebecca
Brown, and a commentary.

Edited by Norman Sanders

With an introduction by Michael Taylor

General Editor: Stanley Wells

Read more in Penguin

PENGUIN SHAKESPEARE